SECDEF

Also by Charles A. Stevenson

The End of Nowhere: American Policy Toward Laos Since 1954

SECDEF

The Nearly Impossible Job of

SECRETARY OF DEFENSE

Charles A. Stevenson

Potomac Books, Inc.
Washington, D.C.

Library of Congress Cataloging-in-Publication Data
    Stevenson, Charles A., 1942–
      SECDEF : the nearly impossible job of Secretary of Defense / Charles A. Stevenson.—1st ed.
        p. cm.
      Includes bibliographical references and index.
      ISBN 1-57488-794-7 (hardcover : alk. paper)
      1. United States. Dept. of Defense. I. Title.
    UA23.6.S74 2005
    355.6092'273—dc22
                         2005029491

Printed in the United States of America on acid-free paper that meets the American National Standards Institute Z39-48 Standard.

Potomac Books, Inc.
22841 Quicksilver Drive
Dulles, Virginia 20166

First Edition

10 9 8 7 6 5 4 3 2 1

The views expressed herein are those of the author and are not intended to represent the U.S. Government or the National War College.

To Sue

Contents

Illustrations ix

Preface xi

I: Background and Evolution of the Office

1. The Nearly Impossible Job 3

2. The Cemetery for Dead Cats 7

II: Politics and Personalities

The Revolutionaries 21

    3. McNamara: The Numbers of Power 23

    4. Schlesinger: The Independence of Ideas 45

    5. Weinberger: The Power of Tenacity 59

The Firefighters 75

    6. Laird: The Power of Politics 77

    7. Aspin: The Politics of Failure 91

    8. Cohen: The Politics of Defense 105

The Team Players 119

    9. Brown: The Technology of Power 121

    10. Cheney: The Power of Decisiveness 135

    11. Perry: The Power of Decency 147

    12. The Rumsfeld Transformation 159

III: Roles and Performances

13. Manager of the Pentagon   181

14. War Planner   189

15. Diplomat   199

16. NSC Adviser   207

17. Successes and Failures   213

Appendix A: Secretaries of Defense   216

Appendix B: Foreign Travel by Secretaries of Defense   217

Notes   219

Bibliography   237

Index   245

About the Author   249

Illustrations

1. James Forrestal at his Pentagon desk   10

2. Louis Johnson with President Harry Truman
   and Gen. Harry Vaughan   12

3. Robert McNamara at a cabinet meeting   27

4. James Schlesinger at a news conference   47

5. Caspar Weinberger visiting U.S. troops   62

6. Melvin Laird and Adm. Thomas Moorer   88

7. Les Aspin with President Clinton   102

8. William Cohen with Gen. Hugh Shelton   115

9. Harold Brown in his office   131

10. Richard Cheney testifying with Gen. Colin Powell   141

11. William Perry speaking to U.S. troops   154

12. Donald Rumsfeld at a Pentagon press conference   173

Preface

Why do secretaries of state each get at least one book written about their term of office while secretaries of defense usually retire to oblivion? That question struck me one day as I prowled through the library stacks. Why don't the Pentagon leaders ever write their own memoirs? Why do scholars relegate them to the corner reserved for management studies, without emphasizing that secretaries of defense are key figures in foreign policy, especially that most serious action of foreign policy, the use of force?

These questions, and the dearth of literature about Defense Department leaders, prompted me to try my hand. I had enjoyed books written in the 1980s that had biographical chapters about several former secretaries–Richard Stubbing's *The Defense Game* and Douglas Kinnard's *The Secretary of Defense*–and wanted to follow the same format while bringing the story up to date. I was also struck, in that naïve summer of 2001, by the extraordinary parallels I saw between Donald Rumsfeld and Robert McNamara, especially in the ways each sought to impose his will on a reluctant Pentagon.

What interests me most is not how the defense secretary manages the department and spends its money, but rather, how the secretary functions in the broader world of national security policymaking–how he handles civil-military relations in planning strategy and wars, how he functions on the National Security Council and deals with the president and the secretary of state, how well he performs as a politician, especially in dealing with Congress. This book is organized around those issues.

I am lucky to have seen several defense secretaries in action, primarily from my position as a national security adviser to four senators, two of whom served on the Armed Services Committee. I also dealt directly with Pentagon officials during my sabbatical year working on the secretary of state's Policy Planning Staff. Several former officials, from the Pentagon, State, and National Security Council, some military and some civilian, have answered my questions and told of their experiences, although most prefer anonymity when discussing personalities. I also have the benefit of a dozen years as a faculty member of the National War College, where I have learned and heard from very experienced professionals—both faculty and students—about the people and processes in which they were deeply involved. I have supplemented these personal contacts with the usual library research, which is reflected in the endnotes.

These chapters are written for students like my own, who sometimes forget that personalities and politics drives much of what government does, and for people interested in American defense and foreign policy, who may not appreciate the important role often played by the person informally labeled the SecDef.

I am grateful to everyone who has helped me understand these issues better and express them more cogently, especially my colleagues at the National War College and at the National Defense University. My greatest debt, however, is to the woman who encouraged me from the start, tolerated my long hours stabbing at the keyboard, and always gave me friendship and love—my wife Sue.

I

BACKGROUND AND EVOLUTION OF THE OFFICE

1

The Nearly Impossible Job

Of the 14 Secretaries of Defense [as of 1980], six were fired and five others dismissed after Presidential elections. It is a post that has been called "the graveyard of political ambitions."

–F. J. West Jr.[1]

The list of secretarial responsibilities is so imposing that no single individual can totally fulfill them all.

–James Schlesinger[2]

The secretary of defense has one of the most difficult jobs in Washington. Many holders of the office served short tours and left frustrated and disappointed. Of the twenty men who have held that office since the post was created in 1947, only half served more than eighteen months; at least seven were fired or allowed to resign gracefully after losing the confidence of the president; one committed suicide soon after leaving the Pentagon. Few retained the celebrity and esteem they held while in office.

Why has there been such a high failure rate? The men selected were talented and experienced, and they found themselves surrounded by consummate professionals, running a responsive bureaucracy. Most understood the ways of Washington, the process of politics that lubricates the U.S. constitutional system. Most were good managers, of their own time and of the people and resources under their control. They set priorities and had clear missions and objectives. So why did so many fail?

Many, of course, succeeded. They survived the programmatic and budgetary storms and the slings and arrows of political opponents, and

3

they served as respected leaders of the defense establishment. Several wrought revolutionary changes on the traditionally conservative Pentagon, imposing their innovative visions and plans on reluctant bureaucracies. Many others did what they could in the short time available between their appointment and the advent of new presidential administrations. They did not fail but they lacked time to make much of a difference; their successes were necessarily limited by their short tenure in office.

The scorecard on secretaries of defense is mixed. As the subsequent chapters will show, there is no one ideal type of SecDef, no checklist of qualifications that predicts success, no menu for aspirants. Political experience is helpful. Managerial experience is useful. Close personal ties to the president and other senior officials are quite valuable. But none of these is sufficient to assure a satisfying and effective term of office. Only a few secretaries have had all three attributes.

Originally, the job was designed for weakness. The 1947 act creating the post did not even create a Department of Defense (DOD), only a "National Military Establishment" over which the secretary had limited powers. While subsequent laws strengthened the authority of the secretary, they also strengthened the senior military, especially the chairman of the Joint Chiefs of Staff, and left all Pentagon officials dependent on the changing demands of Congress.

Even a strong secretary has enormous, sometimes overwhelming, responsibilities. The secretary heads the military establishment and controls its over two million personnel, about eight out of every ten U.S. government employees. These subordinates are spread across the globe, in more than six hundred thousand individual buildings or structures in over six thousand different locations at home and in 146 countries abroad.[3] The secretary also manages a budget larger than the central government budget of any other nation—and higher than the total gross domestic product of all but a dozen countries in the world.[4]

At least sixteen different civilian officials report directly to him, and the chairman of the Joint Chiefs of Staff, along with the senior military officers and the Joint Staff, serve as his military advisers and are legally under his command. Such a broad span of control would tax any decision maker, and even the best secretaries have to limit their purview to only a handful of major issues.

Patterns of Leadership

The men chosen to head the Defense Department have had quite varied backgrounds. Six, primarily in the early years, came from banking or industry. Eleven—over half—were active in politics, with either elective or appointive positions. Three had scientific or technical backgrounds. One, George C. Marshall, was a career military man who had also served as secretary of state. All but six of the others had some prior military service, usually in the junior officer or enlisted ranks.

In office, these men have tended to fall into one of three general roles for carrying out their responsibilities: Revolutionaries, Firefighters, or Team Players.

The Revolutionaries were bold innovators who sought to change the Pentagon in far-reaching ways in order to fulfill their inner vision. These men were political appointees, of course, but they were also advocates for new approaches, and each ultimately persuaded his presidential boss to follow his lead. Of the twenty secretaries of defense, I would count five as revolutionaries: the first, James Forrestal, Robert McNamara, James Schlesinger, Caspar Weinberger, and Donald Rumsfeld. Each saw himself as an agent of change. Each moved aggressively from the first day in office to pursue his planned agenda. Each had a major impact on the Defense Department and should be judged at least partially successful; however, the first three were driven from office, brought down by the same qualities that made them so bold.

The Firefighters were those who were pulled away from their planned course, diverted from the tasks which they considered most important, in order to deal with immediate problems. These matters were sometimes truly significant, sometimes trivial, but all were in the public spotlight and therefore had to be handled. These officials who became preoccupied to a major extent by political controversies included Louis Johnson, Clark Clifford, Melvin Laird, Les Aspin, and Bill Cohen. Two of these men failed to contain the major conflagration of their term and lost their posts. The others were more adept, and left office with their heads held high.

The most common role, adopted by at least half of the men who have served as SecDef, was that of Team Player. They were diligent and supportive members of their administration, helpful in how they handled their jobs and in how they worked with their colleagues. They concentrated on their DOD duties, and tended to be supportive rather than obstructionist on broader national security and foreign policy matters. They got along with the president, with their cabinet colleagues, with Congress, and with the senior military. These men were usually well-regarded during their tenure and afterward. They earned those plaudits by quiet competence.

The following chapters tell the stories of several of these men, what they brought to the job, what they sought to accomplish, and how well they succeeded. Additional chapters describe the key roles of any secretary of defense—not only the manager of the Pentagon, but also the war planner, the diplomat, and the National Security Council member and adviser. Together they describe the challenges facing anyone put in charge of the Defense Department and seek to explain why the job is nearly impossible to perform.

2

The Cemetery for Dead Cats

*This office will probably be the greatest cemetery for
dead cats in history.*

–James V. Forrestal, First SecDef[1]

*The peacetime mission of the Armed Services is to destroy
the Secretary of Defense.*

–Forrestal[2]

The job of secretary of defense was originally shaped by a man who
didn't think it should exist, and who then was given the task of making it
work. The first seven men who held the office represented varied backgrounds and quite different political skills, and they achieved only limited success.

Soon after taking office as president, Harry Truman began pressing
for a fundamental reorganization of the postwar armed forces. "We must
never fight another war the way we have fought the last two," he told his
aide, Clark Clifford. "I have the feeling that if the Army and the Navy
had fought our enemies as hard as they fought each other, the war would
have ended much sooner."[3] Truman favored a proposal first offered by
Army Chief of Staff General George C. Marshall in October 1943, calling
for a single Department of National Defense and a single military chief of
staff over all the armed services.

Navy Secretary James Vincent Forrestal, backed by tradition-inspired
admirals and the Navy's strong allies on Capitol Hill, led the two-year
fight to scuttle Truman's plan, and he largely succeeded. A New York
investment banker, Forrestal had taken flight training in the Navy dur-

ing World War I and was named Under Secretary in 1940 and Secretary in 1944.

Instead of the unification of the military departments, Forrestal proposed a war cabinet committee consisting of the president, the secretary of state, the service secretaries, the Joint Chiefs of Staff, and the head of a board charged with overseeing industrial mobilization. He wanted this new National Security Council to be housed in the Pentagon, not the White House. He thought that the wartime model of unity of command in theater and cross-service coordination in Washington had been successful, and he and his allies feared Army domination of any centralized organization. He wanted an established structure to coordinate policy and advise the president, "but without sacrificing the autonomy of the Navy," as he confided to his diary.[4]

Truman played a deft political game, pushing Forrestal and his Army counterpart to reach some kind of agreement but never making demands that might force his Navy secretary to resign in protest, since he knew that that would jeopardize the unification effort. In December 1945, when he formally sent to Congress his proposal for a Department of National Defense combining the war and Navy departments, he agreed to let the Navy retain its own aviation and to keep the U.S. Marine Corps as a separate military branch. He also called for rotation of the chief of staff position among the military branches. Most significantly, he granted Forrestal and other Navy witnesses permission to "express their personal views on this subject without restraint" when called before congressional committees.[5]

Inter-service negotiations dragged on throughout 1946, with Forrestal suspicious at every turn. The day after the Army capitulated to another series of Navy demands, he warned, "We are going to have to watch them [the Army] very carefully."[6] Finally in February 1947, the president sent a revised proposal to the newly elected, Republican-led 80th Congress. It called for a secretary of national defense presiding over three independent services and a chairman-less Joint Chiefs of Staff as advisers to the president and the new National Security Council.

The final version of the National Security Act of 1947 was signed into law by Harry Truman on July 26 on board the presidential aircraft at National Airport, as he waited impatiently to fly home to Missouri to see his dying mother. Besides creating the National Security Council (NSC) and the Central Intelligence Agency (CIA), the new law established the position of secretary of defense, with the quite limited authority to "establish general policies and programs" and "exercise general direction, authority and control" over the awkwardly-named National Military Establishment.[7] The secretary of defense was allowed only a small staff, none of a rank requiring Senate confirmation, and thus with no real power over the services. The service secretaries retained cabinet rank and seats on the NSC, as well as control over their departments and their budgets.

The First Secretary

Forrestal, like many of his successors, was not his president's first choice for secretary of defense. But when the secretary of war insisted on returning to civilian life, Truman turned to Forrestal. Perhaps this was in recognition of his Navy secretary's skill and experience and in reward for his loyalty despite his disagreements over defense reorganization. But Clark Clifford, Truman's aide on this issue starting in 1945, cited a different presidential motive: "If Forrestal remained secretary of the Navy, he would make life unbearable for the secretary of defense; if, on the other hand, *he* was the secretary, he would have to try to make the system work."[8]

Forrestal brought to his new post significant Washington experience, good political connections both with the president and on Capitol Hill, and an appetite for hard work. One Sunday evening, after having worked his staff for seven straight days, he finally headed home, telling the staff, "Well, have a nice weekend."[9] His standing with the president suffered during 1948, however, as he pressed for more money than the White House was willing to allocate to defense, kept the Pentagon out of the political fray, and at times even seemed to be cozy with Republicans.[10]

The first secretary of defense saw his job as coordinating, planning, and integrating military matters, not running operations. His objective was "unifying the mentality" of the members of the armed forces, of "getting a common mental attitude toward a common problem."[11] He forced the Chiefs to agree to a delineation of roles and missions; he cajoled them to submit budget requests in between what they wanted and what the president was willing to recommend; and he tried to mediate the fundamental strategic rivalry between the new Air Force and the Navy over countering the Soviet threat. He lacked the authority to impose centralized civilian control over the U.S. military. Within a few months of taking office, and despite his most diligent efforts, he concluded that he had failed—indeed, would continue to fail—unless his position were strengthened with new legislation. By the summer of 1948, he told Clifford, "I was wrong, I cannot make this work, no one can make it work."[12]

While trying to establish some measure of control over the National Military Establishment, Forrestal was an active participant in Truman's cabinet discussions of foreign policy. Even though he strongly supported some administration policies, including aid to anti-Communists in Europe and the creation of a new treaty alliance, NATO, he garnered public criticism over his opposition to Truman's support of recognizing the new state of Israel. He was increasingly bedeviled by a mental illness that made him moody, erratic, and paranoid.[13] Truman felt compelled to request his resignation early in 1949, and the ailing Forrestal committed suicide a few months later.

Soon after Truman's surprise reelection victory in 1948, the president sent the new Democratic-controlled Congress legislation merging the three departments into a Department of Defense under a secretary with the authority to "exercise direction, authority, and control" over its components. The measure sailed to passage on a surge of concern over waste and inefficiency in military spending. The 1949 law also created the posts of chairman of the Joint Chiefs of Staff (JCS), deputy secretary of defense, and three Senate-confirmable assistant secretaries.

The Second Secretary

By then, the man in charge of the Pentagon was Louis Arthur Johnson, "a bald bear of a man, weighing two hundred pounds, with a disposition to match."[14] Prior to his selection as the second secretary of defense, Johnson had been a strong advocate for military benefits and preparedness. An Army officer in World War I, he helped found the American Legion and was its national commander in 1932–33. As assistant secretary for war during 1937–40, he repeatedly clashed with his boss by advocating rearmament and universal military training. After several years practicing law in Washington, he became Truman's chief fundraiser for the 1948 campaign, and eagerly sought a cabinet post as a reward for his efforts.

Johnson took office determined to help the president balance the budget by squeezing every last possible efficiency out of the Pentagon. He boasted that he could save a billion dollars a year–from a $14.2 billion

James Forrestal at his Pentagon desk. *National Archives*

defense budget—by consolidating functions. He also believed that the Air Force should get the lion's share. Early on, he issued several orders fraught with symbolism in order to demonstrate his enhanced powers. He ordered the Army secretary to vacate his office, the largest and most elegant in the Pentagon, so that he could refurbish it for his own use. He cancelled the annual service birthday celebrations. And, barely three weeks after his swearing-in, he cancelled the Navy's new sixty-five thousand ton, $189 million super carrier, the *United States,* for which the keel had just been laid.[15] The Navy secretary resigned in protest in April, and the recalcitrant chief of naval operations was fired in October.

Jealous of his powers and suspicious of his cabinet peers, Johnson refused to allow Pentagon officials to work with State Department counterparts. He feared that people from State would interfere with his control of military policy. He participated grudgingly and minimally in the development of what became NSC 68, the blueprint for rearmament to contain the Soviet Union. That document was developed after the surprise Soviet detonation of an atomic bomb and the consolidation of power by the Chinese Communists in October 1949, and accepted by Truman in April 1950. But he sent it on to the Budget Bureau for cost estimates—which had deliberately been left out of NSC 68—saying, "I will not buy a pig in a poke."[16] The huge price tag on rearmament became clear just as war broke out in Korea in June. NSC 68 then became the blueprint for the subsequent U.S. military buildup. By the summer of 1950, however, Louis Johnson was a political liability for President Truman—the symbol of military cutbacks which left American forces ill prepared for war against the Communists.

Johnson also undercut his own standing with Truman by cultivating conservative columnists, leaking them information damaging to Secretary of State Dean Acheson, and openly praising Republican critics of Truman's policies.[17] The president finally asked for his resignation in September. He lamented privately, "I've never had anyone let me down as badly as he did. I've known for months—ever since May—that I would have to fire him, but I just couldn't bring myself to do it. . . . The terrible thing about all this is that Johnson doesn't realize that he has done anything wrong."[18]

Elder Statesmen

To replace Johnson, Truman again summoned George C. Marshall back from retirement, thus naming a widely respected military leader as the civilian head of the Department of Defense. Before he could be confirmed, however, Congress had to pass a law waiving the prohibition against anyone serving as secretary who had been an active duty military officer within the past ten years. While Marshall was still widely respected for his wartime service as Army chief of staff, his nomination was opposed by some conservative Republicans who blamed him for the Communist takeover of China.

Marshall insisted on bringing as his deputy Robert Abercrombie Lovett, who had been his deputy when he served as secretary of state (1947–49) and who was then groomed to succeed him a year later at Defense. As he told a reporter, "Lovett carries out the policies I have announced. He is in complete charge of operations."[19] They presided over three significant events: the Korean War as it turned into a military stalemate; the military buildup in Asia and Europe pursuant to NSC 68; and the firing of General Douglas MacArthur and consequent loss of political support for Harry Truman.

Marshall cancelled Johnson's restrictions on contact between the Pentagon and State Department and reopened an active political-military dialogue. In some respects he spent more time on foreign policy matters than on strictly military ones, for he was reluctant to use his prior service as a trump card against the recommendations of the Chiefs. He maintained close contact, including daily meetings with General Bradley.[20]

Louis Johnson with President Harry Truman and Gen. Harry Vaughan. *Library of Congress*

Marshall and the Joint Chiefs were forced–by the ego and political stature of MacArthur–to play a supporting but backbench role as the five-star commander launched the daring but successful Inchon landing and drove North Korean forces toward the Chinese border in the fall of 1950. When Chinese forces intervened and drove U.S. and South Korean troops back, Marshall and the Joint Chiefs concurred with Truman's limitations on military activity. The president did not want to strike inside China for fear of an even wider war. And he believed that the Soviet Union might challenge America in Europe if the U.S. became too bogged down in Asia.

When Truman could no longer tolerate MacArthur's public criticism of his policies, he relieved him of command in April 1951. In the ensuing political firestorm and congressional hearings, Marshall and the Chiefs defended the president's action, thus providing crucial political support. Nevertheless, Truman's public approval plunged, never to recover, ultimately forcing him not to seek renomination or reelection.

After one year at the helm, Marshall stepped down, leaving Lovett in charge. Lovett had a long record of public service. A highly decorated naval aviator in World War I, Lovett left New York investment banking in 1940 to be the assistant secretary of the Army for air, and later Marshall's deputy at the State Department. In 1961, John F. Kennedy asked if he would be willing to return to the Pentagon, but Lovett declined and recommended instead a rising business executive, Robert McNamara.

Lovett was the quintessential public servant: fiercely loyal to his superiors, effective, focused on the big picture, congenial to his peers, and nurturing to his subordinates. He served only sixteen months as secretary, presiding over a continuing military buildup but enduring political controversy as Republicans hammered the administration over the perceived failures–Korea, corruption, and communism. But he left a record of interagency cooperation on foreign policy issues and gentle but effective coordination of the military departments.

Businessmen in Charge

Dwight Eisenhower didn't want or need a strategic thinker in charge of the Pentagon; he wanted a savvy businessman who could wring efficiencies from the enlarged war machine. He picked the president of General Motors, "Engine Charlie" Wilson, and let him stay in office, despite some embarrassing episodes, for nearly five years.

Charles Erwin Wilson never served in uniform, for he took an engineering job soon after graduating from Carnegie Tech at age nineteen and worked developing radio generators for the Army in World War I. He became president of GM in 1941 and presided over that company's massive defense production activities during World War II. By 1953, he was successful and well-regarded, despite sloppy dressing and being "loud, gregarious, opinionated, stubborn, [and] sometimes insensitive."[21] He was much less aloof than his predecessors. He enjoyed meeting people, walking around the Pentagon, and even got his hair cut in the public barber shop.[22]

His relations with Congress, however, went, as one observer put it, "from atrocious to poor."[23] He got off on the wrong foot during his Senate confirmation hearing by saying, "For years I thought what was good for our country was good for General Motors, and vice versa."[24] His attempt to deny any potential conflict of interest between his new duties and his former corporate ties was instantly inverted in public perceptions, and retained forever in that less flattering form.

With the press, too, he was outspoken to a fault. An aide said, "He could put his foot in his mouth easier than any secretary of defense we've ever had."[25] One of his more notable statements was when he argued against government spending on basic research such as "finding out why the grass is green, things like that."[26] Another time he said that the National Guard was full of draft dodgers. And when the White House failed to back him up, he commented, "The White House is not my dunghill."[27]

Eisenhower felt comfortable as his own defense minister in terms of strategic policy, but he wanted Wilson to manage the Pentagon. He told Wilson, "Charlie, you run defense. We both can't do it and I won't do it. I was elected to worry about a lot of other things than the day-to-day operations of a department."[28] The president also developed close ties with the chairman of the JCS, Adm. Arthur Radford, for strategic analysis and advice.

Besides ending the war in Korea, which was accomplished by an armistice agreement in June 1953, Eisenhower had campaigned with a clear promise to reduce government spending and balance the budget. To that end, he ordered significant reductions in Pentagon spending, which Wilson had to enforce on reluctant military chiefs. Eisenhower defended the "New Look" as a shift from war-fighting to deterrence, based on a reliance on nuclear weapons. This meant more money for the Air Force and much less for the Army.

Eisenhower did order significant changes in DOD organization, however, using reorganization authority then in law. His June 1953 plan tripled the number of assistant secretaries, from three to nine; gave the JCS chairman control over the Joint Staff; and specified that "no function . . . should be performed independent of the direction, authority, and control of the secretary of defense."[29] This was meant to strengthen the secretary against challenges by the service secretaries or Joint Chiefs.

While Wilson tried to manage the inevitable fights over scarce resources, he could not eliminate the inter-service rivalry which seemed to the press and the political opposition as the cause of needless waste. In fact, the president was quite willing to fund competing weapons and technologies in the nuclear area, but he vigorously denied that the Soviet Union was gaining on America militarily.

Wilson was succeeded by another businessman, Neil Hosler McElroy, in early October 1957. McElroy had been too young for the first world war and too old for the second. He spent his whole career at Procter & Gamble, rising to the presidency in 1948. On taking public office, he declared his role was to be "captain of President Eisenhower's defense team."[30]

Tall (six feet four inches) and handsome, McElroy had a photographic memory and an ability to comprehend—and locate errors in—pages filled with numbers. He recognized his inexperience in defense issues and relied heavily on the Chiefs and on talented subordinates like Deputy Secretary Donald Quarles. He also worked to maintain close and good relations with Congress, testifying so often that his scheduler would list days without testimony as "free."[31]

Just four days before he took office, however, the Soviet Union delivered a powerful psychological blow that undermined American self-confidence and sense of security. On October 4, the USSR launched the world's first space satellite, Sputnik, thereby provoking fears that the Communists had opened a dangerous missile gap. Those fears were shared by a special panel chaired by the head of the Ford Foundation, Rowan Gaither. The panel had been named by the president to study national defense and gave its top secret report to him on November 6. Gaither's report said the Soviet Union was getting stronger militarily while the United States was getting weaker. A few members of the panel were so worried about growing Soviet capabilities that they recommended an immediate preventive war. The group recommended new measures to assure the survivability of U.S. strategic bombers in case of a surprise Soviet attack, increased procurement of nuclear missiles, and building fallout shelters for a more effective defense of the population. "Do something," Gaither pleaded. But Eisenhower saw no need for panic, or for massive new expenditures. A week later, the classified report was leaked to the press, fueling a political debate that continued until a new president who promised to close the missile gap was elected in 1960.[32]

Seeds of Reform

While Eisenhower approved only modest increases in spending to accelerate missile development and disperse strategic bombers, he did seize the opportunity to press for—and receive—new legal authority to reorganize the DOD. McElroy became a vigorous advocate as he came to understand some of the problems of running the Pentagon. He was particularly upset by the frequency of JCS disagreements and their inability to provide consensus advice. Once he told them, "You have spent your lives in the military, you are the top men in the field. I am an industrialist from the soap works. Yet I ask you what should be done on a military matter, and you say you can't agree. So I have to make the decision."[33]

Despite opposition from the Navy, as in earlier years, Congress willingly passed the Defense Reorganization Act of 1958 to strengthen the authority of the secretary over the services, give the JCS chairman a formal vote, and create a director of research and engineering under the secretary. To prevent the muzzling of dissenters, however, Congress added language permitting the JCS members and service secretaries to appeal to Congress—something Eisenhower grumbled was "legalized insubordination."

The man who made creative use of those new authorities, setting the stage for the more dramatic power plays of Robert McNamara, was Thomas Sovereign Gates Jr., who had been McElroy's deputy and succeeded him when McElroy left office after his promised two years in place. Gates was ideally suited to impose change on the Pentagon, for he knew the inner working of the building and was liked by its senior leaders.

Gates was an investment banker who had served in the Navy during World War II. Eisenhower named him under secretary of the Navy in 1953, rising to navy secretary in 1957. He had resigned and was about to attend a retirement dinner when Eisenhower recalled him to become deputy secretary of defense in June 1959, thus making him McElroy's logical successor five months later. Unlike his two immediate predecessors, Gates had acquired detailed knowledge of the Pentagon and defense issues. He was praised for listening to others before he made decisions.

But he also had strong views on how to unify the Pentagon and reduce inter-service rivalries and parochialism. On his first day in office, he issued a directive requiring line officers to serve a regular tour with a joint, combined, allied, or Office of the Secretary of Defense (OSD) staff before they could be promoted to general or flag officer rank.[34] This important requirement was not rigorously enforced or written into law until the Goldwater-Nichols Act of 1986.

Gates also began the practice, never tried by his predecessors, of sitting regularly with the Joint Chiefs in order to reach immediate decisions.[35] He also believed in closer coordination of defense with diplomacy, met each Sunday with the secretary of state, and fostered closer working relationships with the State Department on political-military issues. In all these ways, he set precedents which enabled his successors to exert strong control over the Pentagon and significant influence over foreign policy.

Each of these seven men started out with high hopes and the strong support of the president who selected them. Only Eisenhower's two businessmen had no prior high level government experience in defense matters, but they brought the management expertise the president most wanted. Despite their illustrious backgrounds, three lost the confidence of the president; two retired early for health or personal reasons; and two of the best-regarded officials had their terms cut short by the election of a new president from the opposition party.

The early secretaries of defense, therefore, left conflicting models, none of which guaranteed success. What are now seen as flaws could just as easily been virtues if other factors had been different. Forrestal's preference for a strong NSC could have provided the coordination which the weak powers of the secretary of defense could not. Johnson's preoccupation with efficiency could have helped his president fiscally and politically if the Korean War had not intervened. Wilson's candor could have deflected criticism of Eisenhower's policies if the president could have pointed to more successful programs and less inter-service rivalry. Marshall's reluctance to impose his own military judgments might have worked better if the Chiefs were better able to achieve consensus.

On the other hand, Lovett set a standard of professionalism and public service that anyone could be proud of today. And Gates used his increased powers deftly, without provoking resentment the way his successor did. By 1960 the secretary of defense was at last empowered to run the Pentagon with few obstacles in his way. Everything was in place for the first long-serving revolutionary, Robert McNamara.

II

POLITICS AND PERSONALITIES

The Revolutionaries

Some secretaries of defense have been revolutionaries, bold innovators who sought to change the Pentagon in far-reaching ways in order to fulfill their inner vision. These men were political appointees, of course, but they were also advocates for new approaches, and each ultimately persuaded his presidential boss to follow his lead.

Of the twenty secretaries of defense, I would count five as revolutionaries—the first, James Forrestal, the three described in the following pages, and Donald Rumsfeld. All saw themselves as agents of change. Each moved aggressively from the first day in office to pursue his planned agenda.

Only those who served for several years were relatively successful, however, for the Pentagon is like a giant aircraft carrier that steers slowly into new directions. It takes time and close monitoring by the commander to move off the established course. The forces of bureaucratic inertia are powerful and durable.

Revolutionaries also provoke enemies, always from outside and sometimes from within. The comfortable conformists fear the disruptions of change. The parrots of orthodoxy resist learning the new catechism. The experienced old hands complain about the inevitable mistakes of the new team.

Not all change is good or necessary. Even wise policies can be implemented unwisely, and even good deeds may be punished. That is also the story here. At least three of the Pentagon revolutionaries described here lost the confidence of their president and were maneuvered into resignation.

How should these officials be assessed? Does forced resignation negate their accomplishments? Should incomplete revolutions be awarded points for boldness and good intentions? Is success the most important criterion? Is it the only one that matters?

3

McNamara:
The Numbers of Power

*Bob McNamara is the most dangerous man in the cabinet
because he is so persuasive and articulate.*

–Robert F. Kennedy[1]

*Almost any decision is better than no decision at all.
No decision is a decision, a decision to maintain the status quo,
and that is nearly always a mistake.*

–Robert S. McNamara[2]

Robert Strange McNamara should have been secretary of the treasury. That was the job initially offered by Sargent Shriver, the president-elect's brother-in-law, on December 8, 1960. That post would have focused the auto executive's keen analytical mind, his insatiable hunger for data, his self-confident decisiveness, and his empathy for the less fortunate, on the economy and on getting the country moving again, as John F. Kennedy had pledged.

"You're out of your mind," McNamara replied. "I'm not qualified for that." Shriver countered by offering the post of secretary of defense. Again McNamara demurred. "This is absurd! I'm not qualified." Shriver asked that he at least meet with the president-elect to discuss the matter.[3]

They met the next day in Washington. McNamara reiterated his misgivings. He argued that he had more influence on interest rates in his job at Ford than he would at Treasury. He noted that his knowledge of defense issues was dated and that others were better qualified. Kennedy responded that there were no schools for secretaries of defense–or for presidents either. McNamara then asked Kennedy directly whether he had in fact written the Pulitzer prize-winning history *Profiles in Courage,* and received an affirmative reply. The two men agreed to meet again after the weekend.

Over the next few days McNamara grew more interested in the Pentagon post and the challenges and opportunities it offered. He hesitated to leave the Ford Motor Company because he had just been named its president, capping a fourteen-year career, and because it would impose a significant financial penalty on his family, as his salary dropped from $400,000 to $25,000 per year and he had to forego several million dollars in stock options. But he also saw the attraction of running an operation with four and a half million people and a budget larger than those of most countries. "I had no patience with the myth that the Defense Department could not be managed," he later recalled.[4]

If he took the job, however, he wanted it on his own terms. He drafted a letter for the president-elect setting forth two conditions: that he be free to run the department as he saw fit, including final approval over all appointments; and that he not have to go to parties or be "a social secretary." The letter even had a line for Kennedy's signature.[5] The first condition showed his instinct for power and the second his naiveté about Washington, where he later became a frequent and much-prized guest.

When he met with John F. Kennedy and his brother Robert the next Tuesday, he presented his letter. Though surprised at McNamara's audacity, the incoming president wanted him in the cabinet and agreed to the conditions. He kept the letter unsigned, however, and insisted on announcing the appointment immediately to the press outside his house.[6]

Kennedy wanted a cabinet of bright, vigorous men and was willing to name well-regarded people, like McNamara and his choice for secretary of state, Dean Rusk, whom he did not even know. Previous political experience, surprisingly, was neither expected nor welcome. He also wanted the symbolism of bipartisanship, which he found in choosing Douglas Dillon, a Republican from Eisenhower's State Department, for Treasury, and McNamara, who had never changed his original GOP registration even though he had supported several Democrats.

While forming his administration, Kennedy sought out Robert Lovett, who had headed the Pentagon in the Truman administration. Lovett declined any cabinet post for reasons of age and ill health, but he recommended McNamara, who had worked for him during World War II. He called him disciplined, with a great analytical ability, and a great hunger for facts. Lovett also described what a good secretary of defense needed: "A healthy skepticism, a sense of values, and a sense of priorities."[7] Other Kennedy talent scouts heard about McNamara and confirmed his reputation.

Background

To the public, McNamara was a successful auto executive who had helped Ford retool and prosper after World War II by imposing modern management controls and stringent cost-cutting. Those actions came naturally to McNamara, who early in life discovered the magic of numbers and practiced extraordinary frugality. In college, his professors taught him to see math as a process of thought. "It was a revelation," he later wrote. "To this day, I see quantification as a language to add precision to reasoning about the world."[8] Driving to college each day in a 1931 Roadster, McNamara and a friend left the headlights off to conserve the battery and coasted to the bottom of a hill before turning on the engine in order to save on the cost of gas.[9] This was surely the kind of man who could assure, in the words of an earlier secretary of defense, "the biggest bang for the buck."

The American auto industry, led by General Motors, was among the first to embrace new techniques of financial management and statistical control. McNamara learned these disciplines as a student at the Harvard Graduate School of Business Administration and was later asked to teach them to others. In the spring of 1942, a few junior faculty were summoned to join the war effort by teaching courses to newly minted officers. McNamara went to work for Robert Lovett, then the assistant secretary of war for air, and General H. H. "Hap" Arnold, the commanding general of the Army Air Forces. He was one of the so-called "Whiz Kids" in a group headed by "Tex" Thornton, who, after the war, took his team to Ford and later headed Litton Industries.[10]

McNamara taught officers and tried to impose on reluctant bureaucracies a system of statistical control, gathering data from specially formatted reports and analyzing the numbers for deeper meanings. When he found that civilian consultants were more easily ignored than uniformed officials, he was glad to be given a direct commission in the Army, starting as a captain in 1943 and finishing the war as a lieutenant colonel. He did not experience combat, but he learned the military importance of careful planning so that men and equipment were effectively used and inefficient operations were replaced by more efficient ones. He found he had a strong appetite for administration and early on he displayed his hallmark management traits. "Besides arrogance and impatience," his biographer notes, "McNamara also showed his drive for order and results."[11]

Entering the Pentagon on January 21, 1961, he knew what he had to do and was confident he could succeed. He had been instructed to reappraise all U.S. strategy. He wanted tighter civilian control and decisions based on facts, not emotions. His charge from President Kennedy was "to determine what forces were required and to procure and support them as economically as possible."[12] The Democrats had campaigned on America's military weakness and growing Soviet strength and aggressiveness, so the new administration had to rebuild U.S. defenses and close the feared "missile gap." Yet it had to avoid the wasteful inter-service rivalries which had been so evident during the 1950s, leading even President Eisenhower to warn of a "military-industrial complex."[13]

In keeping with the young president's determination to have "arms sufficient beyond doubt," McNamara wanted to speed up the decision processes of the Pentagon and move civilian officials deeper into the management of defense programs. "I considered that we were too slow to develop the alternatives and the decisions as to the numbers and types of forces we really needed."[14] He later recalled, "I was determined to subordinate the powerful institutional interests of the various armed services and the defense contractors to a broad conception of the national interest. I wanted to challenge the Pentagon's resistance to change, and I intended that the big decisions would be made on the basis of study and analysis and not simply by perpetuating the practice of allocating blocs of funds to the various services and letting them use the money as they saw fit."[15]

Defense budgets would increase dramatically under Kennedy, but the allocations would be different than before, and the decisions would be made by civilians and based upon their analyses of the numbers rather than upon the military judgments of senior officers. Though he personally could be overpowered by emotions, McNamara was determined to exclude them from his work. He once told Congress that he was trying to establish "a rational foundation as opposed to an emotional foundation for the decisions as to what size force and what type of force this country will maintain."[16] He believed he derived his power from his numbers.

Political Relations

McNamara also derived his power from his strong support in the White House, first from John F. Kennedy and later from Lyndon B. Johnson. He had ready and easy access to the Oval Office for business, and, as David Halberstam notes, "McNamara was one of the few people working for Kennedy who crossed the great divide and became a part of his social world."[17] He enjoyed partying with the Kennedys and developed close personal ties to supplement his already strong professional ones. Kennedy also admired McNamara's briefing style: He would "come in with his twenty options and then say 'Mr. President, I think we should do this.' I like that. Makes the job easier."[18] McNamara also had a close relationship with the president's national security adviser, McGeorge Bundy, thus smoothing the path between the Pentagon and the White House on procedural as well as substantive matters.[19]

It is revealing to note, in the transcripts of the recordings secretly made during the Cuban missile crisis of 1962, that the president calls McNamara "Bob," while addressing his secretary of state as "Mr. Secretary."[20] Although neither man had known Kennedy before 1960, and Rusk was eight years older than the president, the secretary of state stayed at a professional distance while McNamara became an intimate friend.

Lyndon Johnson also respected McNamara, called him frequently on the phone, and drew upon his talents for a wide range of activities far beyond those of a secretary of defense. McNamara returned the support with unflinching loyalty. Eventually, concerned about his deputy's health and mental stability and troubled by his increasingly dovish views on Vietnam, Johnson orchestrated a shift for McNamara from the Pentagon to the World Bank.

McNamara sought correct if not warm relations with Rusk and the State Department. "We insisted upon cooperation and worked hard to obtain it," Rusk later wrote. "We had our differences, and on rare occasions we took those differences to the president. But Bob and I met nearly every weekend for long talks, usually in my office, where we tried to hammer out our differences."[21] Others at State thought that Rusk achieved this harmony by agreeing too much and being too passive. "I thought [Dean] let Bob run over him," one official concluded.[22] Another State official, Roger Hilsman, praised McNamara's leadership at the Pentagon

Robert McNamara at a cabinet meeting. *National Archives*

but not his judgment. "McNamara was an extraordinarily able man, a brilliantly efficient man. But he was not a wise man."[23]

The problem was that there was a power vacuum on foreign policy which McNamara rushed to fill. When State was slow to produce the requisite paper for interagency consideration, Defense supplied its own. The "little State Department" run by the Bureau of International Security Affairs was more agile, responsive, and creative, and therefore often more effective, than its more ponderous counterpart at Foggy Bottom.

McNamara had his own team at the top of the Pentagon. Immediately after accepting the job offer from Kennedy, he squirreled himself in Ford's Washington office and began calling around to identify and recruit people for the DOD. Unlike Rusk, who had not demanded control over appointments and who had to accept strong and not always compatible personalities foisted on him by the White House, McNamara had the final say regarding Pentagon posts. He even rejected strong presidential hints to name Franklin D. Roosevelt Jr., who had been a key political supporter during the nomination fight, as secretary of the Navy.

Instead, he brought to Washington a large contingent of bright, assertive people who shared his determination to shake things up in the Pentagon: number crunchers like Charles Hitch and Alain Enthoven of RAND; technologists like Harold Brown; and seasoned professionals like Paul Nitze and Cyrus Vance. These men, and the younger people they recruited, formed the defense leadership for more than a generation. They usually started in the Office of the Secretary of Defense (OSD), which grew 50 percent during the McNamara years,[24] and then were farmed out to the services, thereby spreading the McNamara gospel and ensuring more centralized control. Their only career rivals were their Republican equivalents, who came to work for Richard Nixon and Henry Kissinger and stayed on to staff subsequent administrations.

Operating Style

McNamara prided himself on his mastery of facts and his decisiveness. That had been the secret of his success at Harvard, in the Army, and at Ford. He knew more and argued more cogently than anyone else in the room. And when he had the power, he was decisive. "I would rather have a wrong decision made than no decision at all," he declared.[25] He once described two broad philosophies of management, one passive and one very active. The first he labeled "a judicial role," where the secretary "would make the decisions required of him by law by approving recommendations made to him." Instead of this approach, he preferred "an active role providing aggressive leadership—questioning, suggesting alternatives, proposing objectives and stimulating progress."[26]

He worked long hours. He preferred written memos to oral briefings because, he said, he could read faster than anyone else could speak. Yet he could note discrepancies between slides and mathematical errors in those briefing charts. His manner in meetings with subordinates ranged from respectful to hectoring, but rarely warm and friendly.[27]

Knowledge was the source of his power, but the particular knowledge he sought was data, precise numbers that could be manipulated and compared, numbers that had a reality and structure. As he told his biographer, "Numbers, as you know, are a language to me."[28] He knew that numbers had limitations, but he considered them far more valuable than mere impressions or opinions. "I am sure that no significant military problem will ever be wholly susceptible to purely quantitative analysis," he once said. "But every piece of the total problem that can be quantitatively analyzed removes one more piece of uncertainty from our process of making a choice. There are many factors which cannot be adequately quantified and which therefore must be supplemented with judgment seasoned by experience. Furthermore, experience is necessary to determine the relevant questions with which to proceed with any analysis."[29] Note that, to McNamara, judgment is only a supplement and experience shapes relevance, not choice.

McNamara began by naming four of his civilian aides as "commanders" of task forces studying key defense issues: strategic delivery systems, limited war, installations and logistics, and research and development. The ostensible purpose was to recommend ways of implementing the new financial management system, but the secrecy shrouding the membership of the task forces and their recommendations fueled concerns about civilian meddling in military matters.[30]

He followed that up with a series of questions to be studied and answered, called the Trombones because there were ninety-six of them at first, although the list eventually numbered over one hundred. They covered the gamut from threats faced, to force structure to counter the threats, to required weapon systems. This technique has been followed by subsequent administrations, usually centered in the National Security Council staff, either to gather analyses for decision or to preoccupy the permanent bureaucracy while the new team acts.

In fact, McNamara was willingly under the gun to provide major policy recommendations to the president by the end of February, barely six weeks after the inauguration.

Civil-Military Relations

The powers of the secretary of defense had been significantly enhanced even before the Kennedy administration under the strong prodding of Dwight Eisenhower. The 1958 Defense Reorganization Act had given the secretary "direction, authority and control" over the military services, in contrast to the "general direction" language dating from 1947. He also gained greater authority to reorganize the department and more explicit authority over research and development of new weapons. The chairman of the Joint Chiefs of Staff, for the first time, was given a vote in JCS deliberations and coordinate control over the expanded Joint Staff. The service chiefs, by contrast, were removed from the chain of command to regional and functional commanders, although the services institutionally retained strong influence over both military operations and the organization and equipment of the forces.

Eisenhower's final secretary of defense, Thomas Gates, began to utilize the new authorities by consolidating defense communications under a single agency. But he had been in the Pentagon throughout the Eisenhower administration, knew the people and the processes, and was liked by them. By contrast, the new civilian leadership brought by McNamara was brash and abrasive, more determined to change the behaviors of their new colleagues than to understand or accommodate them.

McNamara continued Gates's practice of meeting occasionally with the Chiefs in their special meeting room, the Tank. And he had weekly meetings with the chiefs and service secretaries, as well as top OSD officials.[31] He kept the form but not the substance of the encounters; the words were there, but no music.

This change of style and personalities caused problems with the Joint Chiefs of Staff. McNamara's people were young, arrogant, out to change the world, and imbued with civilian attitudes. The Air Force chief of staff, Gen. Thomas White, who retired six months after the new administration came to power, later articulated the complaints which many of his uniformed colleagues shared toward the new civilian leadership.

"I am profoundly apprehensive of the pipe-smoking, tree-full-of-owls type of so-called professional 'defense intellectuals' who have been brought into this nation's capital," he wrote in 1963. He called them "amateurs," "temporary experts," "termites at work," and doubted that they "have sufficient worldliness to stand up to the kind of enemy we face."[32] White lamented that military judgments were being neglected and that, as a result, the United States was acquiring forces to reach compromises rather than victory. Partly, of course, these complaints reflected a difference of opinion over strategic nuclear doctrine and forces, the wisdom of flexible response and the new concepts of nuclear deterrence. But they also show that there was a profound cultural clash between the Ivy League/ Georgetown civilians and their military colleagues.

Air Force Gen. Curtis LeMay, who had known McNamara during World War II and became Air Force chief of staff in June 1961, later complained that the "Whiz Kids" were "the most egotistical people that I ever saw in my life. They had no faith in the military; they had no respect for the military at all. They felt that the Harvard Business School method of solving problems would solve any problem in the world."[33] LeMay also became angry when the research and development director, Harold

Brown, tried to persuade him of the administration's rationale for canceling the RS-70 strategic bomber. "Why, that son of a bitch was in junior
high school when I was out bombing Japan," LeMay bellowed.[34] Another Air Force general was shocked when Alain Enthoven, McNamara's
leading systems analyst, tried to end an argument over nuclear war plans
by saying, "General, I have fought just as many nuclear wars as you have."[35]

Others complained anonymously to the press, leading military writer
Hanson Baldwin to report in 1963 that McNamara had pressured JCS
members to sign written statements declaring the adequacy of his policies
and that he had imposed a "party line" from which no deviations were
permitted.[36] These tensions became only greater in later years, when the
secretary clashed repeatedly with the JCS over Vietnam.

The new management tools imposed by McNamara reduced the
power of the uniformed military and forced them to communicate in a
different and quite foreign language. Until 1961, the services had broad
authority to choose among spending priorities within their given budget
ceilings. McNamara's system forced nuclear war-fighting weapons into
comparison and competition with one another, with judgments to be based
upon cost-effectiveness rather than service preferences. Instead of service
budgets, he established mission categories. And he forced the Pentagon
to speak in terms of numbers, the numbers of operations research and
systems analysis, the quantification of what many in uniform considered
imponderables. The military leaders were slow to learn these new systems and resented the certitude with which they were being imposed.

Different cultures, different language, and different priorities. The
Kennedy administration came to power determined to increase the size
of the Army and the number and types of long-range nuclear missiles.
This ran counter especially to the Air Force's devotion to strategic bombers. Between 1961-65, McNamara cut the Air Force budget 10 percent in
real terms while increasing resources for the other services. Air Force
dissents from JCS recommendations also increased greatly in the 1960s.
Even when the Chiefs were unified, after 1965, McNamara frequently
rejected their advice.[37]

The new defense intellectuals thought that they could deter a nuclear
war through the proper mix of weaponry and operational plans, and they
wanted to guarantee that the president had multiple retaliatory options, not
simply total nuclear war. These differences also exacerbated the civil-military tensions in the McNamara years.

McNamara also lost confidence in the military leadership he found at
the Pentagon in 1961. Just before the inauguration, he asked the Chiefs
for their suggested changes in the existing Eisenhower budget. Their answers were a rehash of previously submitted requests for increases. "Do
they think I'm a fool?" McNamara cried. "Don't they have ideas?"[38] He
reacted by setting up civilian-run task forces.

The Bay of Pigs fiasco undermined both McNamara's and Kennedy's confidence in the Chiefs. When Senator Albert Gore (D-Tenn) publicly called for the removal of the JCS, neither the president nor secretary spoke out in their defense for more than a week. McNamara later "accepted" responsibility for all DOD actions but did not deny the accusations against the Chiefs. The senior military officers noticed and did not appreciate the lack of support.[39]

Furthermore, the secretary also clashed with the Chiefs over what they said in public. From the early days of the Kennedy administration, he tried to censor their speeches, especially the strident anticommunist rhetoric of Adm. Arleigh Burke, the long-serving chief of naval operations. The reports of censorship provoked outcries from the administration's political opponents, but the process continued.[40]

In addition to controlling the Chiefs' public comments, McNamara also tried to prevent their airing of differences in front of Congress, despite their legal authority to "make such recommendations to Congress relating to the Department of Defense" as they saw fit—provided only that they first inform the secretary. He issued guidance that the officer should indicate that he abides by "the departmental position" despite his personal views.[41]

When challenged over reports of civil-military conflicts, McNamara responded with denials and numbers. The relations were "closer than they have ever been before between secretaries and the Chiefs," he claimed in 1961.[42] "Never have the views of senior military officials been solicited as frequently, nor considered as carefully," he asserted in 1964.[43] His press spokesman documented the numbers of meetings and consultations.

Most significantly, the president totally undermined the formal system of military advice by naming retired Army Gen. Maxwell Taylor as military representative to the president and installing him in the White House with a mandate to call on government agencies for information and then advise on military matters.[44] Kennedy had asked Taylor to study what had gone wrong in the Bay of Pigs and then decided to use him as his liaison to the military, bypassing the chairman of the JCS, Gen. Lyman Lemnitzer. Eventually the president sent Lemnitzer to NATO and nominated Taylor as chairman. When Taylor left to be ambassador to South Vietnam, Army Gen. Earle Wheeler became chairman of the JCS. He worked assiduously to reduce the civil-military friction, both by negotiating away differences and sometimes not even reporting them to McNamara.[45]

Relations with Congress

At first, McNamara impressed the barons of Capitol Hill as he had others, with a barrage of statistics packaged in concise points. The congressional leaders were pleased to see a man of such obvious competence tackle the critical issues of national security. They welcomed the arrival of someone who could end inter-service rivalries by making sound, fact-based judgments on how much is enough. The secretary had a way of rephrasing questions put to him into forms he could more easily and persuasively answer.[46] He did not, however, cultivate members of Congress socially, leaving that task to his deputy secretary, Roswell Gilpatric.

Prior to the Vietnam War, McNamara maintained good relations with Capitol Hill, although he did clash with some key figures, such as House Armed Services Committee Chairman Carl Vinson (D-Ga.) over his decision to cancel the B-70 bomber and Senator John McClellan (D-Ark.) over the controversial TFX aircraft program. It helped that McNamara initially was increasing the defense budget. When he began cutting back and canceling politically appealing programs, he encountered more opposition. For the most part, McNamara won his budget battles in Congress and retained the support of congressional leaders until the Vietnam War turned many against him and his policies.

McNamara had good relations where it counted; he dominated his department and was highly influential in other national security areas. He played his multiple roles vigorously and effectively.

Manager of the Pentagon

The secretary's most pressing job is to manage the Defense Department, to allocate and oversee the expenditure of billions of dollars, to minimize the friction and improve the coordination of several million people in thousands of offices and facilities. McNamara had done that at Ford. He did it with the statistical control devices he had studied and taught at Harvard, and then had used in real-world operations during World War II. He was determined to apply the same analytical tools to national defense.

He began with the budget—the source of bureaucratic power, the indicator of priorities, and the means of control. Until the 1920s, when the president was first required to submit an overall governmental budget, the executive departments dealt directly with the congressional committees that voted appropriations. Presidential budgets remained wish lists, with the key deals still being cut by committee chairmen and cabinet secretaries. In the Pentagon, the practice had been for the services to submit large requests and then cut them to fit within the administration's ceiling on defense spending. There were some shifts, such as the decline of the Army and the growth of the Air Force in the 1950s, but each service's slice of the budget pie stayed about the same from one year to the next.[47] Each service usually had broad discretion on choosing how to comply with the presidential ceilings.

McNamara changed that. He ordered that budgets be reorganized in terms of military missions so that strategic missile programs would compete against each other, and missiles with bombers, and Navy tactical aircraft with those of the Air Force, and warships with ground combat forces. He established a Planning, Programming and Budgeting System (PPBS) to funnel the choices into his office under a regular timetable for submissions, reviews, and decisions. He created a special Office of Systems Analyses (OSA) to second-guess the service requests by using logical models and mathematical tools. These were the "pipe-smoking, tree-full-of-owls type of so-called professional 'defense intellectuals'" so derided by General White and others in uniform.

Ultimately, McNamara's managerial revolution took over the Pentagon and its PPBS system was imposed on the rest of the executive branch. But the changes met resistance and to this day, Congress still approves funds using its historical service-by-service line items. In the Pentagon, however, PPBS meant that military planners had to estimate spending needs for each program for the next five years and then had to receive approval for deviations. This made it harder for new weapons to get started, and more obvious when their costs began to soar.

McNamara claimed, like most of his successors, that he would decide on defense spending without regard to any arbitrary ceilings. He asserted that the budget reflected a rational judgment, based solely on military considerations and without regard to domestic needs. In fact, he had to go to extreme lengths to maintain that fiction. As one officer observed, "McNamara always insisted there was no budget ceiling but regularly made all kinds of cuts to get under it."[48] Proposed changes were submitted at the same time that annual budget reviews occurred. Decision papers on those changes were largely written after budgetary decisions were made. By 1964, McNamara had begun issuing "Tentative Force Guidance" tables, which were treated as hard and fast decisions on force structure. Meanwhile, the Budget Bureau had given all other departments appropriations targets, thus leaving an implicit defense figure.[49]

Every president develops budget ceilings for defense. None has ever really done a zero-based or bottom-up review unconstrained by some notion of limits. Eisenhower argued that too much for defense would weaken the domestic economy, and that was sufficient reason for not building all the weapons requested by the military. McNamara could not allow himself to make such an argument. Wedded to his concept of rational analysis, he had to maintain that all decisions were based on facts, not emotions. But that approach, as Arnold Kanter notes, turned every denial of a military request into a challenge to the military's competence and judgment.[50]

Defense budget requests under the Kennedy administration soared at first, then stabilized, then declined in real terms, most noticeably for the Air Force. After launching a buildup to close the missile gap, which had turned out to be illusory, and to increase the Army's conventional fighting posture, McNamara kept the lid on spending. The PPBS system worked to slow the development process by requiring periodic reviews and approval, and the budgets reflected this with larger portions devoted to research and development and smaller to procurement.

Two months after taking office, the president sent a message to Congress seeking substantial increases in defense spending–a net increase of almost $2 billion, or nearly 5 percent above the final Eisenhower request. The funds went primarily for a larger Polaris missile submarine fleet, airlift, and thirteen thousand more military personnel. Cuts of $750 million were proposed in the B-70 bomber program and the nuclear-powered airplane.[51] When a crisis arose over Berlin in the summer of 1961, Kennedy sought further increases: another $3 billion for defense, two more Army divisions, and the call-up of 150,000 reservists.

The basic changes McNamara sought in U.S. strategic forces and associated budgets were a reduction in bombers–the retirement of the overseas-based B-47 and rejection of a new B-70–and an increase in long-range missiles, starting with the Navy's Polaris missiles and submarine. He also saw no need to keep vulnerable land-based missiles in Europe. These decisions brought him into sharpest conflict with the Air Force and its patrons on Capitol Hill. Congress added funds for the B-70 and insisted that the president spend them. The controversy simmered until the president persuaded Carl Vinson, chair of the Armed Services Committee, in a stroll in the Rose Garden in March 1962, not to press the issue to a constitutional crisis.[52]

Even on minor things, McNamara stressed the importance of cost-effectiveness, such as through greater commonality. "Early on, McNamara held a 'fashion show' in his conference room attended by his civilian and military deputies. The different services' belts and butchers' smocks and women's bloomers were modeled, as were jackets, caps, boots, and other things. As each item was shown, McNamara decided on the spot which of the versions would henceforth by used by all the services." He also used the occasion to stress the value of making quick decisions.[53]

McNamara's approach to cost-effectiveness led to his second major clash with Congress over his insistence that the Navy and Air Force build a common next generation aircraft, the TFX (TFE). This challenged both service prerogatives and operating requirements. Neither wanted to compromise its perceived needs to accommodate those of the other. The Navy, for example, needed low weight for carrier operations, and the Air Force wanted the greater weight required for supersonic dash. The secretary imposed common requirements on the services, then caught flak as the cost estimates rose. He spent much of 1963 defending his decisions in front of congressional committees prodded to act by losing contractors and disgruntled officers. One of the nagging issues was that McNamara had overruled the design review team and had chosen General Dynamics over Boeing, which seemed to have more political than technical advantages.[54] Eventually only the Air Force version was procured, and became known as the FB 111.

He forced reluctant military leaders to accept new organizations and technology as well as previously neglected missions. With the president's strong encouragement, he set up the Green Berets. He pushed air mobility with helicopter cavalry. He insisted on building a new close air support plane, the A-7. He forced unpopular increases in the C-5A for airlift and tried unsuccessfully to launch a program for Fast Deployment Logistic (FDL) ships to carry ground combat equipment.[55] These were not his ideas alone, but his sponsorship enabled them to overcome service resistance. In the Vietnam War, he advocated other technological innovations—remotely piloted vehicles and laser-guided bombs and construction of a physical barrier to block North Vietnamese infiltration into the South, which the press labeled the "McNamara Line."

As manager of the Pentagon, McNamara largely succeeded. Indeed, he engineered a revolution in budgeting and civilian control which has lasted to this day. He seized upon the legal authority to organize and direct activities, brought in his own team of advisers and subordinates, forced everyone to speak in the new language of systems analysis, and added weapons and a force structure which lasted a generation. Where he lost public esteem—and perhaps his own self-confidence—was when he tried to apply the logic of numbers to the jungles of Southeast Asia.

War Planner

The first war McNamara tackled was the one everyone hoped to avoid: a nuclear exchange between the United States and the Soviet Union. The Eisenhower strategy had been called massive retaliation and was based on the idea that the threat of nuclear attack would deter both nuclear and conventional conflicts between the nuclear powers. The Kennedy administration thought that such threats were unbelievable to an enemy and inadequate for dealing with inevitable problems. The new president wanted a flexible response that gave him options other than surrender or annihilation.

Throughout the 1950s, the military services had fought over who should have the lead in nuclear weaponry. Each wanted its own systems—bombers in the Air Force, carrier-based planes in the Navy, and rockets in the Army. Only late in 1960 did Defense Secretary Gates succeed in forcing the services to agree to a single, coordinated nuclear war plan, the Single Integrated Operational Plan (SIOP), developed by a joint service target planning staff. When he got his first briefing on the SIOP, in early February 1961, McNamara was shocked to learn that it was really a first strike plan: it foresaw multiple weapons on each target, held nothing in reserve, and would kill millions of people whose only crime was to be victims of Communist rule. When he asked why Albania, which had shown some independence from Moscow, still had to be destroyed, Gen. Tommy Power pointed to a Soviet air defense radar within its territory and said, "I hope you don't have any friends or relations in Albania, because we're just going to have to wipe it out."[56]

Appalled by what he heard, McNamara set out to change the strategy. The intellectual foundations for an alternative came from civilians who had entered the nuclear fraternity during the 1950s. A RAND study had demonstrated the extreme vulnerability of bombers to attacks on their bases. Others in think tanks were beginning to formulate new concepts for understanding the utility of nuclear weapons–first strike, second strike, counterforce, minimum deterrence, and so on–terms which senior military leaders dismissed as "quasi-military shibboleths."[57] McNamara learned of a study by the Weapons Systems Evaluation Group (WSEG) which also concluded that existing B-47 and B-58 bombers should be scrapped, that the B-70 was too costly and vulnerable, that a new Minuteman ICBM would be better than the existing Atlas and Titan, and that the Polaris missile and submarine would be least vulnerable of all.[58] The WSEG study also argued that a competition to develop counterforce weapons–to attack enemy missiles and bombers–was essentially unwinnable.

These ideas appealed to McNamara on financial and moral grounds. They provided a rationale for limiting the number of nuclear weapons and limiting their likely use to controlled choices rather than spasms of destruction. He asked the JCS chairman, Gen. Lyman Lemnitzer, to "prepare a 'doctrine' which, if accepted, would permit controlled response and negotiating pauses in the event of a nuclear attack." Lemnitzer responded on April 18 saying that the United States should not "risk withholding a substantial part of our effort, once a major nuclear attack has been initiated." He concluded that "attempts at the present time to implement such a doctrine, or to declare such an intent, would be premature and could gravely weaken our deterrent posture."[59]

Rejecting that military view, McNamara drew upon his civilian advisers and worked to fashion a new strategy. Although it was debated in terms of flexible response and the avoidance of attacks on cities, the underlying idea was that of signaling and bargaining in the midst of nuclear war: "controlled response and negotiating pauses." The new nuclear clerisy, the civilian war gamers, believed that nuclear exchanges could and should be restrained. They believed that leaders would recognize and respond to limitations in the attacks against them by reciprocal restraint, while the threat of even worse devastation would compel them to negotiate.

As McNamara explained to the president in a 1961 memorandum, "We might try to knock out most of the Soviet strategic nuclear forces, while keeping Russian cities intact, and then coerce the Soviets into avoiding our cities (by the threat of controlled reprisal) and accepting our peace terms. . . . I believe that the coercive strategy is a sensible and desirable option to have in second-strike circumstances in which we are trying to make the best of bad situation."[60] These beliefs in rational calculation and the possibility of control in nuclear war were fundamental to McNamara and his acolytes, and they ultimately became the assumptions underlying the subsequent debates about arms control and missile defense.

McNamara also seized upon the numbers which proved to him the futility of an unrestrained arms race. One 1964 study concluded that for each dollar the Soviets added to their strike forces, the United States would have to spend three dollars to protect 70 percent of its industry, two dollars to save 60 percent, and at least one dollar to defend 40 percent. Even the JCS analyses acknowledged that the Soviets could add to their offense more cheaply than the U.S. could add to its defense.[61]

Armed with those numbers and determined to find a better way, McNamara spent the next several years developing and implementing the new doctrine that he wanted. He scrapped many of the bombers, accelerated the missile programs, capped the number of Minuteman ICBMs at a politically acceptable one thousand, and tried to educate political leaders at home and abroad of the benefits of trying to avoid attacks on cities and people by concentrating on offensive military forces. He unleashed his civilian aides on this project and provoked in response the anger expressed by General White and others. Through his control of the weapons programs and his power to sign off on the SIOP, he was able to achieve the changes he sought. He also cajoled the Chiefs in meeting after meeting to win their open support for Kennedy's major arms control achievement, the 1963 Limited Test Ban Treaty.[62]

At this distance it may be hard to appreciate how virulent the debates were as the civilian game theorists, enamored of their elegant calculations about the rational ways to fight a nuclear war, challenged the military officers who were convinced that more and bigger and better weapons deterred better than self-restraint and who doubted that the enemy would notice and reciprocate the signals and restraints built into the flexible response. Each side was convinced of the wisdom of its views. Fortunately, neither approach has been tested in nuclear conflict.

Vietnam was the real war that McNamara planned and managed. He applied the same notions he used for nuclear war, fixated on numbers to measure its progress as he did on other Pentagon activities, and dominated the internal and public debates on the subject.

He came to the problem convinced, with the rest of the Kennedy administration, that Communists could and should be stopped from advancing in Southeast Asia. He urged putting troops in Thailand to help defend Laos in early 1961 when some military advisers were more reluctant. He traveled to Vietnam with General Taylor and recommended plans to increase U.S. military assistance. He did not seem to second-guess the military, or impose his own designs, on the conflict until it became a major U.S. war in 1965.

By then Lyndon Johnson was president, a man who respected and trusted McNamara, but who was unwilling to sacrifice his Great Society domestic programs by calling up the reserves or increasing taxes. Johnson wanted victory, but at an acceptable cost, a challenge perfectly suited to the defense secretary's way of thinking.

As Fred Kaplan argues, "By early 1965 McNamara's Vietnam strategy was essentially a conventional-war version of the counterforce/no-cities theory—using force as an instrument of coercion, withholding a larger force that could kill the hostage of the enemy's cities if he didn't back down."[63]

He picked targets for their political and psychological value more than their military value. He supported bombing raids to demonstrate American resolve and punish the aggressors. He supported bombing pauses intended to demonstrate U.S. willingness to de-escalate the conflict. The concept was "graduated pressure," built on images of ratchets and spigots that could be tightened and loosened. It was also described as "squeeze and talk."[64] Target lists were approved one week at a time, to allow such careful calibration.[65] It is wrong to say that Johnson "picked" targets contrary to military advice. Rather, he deselected certain targets—particular those near the Chinese border or the cities of Hanoi and Haiphong—from the military's recommended list. But those deletions sometimes complicated the attack plans and put pilots at greater risk.

While constraining the air war, McNamara generally supported the main local commander's requests for more ground troops. They were part of the arithmetic of the war. From the start he wanted "measurable criteria" to assess the conflict. He counted weapons shipped, enemy weapons captured, strategic hamlets pacified, enemy and friendly dead, bomb tonnages dropped. When he traveled to the war zone, he insisted on briefings filled with those numbers. They were his reality, and the military commanders complied. And he proudly told the world, as he did in May 1962 during his first trip to the war zone, "every quantitative measurement we have shows that we're winning this war."[66] When coups and defeats led to different numbers, they became the new baseline from which to measure progress.

Eventually, however, his views began to differ from those of the Chiefs, and even of the president. The Chiefs and the commander in the field wanted still more troops and more widespread bombing, hitting targets near the big cities of Hanoi and Haiphong and closer to the Chinese border. While more troops were sent over time, the president obviously wanted to limit the commitment. And he rejected on political and diplomatic grounds the targets deemed too sensitive.

McNamara also went to great lengths—some argue that he did so with lies and deceit—to maintain a public appearance of civil-military harmony on prosecuting the war. Many in Congress later felt misled by his strident testimony in the mid-1960s, and the Chiefs themselves came close to mass resignation in the summer of 1967.

Despite his public cheerleading for the war, McNamara became privately dubious about its wisdom and effectiveness. The numbers didn't add up; neither the pain of bombing nor the possibility of negotiation had the desired effect. By late 1965 he was airing doubts in private. The president was concerned about his health and his commitment. Eventually in 1967, Johnson arranged for his defense secretary to depart for a job as head of the World Bank, where McNamara's humanitarian instincts were married to a different set of numbers.

As a war planner, McNamara sought military advice but felt free to make independent judgments and to offer his own ideas. Unlike many in uniform, who believed that the only acceptable goal of the war was total victory, he believed that the war had to be limited in both ends and means. He kept track of the means, calculating and recalculating the cost-effectiveness of various actions. Only in retrospect did he acknowledge his doubts.

Diplomat

Previous secretaries of defense had left foreign policy issues largely to the president and secretary of state. There had been an assistant secretary of defense for international security affairs since 1953, but McNamara empowered this position, named the experienced and assertive Paul Nitze to the post, and let it grow into a "little State Department" that could hold its own, or better, with Foggy Bottom. This office was responsible for coordinating issues with State when the need arose and for following international developments with a DOD perspective.

McNamara took these routine responsibilities to new heights. Nitze provided, and he welcomed, ideas and point papers for use in White House discussions. When State was slow to develop an action plan to deal with Berlin in the spring of 1961, McNamara offered his own, Pentagon-drafted version, and found the president receptive. The DOD team knew and followed the rules of the bureaucratic game: the first paper on the street usually sets the framework for decision and action.[67]

Publicly, McNamara disavowed any DOD role in foreign policy. Indeed, his justification for muzzling his generals and admirals and censoring their speeches was that "it's inappropriate for any member of the Defense Department to speak on the subject of foreign policy." He told a reporter, "That applies to me as well as it does to all of the presidential appointees, all of the military officers, and all of the high civilian officials in the department."[68]

In practice, however, McNamara was very active in foreign policy issues, and not only those with a military dimension. As Roger Hilsman observed from his State Department post, "McNamara's boundless energy and formidable ability . . . sometimes tempted him to use whatever military component there was in a political problem as a beachhead. Occasionally he extended the beachhead until he came very near to dominating the whole affair." Hilsman cites relations with India and Europe, starting with Berlin, as well as Vietnam.[69]

One of his major areas of interest was Europe. NATO was a military alliance, so the secretary of defense was necessarily involved in its meetings and planning. McNamara was particularly concerned about changing NATO's strategy to bolster non-nuclear defenses so that the early use of nuclear weapons could be avoided, and that required numerous meetings and consultations. He worked with State Department officials in fashioning proposals for a multilateral nuclear force for Europe. To a large extent he supplemented the efforts of the State Department and did not run an alternative foreign policy.

His bureaucratic proclivities—generating ideas, offering point papers, responding faster than State to White House requests—made it only natural for him to become a major player on foreign policy. As one official put it, "Rusk believed that doing nothing was sometimes the wiser course; McNamara felt that inaction was almost always a mistake. When Rusk appeared to leave a vacuum, McNamara filled it."[70] He decided that the secretary of defense should issue an annual report explaining and justifying the defense programs. But that required an analysis of threats and objectives, which necessarily raised foreign policy considerations.

An official at State, said to be an admirer of McNamara, recounted, "What happened over here was that everyone went right up the wall. Everyone except the secretary of state." When the diplomats complained of poaching, Rusk "just smiled and shrugged."[71] McNamara took pains to show Rusk what he was proposing to say, but the secretary of state never challenged McNamara's report or offered his own. That would not occur until Henry Kissinger seized the reins of power in the Nixon administration.

So effective was McNamara in all that he did in the early years of the Kennedy aministration that he was given to understand that he was likely to be named to succeed Rusk after the 1964 election.[72]

NSC Adviser

One of the most important roles of the secretary of defense is as one of the statutory members of the National Security Council, along with the president, vice president, and secretary of state. The chairman of the JCS and the director of central intelligence are only statutory advisers. Each president has also designated others to sit in on formal deliberations during his administration. In that capacity, McNamara participated in the White House meetings on the full range of national security issues throughout the Kennedy and Johnson administrations.

After his initial reticence during the Bay of Pigs discussions, he became more assertive during subsequent crises. When Kennedy wanted to be tough on Berlin, McNamara offered the Army expansion and callup of reserves that the president accepted. During the Cuban Missile Crisis, he initially dismissed the threat of Soviet missiles ninety miles from Florida as not affecting the overall military balance, though he acknowledged it was a political problem.[73] Kennedy and others disagreed, seeing the weapons in Cuba as both a political threat at home and in Berlin and as a challenge to the administration's very public red line against any such deployments.

As the senior officials struggled to devise a response, McNamara was one who saw the advantages of a "quarantine," even while preparing forces for a possible invasion of the island. He emerged from that crisis sobered by the prospects of nuclear war and ever more determined to maintain civilian control over military plans and operations. He later deposed Adm. George Anderson, the chief of naval operations, who had challenged his interfering questions about the naval blockade and who later criticized the TFX decisions in congressional testimony.[74]

Many political scientists believe that officials tend to "stand where they sit"; that is, they take policy positions that reflect their organization's interests and preferences. McNamara seems to have done that, in the sense that he represented DOD views and approached problems from a Pentagon perspective by looking for military options to contribute to overall policy. But he ventured opinions on non-military subjects and was forceful in every argument he joined. He could not sit back and be quiet, and his two presidents welcomed his contributions.

Although he had never run for office or been especially partisan, he entered the 1964 campaign with gusto. With Barry Goldwater challenging LBJ's defense and foreign policy as the centerpiece of his campaign, McNamara defended administration policy openly and frequently, including highly political testimony before the Democratic convention's platform committee. He had strong White House encouragement to do so. Perhaps there was no way for partisanship to stop at the water's edge. In any event, McNamara was not one to shrink from the fight.[75]

Evaluation

Robert McNamara engineered a revolution in the Pentagon, a radical change in the structure and processes of the armed forces, in their strategy, even in their language and concepts. He proved that the Pentagon was manageable, that costs could be identified and somewhat controlled, that bureaucratic resistance to change could be overcome. At a time when many were concerned about military influence over policy, he was the "civilian on horseback"[76] who controlled and dominated the uniformed military. He altered nuclear strategy in ways that made the world safer for decades to come and oversaw a conventional war he couldn't win and couldn't escape. He became the model against which all of his successors have measured themselves, not always to emulate but often to judge their own strengths.

4

Schlesinger:
The Independence of Ideas

I don't want to see that guy in my office again.

–Richard Nixon after his first meeting with Schlesinger[1]

He was obviously unsuccessful in dealing with Congress, and his rivalry with Kissinger was making me increasingly uncomfortable. But I must admit that his aloof, frequently arrogant manner put me off.

–Gerald Ford on Schlesinger[2]

James Rodney Schlesinger bungled the first meeting he had with each of the presidents he served. He irritated Richard Nixon in 1970 by the way he discussed some Pentagon budget matters. In his first meeting with the new vice president, Gerald Ford, he was stiff, doctrinaire, and incapable of small talk. He didn't help his standing with these men by his tendency to enter the Oval Office with tie loosened, then sit in an armchair and drape one leg over the armrest.[3]

Although he had prepared most of his adult life to be a secretary of defense, at least intellectually, he never mastered the personal and political skills which are also key requirements for success in the job. Born in New York in 1929, Schlesinger went to Harvard in the same class as Henry Kissinger (though the two did not know each other then) and stayed on for an MA and PhD in economics. He taught and wrote on defense economics, moving to RAND in 1963. One of his most notable, or notorious, academic works was a 1963 article criticizing the heavy reliance on quantitative analysis of national security issues–and thus challenging what McNamara with his stable of RAND analysts was doing at the time. He wrote, "One ought not deceive oneself: when choosing among weapon systems, one is selecting a strategy—a decision into which, under the best of circumstances, some degree of prayer and hope must be infused."[4]

His hobby was bird-watching, and he had logged over six hundred different species by the time he became secretary of defense.[5] He had eight children and little interest in Washington social life. He smoked a pipe, spoke in paragraphs and sometimes whole chapters, and showed disdain for lesser mortals. He was rumpled in dress though sharp in mind and argument.

A self-described "Taft Republican," he joined the Nixon administration as the assistant director of the Bureau of the Budget for defense and intelligence programs. His Washington career was almost cut short when his name was linked to a *Wall Street Journal* article laying out arguments against the defense budget, especially the B-1 bomber. Defense Secretary Laird sent word: "Keep quiet, Schlesinger, or you'll find yourself back at RAND."[6]

Despite that misstep, his otherwise strong performance there impressed the White House, which began considering him for higher posts. He was in line to be undersecretary of the interior until blocked by objections from western senators who wanted someone from their region. He was then named head of the Atomic Energy Commission (AEC), the agency that designed and built America's nuclear weapons. At the AEC, Schlesinger showed his management talents and budget-squeezing proclivities in implementing well-received reorganization plans. He cut hundreds of personnel, fixed problems in weapons production, and streamlined licensing procedures for nuclear power plants.[7] At AEC and later at the CIA he seemed to relish firing people. When an aide suggested his cuts appeared ruthless, he replied, "Ruthless? I'm just trying to clear the aisle so I can walk."[8]

Such displays of managerial toughness endeared him to his political superiors even as they angered many subordinates. In July 1971, he earned even greater admiration at the White House by his gutsy response to environmentalists protesting the planned underground testing of a nuclear weapon in the Aleutian island of Amchitka. Schlesinger took his wife and two of his children to the island during the test to prove his confidence in its safety.[9]

In January 1973 Nixon named him the new director of central intelligence, replacing Richard Helms. Knowing the costs and benefits of intelligence community activities from his time in the Bureau of the Budget, Schlesinger applied his proven managerial approach of reorganization and layoffs. "The trouble with this place," he said, "is that it has been run like a gentleman's club."[10] In his first four months he asked over one thousand CIA employees to resign or retire, prompting such an angry backlash that his personal security detail had to be increased. At the same time, he was open and forthcoming to Congress regarding CIA misbehavior, including its involvement in the Watergate scandal.

Despite that additional, though minor, wound to the Nixon administration, the president elevated Schlesinger to Defense when he needed to shift Elliott Richardson to Justice. In the Pentagon, Schlesinger found an intellectual home, the place where his intelligence and energy could best be spent.

In fact, except for Charles Wilson, who was already a business executive at the time of World War I, and Neil McElroy, who was too young for that war and too old for the next, Schlesinger was the first secretary of defense who had never served in the armed forces, although many of his cohort had spent time in uniform. He was the prototypical pipe-smoking, ivory tower civilian defense intellectual who thought his ideas about nuclear strategy were at least equal to those of anyone else. He had the arrogance of a brilliant man and the self-confidence to resist the views of others. He was fiercely independent because of the strength of his ideas.

As secretary of defense, he did not really see himself as the deputy commander in chief—as his position in the chain of command suggests—but rather as the guide and supporter of the armed forces, providing strategic guidance and resources without interfering in the details of military organization and planning. With America's combat role in Vietnam ending, he saw himself as a "revivalist" for the postwar military, one who had

James Schlesinger at a news conference. *Washington Post*

"to buoy up the Department."[11] He considered the office weak, providing the secretary "simply with a *license to persuade* outside parties."[12] He regarded himself as a strategist, not a politician.[13]

He had no specific written or oral directions from President Nixon as to how to run his department or what issues to tackle. So Schlesinger concentrated on those areas where he had special interests and expertise: "strategy and deployment and weapon system selection," particularly the strategic nuclear forces and issues.[14] He was forced to deal with other problems as they arose, of course, but he always returned to his priorities.

He drew important lessons from his predecessors. He admired McNamara as "a great secretary of defense and a terrible secretary of war." He praised Laird's political skills but criticized his limited attention to substantive policy matters.[15] Schlesinger sought to tip the balance back under his tenure, to focus on the substance rather than the politics of issues.

Yet he acknowledged, years later, that the job is nearly impossible. In 1983 "ruminations" on the office he had held, he said that "the list of secretarial responsibilities is so imposing that no single individual can fulfill them all."[16] He should be counted as one of the "Revolutionaries" because he consciously sought and partly succeeded in imposing major changes on the Pentagon. He never let the inevitable "fires" distract him from his strategic goals.

Political Relations

The Nixon White House was under siege during Schlesinger's first year in office. Distracted by Watergate, bereft of his key aides, and preoccupied with limiting the damage from congressional hearings, newspaper exposes, and court proceedings, Nixon had no time either to oversee or support Schlesinger in his quest. His chief of staff, however, was one of Schlesinger's chief patrons in Washington. Alexander Haig had been instrumental in pushing his name for ever more important posts.[17]

Nixon was aware of Schlesinger's limitations, especially his political inexperience and ineptitude. While at the Budget Bureau, he frequently got instructive notes from the White House scheduler: "Schlesinger is to be here for the substantive discussion, but is not to be here for the political discussion." Despite the rebuff, Schlesinger respected Nixon for his broad knowledge and deep involvement in policy issues and his ability to be reflective. He often found it hard, however, to figure out precisely what was on the president's mind or what he was really thinking about a particular policy.[18] Nixon mentions Schlesinger only four times, and only in passing, in his thousand-page memoir.

When Gerald Ford became president upon Nixon's resignation, he already had doubts about Schlesinger, but since he believed that America needed stability and continuity, he said he did not want and would not accept any resignations from his cabinet. But he later wrote of his defense secretary, "Our personal relationship, which had never been good, slid downhill after I became president."[19] The problem was that Schlesinger had tried to solve a dispute between two House committee chairs by siding with one and publicly lambasting the other, who happened to be the chairman of the Appropriations Committee. Ford had to step in and resolve the conflict, which he blamed on Schlesinger. Ford then made disparaging comments on background to a reporter. Since he couldn't deny that he was the source, he apologized to Schlesinger for the adverse publicity, but not for any inaccuracy. "Jim, that's the way I feel," he said. He urged the defense secretary to broaden his base of congressional support.[20]

Despite Ford's admonition, Schlesinger developed only mixed relations with Congress. He found some allies on policy grounds, including his strong supporter and patron, Senator Henry M. "Scoop" Jackson (D-Wash.), but also managed to alienate some of the Hill barons, such as House Appropriations Committee Chairman George Mahon (D-Tex.). Democrats were strongly in control of Congress, particularly after the 1974 "Watergate elections," so the administration necessarily needed to build bridges to the political opposition. In Schlesinger's case, however, he probably overstepped the line by his close relationship to Scoop Jackson, who since 1972 had been an active opponent of the Kissinger policy of arms control and détente with the Soviet Union. Schlesinger later acknowledged that he regularly supplied information to Jackson to help the senator's efforts to challenge administration policy.[21]

His basic political problem with Congress was that the legislative branch wanted a peace dividend after Vietnam, and it seized upon the Nixon-Ford strategy of détente with the Soviet Union as proof that defense spending could be cut back. There were some advocates of military modernization in Congress, but little enthusiasm for the whole panoply of new systems the Pentagon was pushing. So the most he could achieve was tactical alliances on particular programs rather than full-spectrum cooperation on increases.

For over a year, Ford tolerated Schlesinger, his pontifications, his disrespectful habits, such as sprawling over Oval Office furniture while leaving his tie askew, and his public disputes with Henry Kissinger. Eventually Ford sided with his secretary of state on substance and politics, and fired his secretary of defense. The personal chemistry became too volatile. Schlesinger later acknowledged his prickly personality. "I tended to be self-righteous, a quibbler. Stubborn, too. It took me a while to understand how hard I must have been to deal with."[22]

While most secretaries of defense have the dual challenge of maintaining good relations with the secretary of state and the national security adviser, Schlesinger faced the singular challenge of Henry Kissinger, the man named to both jobs by Richard Nixon and kept there by Gerald Ford. Both presidents—and a fawning press corps—admired the intellectual and bureaucratic skills of the German-born, former Harvard professor. Henry—as he was known to all by that Washington shorthand which few achieve—so dominated national security policy that *Time* magazine considered him the equal of the president when it named both "Men of the Year" for 1972. There was another secretary of state during Nixon's first term, and a State Department, but they didn't matter. Policy was devised and implemented in the White House by Kissinger and Nixon.

By 1973, Schlesinger could expect only to be a bit player in the great drama. No one else considered him Henry's rival, despite his own accomplishments as an academic and defense intellectual. Yet he eventually came into conflict with Kissinger, traded punches, and held his own during a series of policy debates until he finally lost the confidence of the president. One Kissinger aide note that "their views were not as far apart as their conflicting vanities would indicate."[23]

Kissinger viewed Schlesinger as an annoyance. By 1974, he wrote, "Our internal disputes were no longer geared to substance; they had become a struggle for preeminence. Schlesinger and I battled over turf continually; every issue, whether it was the Strategic Arms Limitation Agreement (SALT) or human rights or Cyprus, became a source of tension between us."[24] These constant clashes reached the press since each man had incentives and skills to press his views publicly, and they frustrated Ford, who felt that the bickering conveyed an image of administration disarray and presidential weakness.

Civil-Military Relations

Schlesinger had additional problems within the Pentagon. He did not like and repeatedly tried to remove his deputy, Texas oilman William Clements, who had been named six months before Schlesinger moved into place. He said Clements had "a strong personality that was somewhat unguided," and was "forceful but lacking in judgment."[25] He thought that Clements coveted his own job. He also suspected the oilman of violating his pledge to recuse himself from any matters relating to oil.

Given these suspicions, Schlesinger had a tense relationship with his deputy and refused to give him much authority. Most secretaries treat their deputy either as an alter ego who can substitute for them in any role, or as the "inside man," managing the Pentagon while the secretary is the public face before Congress and in the NSC. Schlesinger was reluctant to give Clements either role, preferring instead to limit him to working out lesser problems that arose between the services over programs and budgets.[26]

With military leaders, he tried to maintain close and cordial relations.

He had weekly meeting with the Chiefs in their Tank, but with a difference. He sometimes served as briefer, lecturing them at length with his views and his own slides, rather than sitting as a recipient of their views.[27] He had grudging respect for the chairman of the JCS, Adm. Thomas Moorer, but was eager to name a successor with expertise and enthusiasm for dealing with strategic nuclear issues. He picked Air Force Gen. George Brown, to whom he became especially close, and named Gen. David Jones as Air Force chief of staff. He had strong political and programmatic ties to the outgoing chief of naval operations, Adm. Elmo Zumwalt, and named his successor. He greatly admired the ailing Army chief of staff, Gen. Creighton Abrams, and settled a major force-sizing issue with him as part of his grand strategy.[28]

He picked the people for the JCS and negotiated grand bargains with them on manpower and budget issues, described below. But they still remained somewhat skeptical of him. In the days before Nixon's resignation, he took steps which puzzled and troubled them. Concerned that the besieged president might resist the constitutional removal from office as the impeachment process played out during the summer of 1974, Schlesinger instructed the JCS that "any emergency order coming from the president" be shown to the other Chiefs and to the secretary of defense.[29] The Chiefs were puzzled–and offended that their civilian boss would doubt their fidelity to the Constitution. As things turned out, Nixon issued no bizarre orders and the transfer of power occurred smoothly. But Gerald Ford was also offended by Schlesinger's actions, viewing them as a stab in the back of the military.[30] Perhaps, too, Schlesinger seemed unduly disloyal to the man who had named him to high office.

Operating Style

Unlike business executives or military officers, who set up regular processes for staff advice and line management, Schlesinger ran his office informally and non-hierarchically. He had a "kitchen cabinet" of aides he had previously worked with, and he met most often with them to hash out courses of action. He did not have systematic senior staff meetings, but met only occasionally. He had the regular habit–quite annoying to his schedulers–of getting involved in intellectually fascinating conversation about a subject for hours at a time. His daily schedule often was totally ignored as he pursued conversation with someone about a subject of interest to the secretary–often an arcane concept of nuclear strategy. Some of his subordinates learned their lesson and did not even leave their offices for a planned meeting until they were sure that Schlesinger was in his office and available. As with another engaging intellectual who became SecDef, Les Aspin, Schlesinger lost some respect from others in the Pentagon because of his lack of organization and punctuality.[31]

Civilian control to him meant the right to lead and, if necessary, to choose. But he did not want to interfere in nonstrategic matters. Where nuclear weapons or the U.S.–Soviet military balance were concerned, he wanted to be on top. But on programmatic questions like Army tanks and Air Force bombers, he was indifferent. He had some ideas for efficiencies, but little passion for nonstrategic issues. Sometimes he quoted McNamara: "One can only slay so many dragons each day."[32]

Schlesinger trusted his own judgment on nuclear matters and was unafraid to espouse and defend his positions, even against Henry Kissinger (or perhaps one should say, especially against Henry Kissinger). He had stronger ideological loyalty than personal loyalty, a stronger commitment to his co-believers than to his colleagues, as he showed in the arms control disputes during the Nixon and Ford administrations. Where he cared deeply, he was rigid and unyielding; where he did not see fundamental issues at stake, he was quite willing to bargain.

Manager of the Pentagon

With Vietnam winding down, Schlesinger knew that Congress would want to cut back military spending. In fact, he got his presidents to propose increases which the legislative branch pruned sharply. He knew that budgetary success required a compelling case demonstrating urgent need coupled with evidence of sound management and cost control. He also knew that the military services were anxious and needed strong and effective civilian support.

So he bargained. Starting with Army Chief Abrams, he offered a giant carrot and stick. If the Army would stay within the manpower ceilings Schlesinger wanted for budget reasons, it could have three more divisions, going from thirteen to sixteen, and could reorganize the people as it chose. He also agreed to support several big-ticket Army weapons programs. This deal gave the Army two things it desperately craved: a manpower floor against deeper cuts and management flexibility instead of OSD interference. It gave Schlesinger the budgets he could sell, along with a strong argument: more teeth and less tail.[33]

The Air Force was offered a similar "golden handshake." It could add four additional fighter wings, from twenty-two to twenty-six, provided that it agreed to a "high-low mix" of F-15s and the new F-16s.[34] The Air Force agreed because it wanted more force structure and was willing to tolerate large numbers of the less "sexy" F-16.

Working with his friend and fellow arms control skeptic, Admiral Zumwalt, he tried to encourage the Navy to move toward a larger number of lower-cost ships. They were in agreement, but many in Congress doubted the value of small ships.[35]

In each case, Schlesinger showed his management style: offer incentives to do what he wanted, force tradeoffs, but grant autonomy of execution. The services welcomed this approach, at least so long as it proved an effective strategy for winning congressional support as well. On Capitol Hill, however, the outcomes were less clear-cut because Congress as a whole sought peace dividend reductions in defense spending.

Schlesinger also stressed improvements in near-term combat capability, for he believed that only the secretary of defense could be the "patron of readiness." Faced with force structure and modernization demands, he feared pressure to skimp on readiness, but he insisted that such pressures should be resisted.[36] This fear reflected the political reality that Congress was more responsive to arguments about force structure and weapons procurement, because each related to jobs back home, and used cuts in operations and maintenance accounts, which affected readiness, as bill payers for legislative cuts or add-ons. In fact, military readiness continued to decline after Vietnam and became a major political problem for President Carter in the 1980 presidential campaign.

War Planner

Schlesinger's primary personal goal as secretary was to change America's nuclear war strategy.[37] The SIOP was essentially the same one that McNamara fashioned a decade earlier, but the strategic balance seemed more perilous because of the development of Soviet missiles that could destroy even hardened Minuteman silos. Schlesinger believed that the United States needed both a more survivable retaliatory force and a more credible capability to attack Soviet military targets. Like McNamara, Schlesinger embraced the game theorists' notions of graduated reprisals, questioned the morality of threatening Soviet cities, and favored the development of multiple options so that the United States could respond to any sort of attack flexibly and commensurately. But he distanced himself from McNamara's criterion of "assured destruction" (usually seen as the ability to survive a Soviet first strike and still destroy at least 25 percent of Soviet population and over half its industry) by joining the critics who renamed it "mutual assured destruction" so that they could call it MAD. Like McNamara, he concluded that Soviet conventional forces were not nearly as formidable as their numbers would suggest and he sought to strengthen allied forces in Europe. But his willingness to actually plan fighting a nuclear war in Europe made allied officials and their publics nervous.

While he was instrumental in advocating and articulating the revised nuclear warfighting strategy, he built upon work already under way in the Nixon administration. Kissinger had commissioned a broad strategic review in 1969 and later a nuclear weapons employment plan (NUWEP). Developed by a coterie of civilian theorists working in the Pentagon and for the NSC, this new approach was contained in a draft presidential policy paper that languished for months in the NSC staff. To force the issue, Schlesinger went public in a speech to the Overseas Writers Association on January 10, 1974, and announced that there had been "a change in the strategies of the United States with regard to the hypothetical employment of central strategic forces, a change in targeting strategy, as it were."[38] A week later the president formally signed National Security Decision Memorandum 242 codifying the policy.[39]

To help him explain the new strategy, Schlesinger brought back to the Pentagon MIT professor William Kaufman as a speechwriter, consultant, and general adviser, who had done some similar work for McNamara.[40] Schlesinger coupled this declaratory policy of flexibility with new programs designed to enhance U.S. capability to implement it, especially greater missile accuracy for hitting hardened targets and a maneuvering reentry vehicle (MaRV) that could evade Soviet missile defenses.

His nuclear theories shaped Schlesinger's responses to a broad range of foreign policy issues facing the Nixon and Ford administrations. His fears of Soviet capability made him dubious of arms control agreements that codified equality, especially since the parity was in numbers of weapons rather than in fighting power, particularly megatonnage and warheads. His conviction that the Russians had aggressive intentions and superb deceptive skills made him reluctant to conclude even supposedly verifiable agreements. His sense of history, of a Soviet Union gaining momentum while the United States drifted in complacency, made him an ardent voice for rearmament. These views put him at odds with Kissinger and with the détente policies of Nixon and Ford, but they drew him closer to the growing chorus of hardliners within and outside the administration.

Schlesinger also had to manage some military operations in the final weeks of the collapsing South Vietnamese government. His conduct was unsurprising, consistent with the military advice he received. He pressed Kissinger to begin the evacuation of U.S. personnel from Vietnam for practical reasons, but the secretary of state and his ambassador in Saigon resisted for symbolic reasons: they knew evacuation would signal American loss of faith in the survival of the government.

When Cambodians seized an American merchant ship, the *Mayaguez*, and held its thirty-nine-man crew hostage, everyone favored diplomatic demands and a rescue mission, if possible. But they disagreed on the larger implications of the incident. Kissinger argued that this was a test of U.S. resolve, requiring a strong response, including B-52 strikes against Cambodia. Schlesinger minimized the global significance and said that bombing was not necessary militarily or symbolically.[41]

A rescue mission went to find the crew just as the Cambodians were announcing their willingness to release the ship. Meanwhile, the crew had been moved to another ship, which then was located and the captives freed. As part of the operation, Kissinger and Ford expected that a planned bombing raid on the mainland would still be carried out as a sign of U.S. determination not to be cowed by the collapse of Vietnam. But Schlesinger apparently cancelled the attack, further feeding Ford's suspicions of his reliability as a team member.[42] The president believed there had been "high-level bumbling at the Defense Department" and that someone "had contravened my authority."[43] It is ironic that the defense secretary who saw the value of signaling intentions with nuclear weapons was unwilling to do so in the heat of conventional battle.

Diplomat

Schlesinger believed that he needed to be more active than his predecessors in foreign policy, particularly in Europe: "In alliance relations, quite frequently the secretary of defense must play a larger role than does the secretary of state."[44] NATO was America's keystone military alliance, and its success required military and diplomatic strengthening, which he sought to promote. He saw no reasons to be deterred from that mission by the sometimes conflicting views of Henry Kissinger.

In the summer of 1974, he clashed openly with the secretary of state over Turkey. When Greek Cypriots staged a coup and Turkey sent its troops into Cyprus, Schlesinger publicly suggested reassessing U.S. aid. The State Department opposed an arms embargo and fought unsuccessfully to prevent Congress from imposing one on a reluctant administration.[45]   The two officials also got into a dispute over the resupply of weapons to Israel during the October 1973 war. Kissinger wanted to aid Israel but insisted on using civilian aircraft so as not to trigger Soviet concerns about U.S. military intervention in the conflict. U.S. airlines were understandably reluctant to run the risks, so the administration had to authorize military transport, which Schlesinger promptly arranged. When Israel's supporters criticized the delays in delivering equipment, anonymous sources pointed the finger at Schlesinger.[46] This was just another in the ongoing turf battles between the two officials.

Although Kissinger had declared 1973 to be "the year of Europe," he wound up being distracted elsewhere that year and subsequently. But Schlesinger saw the need and the opportunity to engage with alliance members, especially on security issues. The defense secretary prepared a lengthy briefing, complete with highly classified satellite photos and other intelligence information, which he took to European leaders in order to convince them that the Soviet forces were not as strong as feared and that they could be countered by a conventional buildup in the alliance.[47]

Besides pushing for increased defense spending by the Europeans, Schlesinger advocated concrete steps to improve the standardization and interoperability of NATO weaponry. National procurement systems had led to a situation where, for example, many alliance aircraft could not refuel or rearm at neighboring country airfields. He signed an agreement with the Germans to evaluate their new Leopard tank against an American design, hoping that the two nations would eventually agree to procure a common system, regardless of its provenance. That approach ran into a buzz saw in Washington from members of Congress who always wanted to "buy American" and from many in the Army who didn't want anything not invented here.[48]

Schlesinger saw his greatest political challenge, throughout his tenure as secretary, as defeating congressional efforts to force a significant withdrawal of U.S. forces from Europe. The key measures were sponsored by the majority leaders in Congress, Representative Tip O'Neill (D-Mass.) and Senator Mike Mansfield (D-Mont.), thus demonstrating the strength of sentiment for troop cuts. In 1974, and only after vigorous administration lobbying, the Senate narrowly defeated a seventy-six-thousand-person cut in European troop deployments (about 17 percent) while the House more easily defeated an amendment calling for a one-hundred-thousand-person cut. The administration did have to accept a cut of thirty thousand—twelve thousand five hundred in combat troops and eighteen thousand in noncombatant support troops.[49] The post-Watergate Congress was more assertive of its prerogatives and of its domestic policy priorities.

NSC Adviser

In deliberations with the other members of the National Security Council, Schlesinger was often the contrarian, the one challenging the consensus Kissinger had already achieved with his presidential boss. The most notable and sustained dispute was over the policy of détente toward the Soviet Union and the associated negotiations for arms control agreements.

Nixon had concluded two major agreements in 1972—the Anti-Ballistic Missile (ABM) Treaty forbidding the development or deployment of national ballistic missile defense systems, which enshrined the doctrine of assured destruction and precluded much effort at damage limitation, and SALT, capping the number of strategic missiles. Schlesinger had personal doubts about the wisdom of these agreements and of the underlying policy of accommodation, and he felt few inhibitions about expressing his concerns once he joined the NSC.

Meanwhile, Kissinger was proceeding to conclude additional agreements further limiting ABM, imposing controls on long-range bombers and offsetting the Soviet advantages in missile throwweight and megatonnage that so troubled Senator Jackson, Schlesinger, and other SALT critics. The arguments may seem quaint today, couched as they were in the arcane language of nuclear weapons and based on firmly believed assumptions about rationally calculating leaders in the midst of nuclear exchanges, but they were the coin of debate and an inescapable part of public discourse. What is important for our purposes is not the details, but their pattern.

Schlesinger used the internal debates to resist any rush toward a new agreement. He raised concerns and counterproposals within the councils of government, and provided information to congressional critics which led them also to raise doubts about possible agreements. He had allies within the Executive Branch as well as on Capitol Hill. Many Pentagon civilians and military officers shared his views about the USSR and about particular restraints on weaponry. They resisted agreements which would limit American technology and capability, regardless of whether they imposed similar limits on Moscow. In this sense, Schlesinger was simply the chief point man for a phalanx of opposition to Kissinger's policies.

In June 1974, Schlesinger publicly praised a proposal by Senator Jackson that went beyond U.S. negotiating plans and was personally called on the carpet by the president. But the defense secretary stood firm and raised objections to Nixon's proposals, thus dooming the mid-summer summit with Brezhnev, the final diplomatic event before Nixon's resignation.[50]

The same battles occurred in the Ford administration as Schlesinger fought a rearguard action that made it harder for the new president to achieve the foreign policy success he desperately wanted as he fought for a full elected term. Ford came under attack not only from Democrats like Jackson but also from Republicans, most prominently Ronald Reagan, who came close to defeating the incumbent in the 1976 fight for the GOP nomination. So damaged was Ford by the conservative attacks that he had to dump his vice president, Nelson Rockefeller, and downplay his foreign policy accomplishments under Kissinger.

By October 1975, Ford had decided to get rid of Schlesinger. He certainly had cause. The defense secretary's public disputes with Kissinger created the impression that the administration was in disarray and Ford was incapable of showing strong leadership. Ford never felt comfortable with Schlesinger, and he became particularly angry when his subordinate threatened to resign if the forthcoming defense budget was not increased. The next day Schlesinger was summoned to the White House and told that he would be replaced. The stunned defense secretary argued with the president for an hour, refusing to resign when he was really being fired.[51]

Ford used the opportunity of Schlesinger's ouster to make additional changes in his administration. He also dumped CIA director William Colby and forced Kissinger to surrender his NSC hat to Brent Scowcroft. He named his chief of staff, Donald Rumsfeld, as the new defense secretary, the youngest ever appointed to that post. Rumsfeld, too, eventually came to fight with Kissinger and he succeeded in blocking any further movement on arms control prior to the elections. Schlesinger became a vocal critic of administration policy and was even brought into the new Carter administration, though in the more limited role of energy secretary.

Evaluation

Schlesinger sought to make major changes in U.S. strategy and in the Pentagon, and he succeeded to a notable degree. He was justifiably proudest of altering strategic doctrine and rebuilding NATO.[52] His operating style, however, generated opposition even from people who agreed with him in substance. He ultimately failed to keep his job because he never developed enough rapport, confidence, or support with people who could defend him when controversy arose. In particular, he failed to solidify his relationship with his two presidents. Thus, like McNamara, he left the Pentagon prematurely, a revolutionary stopped short of final victory.

5

Weinberger:
The Power of Tenacity

The minute you start making deals, they'll nibble you to death.
If you don't dig your heels in and fight, you're just going to get wasted. No deals.
No compromise. No way.

—Caspar Weinberger to Bud McFarlane[1]

I know there's always been this thing between Cap [Weinberger] and George
[Shultz]. I don't know why, but it's there. I wish they could get along with each
other better. But at my age and their age, people don't change very much. And
they are both my friends. I don't want to fire either one of them.

—Ronald Reagan to McFarlane[2]

Caspar Willard Weinberger wanted to be secretary of state in Ronald
Reagan's cabinet. The leading candidates for secretary of defense were
Al Haig and George Shultz. But the president-elect told his kitchen cabinet of longtime advisers, meeting to discuss recommendations for various
posts, that Weinberger had done so well managing California's finances
that he was needed in the Pentagon. It seemed logical to Reagan that "Cap
the Knife" should preside over his planned buildup of U.S. military forces.[3]

And he did. For six years and ten months, the former budget cutter
was a steadfast advocate for ever-higher defense spending. The second-
longest serving secretary of defense presided over a massive rearmament
program but repeatedly urged restraint in the actual use of the armed
forces. He was not a team player, nor was he content merely to fight the
fires that flared in his in-box. I count him one of the "revolutionary" secretaries of defense because he sought—and largely achieved—major changes

in the Pentagon, not in the structure or strategy of the armed forces but in their financial resources and capabilities.

Born in San Francisco in 1917, Weinberger grew up an avid reader, fascinated by history, and deeply interested in public affairs. His father told him bedtime stories about the Constitutional Convention and took him to campaign events for Herbert Hoover, whom the young boy considered a hero. Not content with the local press coverage of the New Deal, the teenage Weinberger asked his congressman to send him copies of the *Congressional Record*, which he then read assiduously.[4]

He went east to Harvard College, where he wrote "fierce, biting, heavily ironic" and one-sidedly conservative editorials for the *Harvard Crimson*, of which he became the president.[5] He stayed on for Harvard Law, finishing in 1941. A few months later, even before Pearl Harbor, Weinberger enlisted in the Army as a private and was sent to the South Pacific, where he won a Bronze Star and served on General MacArthur's staff. He was sent home as a captain in 1945. The chief lesson he derived from his military experience was the danger of inadequate preparedness.

Returning to California, he became active and successful in state politics. He served three terms in the state assembly, lost a primary fight for attorney general, hosted a public affairs program on local television for nine years, wrote frequent newspaper columns, and was chairman of the California Republican State Central Committee from 1962–64. Ronald Reagan recruited him as director of finance despite the fact that Weinberger had supported another candidate in the gubernatorial primary. The two men formed a close working relationship, and Weinberger became one of Reagan's political advisers in his subsequent campaign for the White House.

He gained significant Washington experience after Richard Nixon named him to head the Federal Trade Commission in 1970, and a few months later made him deputy to George Shultz at the Office of Management and Budget (OMB). He moved up to be director of OMB in 1972 and was then made secretary of health, education, and welfare in 1973. His skill at paring budgets earned him the label "Cap the Knife." He returned to private life in California in 1975 and eventually became general counsel at Bechtel Corporation, again under George Shultz, who was company president.

As part of Reagan's kitchen cabinet, he was involved in discussions over staffing the new administration. He didn't want to go back to OMB or the renamed Department of Health and Human Services, as some of his colleagues urged. For Defense, the group considered John Connally, Bill Clements, Al Haig, and Senator Sam Nunn (D-Ga.). The Texans were ruled out; Haig was deemed legally ineligible, and Weinberger suggested that Nunn might not feel comfortable in a Republican administration. The group ultimately added Weinberger's name to the list of possibles.

The list for secretary of state was even longer at one point, and included Weinberger, Donald Rumsfeld, and Henry Kissinger, though it was eventually pared to Shultz, Haig, and Senator Howard Baker (R-Tenn.).[6]

Reagan picked Haig for secretary of state and Weinberger for secretary of defense and downgraded the National Security Council staff by putting its first director, Richard Allen, underneath his troika of senior White House aides. These arrangements led to early and continuing problems for the administration, for there was no mechanism to coordinate the strong-willed cabinet officers.

The Weinberger appointment provoked criticism from some very conservative Republicans, especially on Capitol Hill. They feared that Weinberger, knowing little about defense and much about trimming budgets, would not fight for the massive buildup they favored and thought the new president intended. The new secretary reinforced those concerns by naming as his deputy another person with no DOD experience, Frank Carlucci, a career Foreign Service officer who had served with him at OMB and Health, Education, and Welfare, but who had also served as deputy director of the CIA under Jimmy Carter. Weinberger further enraged zealous conservatives by abruptly dismissing the well-connected nuclear strategy expert who headed the Defense transition team and by hiring only a few of its members.

In fact, Weinberger had been critical of some defense programs, including the B-1 bomber, in his earlier time at OMB, and had recently criticized a Laird proposal for a $10 billion hike in Pentagon spending as too much too fast. But once in office, he readily embraced a tripling of that figure in the first Reagan budget.[7] As he told his confirmation hearing, his two highest priorities were to "improve all aspects of the readiness of the forces we now have" and "to begin to improve the strategic balance between ourselves and the Soviet Union." He argued that these actions would also help "to regain the respect and the honor and the appreciation that I think we should all feel for people in the uniformed services."[8]

Behind the scenes, he became an implacable advocate and skillful bureaucratic infighter for increased defense spending. The new director of OMB, David Stockman, found himself outmaneuvered at his planning sessions with Weinberger. Reagan had promised "5 percent real growth" above inflation for the Pentagon during the campaign, but the outgoing Carter administration had already proposed that figure. The new administration could do no less and wanted to do more, deciding on an extra 7 percent, starting in fiscal year 1982. Only later did Stockman realize that he had agreed to additions to a baseline already increased by 12 percent real growth on top of congressional add-ons of 9 percent real growth. The net impact was a doubling of the funds that candidate Reagan had promised in his campaign budget plan.[9]

What accounts for Weinberger's unwavering commitment to defense budget increases? Intellectually and emotionally, he was in favor of military superiority. The threat briefings he received as incoming secretary reportedly shocked him. He probably also wanted to persuade any doubters—especially conservative Republicans—that he had left his budget squeezing days behind. He certainly believed that the new president intended to remedy the problems in the Carter defense posture cited during the campaign. And as a good lawyer, he believed that he owed his client the strongest possible advocacy, giving no ground until ruled against. It wasn't his job to worry about the effects on the economy of large tax cuts, defense boosts, and resulting deficits.

Curiously, Weinberger's agenda for the DOD did not go much beyond obtaining increased resources. He wanted to decentralize administration, not pull more into his office. He wanted to strengthen the service secretaries and let them manage the buildup. He was indifferent to management reforms and to growing pressures to reduce service parochialism and separateness. Although he came to endorse some strategic policy changes, he did not set out to revise the existing strategy. While he remained deeply interested in foreign policy, he did not push the Pentagon into new arenas. On the contrary, he preached a new doctrine of military restraint, codifying the lessons he and many military officers derived from the Vietnam War.

Political Relations

Weinberger's power and longevity in office derived from his closeness

Caspar Weinberger visiting U.S. troops. *Department of Defense*

to the president. The two men admired and respected each other. No cabinet member was more loyal. Even during the Nixon administration, Weinberger had kept a picture of Reagan on his desk. Later, he regularly wore presidential cuff links and a tie bar with Reagan's signature. He had access to the president when he wished, but he did not have regularly scheduled meetings until 1986, long after his rival George Shultz had demanded and received them.[10]

Reagan apparently thought that his proposed military buildup would be more prudently done by someone as skilled as Weinberger at cutting budgets. As he told a group of local officials a few weeks after his inauguration, "I can assure you that Cap is going to do a lot of trimming over there in Defense to make sure the American taxpayer is getting more bang for the buck."[11]

There are few examples when Reagan overrode the advice of his defense secretary on security issues. The president was convinced of the need to send U.S. troops into Lebanon despite strong Pentagon opposition, and he pursued better relations and arms control agreements with the Russians despite Weinberger's cautions. On military spending, the secretary had a free hand.

The senior White House leadership—Ed Meese, James Baker, and Mike Deaver—also did little to challenge Weinberger. One notable exception came in August 1981, when OMB Director Stockman sought Reagan's approval for a slower rate of increase in defense spending and Chief of Staff Baker told the press that there would be a $30 billion reduction. Weinberger convinced the president to cut only a token $13 billion from future programs.[12]

The National Security Council staff was deliberately subordinated by Reagan. Director Richard Allen did not see the president regularly, for he had to report through Ed Meese. Since Meese was not adept at handling the volume of paperwork, many items needing presidential action languished for weeks in Meese's briefcase. Weinberger had friendly relations with Meese and Allen and his successor William Clark, but not with all of the top NSC officials during the rest of the Reagan administration.

His most tempestuous relations were with Reagan's two secretaries of state, Al Haig and George Shultz. Haig viewed his cabinet colleague as "a capable man, immensely likable and honest, a talented administrator, and a stubborn fighter for what he believes is right."[13] Shultz, even after their cabinet clashes, called him "able, charming, and stubborn."[14] In return, Weinberger saw Haig as always passionate and intense about policy issues and intolerant of those who disagreed with him.[15] He treated disagreements with Shultz as policy differences, not clashes of personality.

Time and again in the early months of Reagan's presidency, Haig spoke out forcefully and Weinberger quietly disagreed. At the first meeting of the incoming cabinet, Haig spoke at length about the Communist threat in the Western Hemisphere and said that the United States would have to invade Cuba. Weinberger countered that any such action would require convincing the American people first and then acting with an unshakable will to win. These became themes he uttered throughout his service in the Pentagon. When Reagan was shot and Haig claimed that he was next in succession pending the return of the vice president, Weinberger pointed out that the law had been changed.[16] Although the two men agreed on Haig's proposal for a presidential directive delineating responsibilities in the NSC system, it was seen by the president's inner circle—and portrayed to the press—as a power grab by the secretary of state.

When Haig was forced from office in the summer of 1982, George Shultz was put in charge of the State Department. He and Weinberger disagreed frequently and vociferously on a broad range of policy issues, notably the use of force and relations with the Soviet Union. The president tolerated the very public clashes between his cabinet members, noting that "they are both my friends."[17]

Toward the Joint Chiefs of Staff, the secretary was friendly and solicitous. Although he was under pressure from conservative Republicans to fire the senior leaders appointed by Jimmy Carter, particularly JCS Chairman Gen. David Jones, he let them serve out their respective terms. He had a strong antipathy toward Jones, however, fueled in part by the chairman's disparaging comments in front of other officials on the secretary's suggested new basing scheme for the MX missile—putting them on surface ships.[18] The Carter administration had studied and rejected over thirty basing plans before settling on moving them between protected shelters. Candidate Reagan criticized this "racetrack" plan and promised something different. What Weinberger eventually proposed, bunching the inter-continental ballistic missile silos so that attacking missiles would destroy each other by fratricide, earned its own label, "Dense Pack."

To replace Jones in the summer of 1982, Weinberger recommended Army Gen. John W. Vessey Jr., who had enlisted as a private in World War II, was commissioned in 1944, and went on to serve in Vietnam and Korea.[19] "He and I were the last two people in the Pentagon who had active service in World War II," Weinberger told Jim Locher. "His judgment was extraordinary and his understanding of the whole military was invaluable."[20] When Vessey retired in 1985, Reagan named Adm. William J. Crowe Jr., who had impressed him during an Asian visit.[21]

Crowe came to like Weinberger, whom he considered smart, stubborn, and quite humorous in private. The secretary insisted that the admiral not disagree with him in public, since that would weaken his hand in dealing with others. He also tolerated but did not like the fact that

Crowe would meet regularly with Shultz and provide his advice on issues.[22] Crowe was also concerned by what he saw as the secretary's tendency to pander to the extreme conservatives.

> "Weinberger considered himself the guardian of the right in the Reagan administration, and he applied the political test to every major question: 'What will the right think about this?' If the right didn't have any views on it, then you could talk to him about it. But if it was something that was dear to their hearts, you were dead. He carried around some ideological baggage that was pretty fierce."[23]

Where Weinberger had the most trouble was with Congress, where even members who supported his huge defense budgets found him an inflexible ally. Defense hawks like Senate Armed Services Committee Chairman John Tower (R-Tex.) doubted his knowledge and commitment and readily offered their own advice on programs, personnel, and the budget. Tower was unhappy with the administration's decisions on strategic programs, particularly its rejection of "racetrack" basing for the MX missile, as well as Weinberger's personal style.

As NSC official Robert "Bud" McFarlane observed, "Cap Weinberger's contemptuous attitude toward Congress made his dealings with that body fractious and troublesome at all times. For its part, the Congress had no confidence in Weinberger as a spokesman for defense issues."[24]

Senate Majority Leader Bob Dole (R-Kans.) quipped that "Cap Weinberger is the first person in history to overdraw a blank check."[25] Senate Budget Chairman Pete Domenici (R-N.Mex.) said, "His 'sky's-falling-in' theory was no more than a theory, and so it cemented the mood into an absolute majority who had become extremely skeptical" toward the Pentagon.[26] As even Republicans in Congress became concerned about the sustainability of the ever-higher defense budgets, especially when facing mounting deficits and economic recession, the defense secretary was steadfast, unyielding, repetitive, and uncompromising. Republican Senator Bill Cohen of Maine said, "He [Weinberger] has a mind-set which precludes, for the most part, taking into account diversity of opinion or at least recognizing the legitimacy of diverse opinion. That may be unfair, but that's the perception. And so as a result, he doesn't have anybody who can carry the water for him."[27] As *New York Times* reporter Hedrick Smith concluded, Weinberger "never really built the essential political networks. He was tireless in testifying and in after-hours socializing, forever arguing his case. But his geniality could not overcome his rigidity."[28]

Weinberger believed that concessions only invited more concessions: "The minute you start making deals, they'll nibble you to death. If you don't dig your heels in and fight, you're just going to get wasted. No

deals. No compromise. No way."[29] As a result, by 1983 he had lost credibility on Capitol Hill. The Republican-led Senate Budget Committee
adopted a much lower spending ceiling than the administration wanted
because Weinberger refused to agree to a smaller reduction. The secretary was also reluctant to provide guidance for where congressionally
mandated cuts would have the least impact. To him, any cut was a danger for U.S. security.

Weinberger's obstinacy also helped solidify congressional support
for defense reorganization. When General Jones retired in 1982, he
warned that the JCS system was broken and needed major repairs to
reduce service parochialism. Weinberger defended the status quo and
stubbornly resisted any change. As one of the leading figures in the campaign to reform the Pentagon notes, "His in-your-face rigidity created
both the incentive and the ideal environment for the reformers to mount
a crusade. Had Weinberger shown some flexibility during the first four
years of debate, he could have undermined, if not curtailed, congressional efforts. Had he agreed to a few meaningful reforms and then asked
Congress for three or four years to evaluate them before taking further
steps, Weinberger could have defused the issue."[30] But he didn't, and the
Goldwater-Nichols Act became law in 1986. While that measure sought
mainly to improve the quality of military advice by strengthening the
chairman of the JCS and to improve the combat effectiveness of multi-
service operations, it had the unintended consequence of weakening the
civilian authorities in the Pentagon.

As with many leaders, the qualities which lead to success—such as
Weinberger's steadfast advocacy and refusal to compromise—may also
lead to failure. The defense secretary ultimately encountered serious problems with everyone else in his policy environment except the most important person, the President. Following bitter debates at the White House,
he often told his staff, "There was only one vote in the room that was on
my side, and that's the one that mattered."[31]

Operating Style

Throughout his professional life, Weinberger followed the same pattern when confronted with new responsibilities or new issues. "You do
what you do when you take on a new client or prepare for trial. You just
read everything you can find and talk to everybody you can find and try
to absorb as much as possible."[32] He was a quick study, impressing others
with his photographic memory and total recall of details and complex
arguments.

As befitted a former journalist, he began his daily staff meetings by
discussing the items in the daily compilation of newspaper articles about
military programs and issues, the *Early Bird*. "Cap's management control
system was the newspaper," said a former official.[33] He received regular

reports and briefings, of course, but was particularly sensitive to matters which reached the press.

His staff praised his even-tempered civility, his courtesy and graciousness. He didn't raise his voice in anger or berate the hard-working people around him.[34] His style was formal and orderly, with the morning staff meeting an important venue for gathering information and focusing senior officials' attention on matters of significance to the secretary.[35] As one of his military assistants, Colin Powell, later wrote regarding his workday rituals and punctuality, "Cap Weinberger was a man who worked grooves into his life and then stayed in them."[36]

He believed in delegating authority in the Pentagon in what was called his "laissez-faire management style."[37] He wanted the service secretaries to have more power, so he added them to the Defense Resources Board that had been set up to review major programs. He asked the services for their suggestions for using the dollars the president was willing to add to defense. For the most part, he did not push his own preferences down onto the services. Having delegated management while he busied himself with fund-raising, he found it hard to re-centralize authority to deal with problems.

Manager of the Pentagon

Weinberger followed the usual pattern of letting the deputy secretary handle day-to-day management, freeing himself for his advisory and outreach roles. His deputies ranged from the skilled bureaucrat Frank Carlucci, to defense industry executive Paul Thayer, to his longtime subordinate William H. Taft IV. Each tried to make the Pentagon more businesslike in its procedures, but each faced the added problems of disciplining spending when there were few pressures or limits on defense budgets.

In the early months, service budget planners had to reach to low priority programs to fill their quotas. When the torrent of money exposed some embarrassing examples–like a $640 toilet seat and $7,622 coffee maker[38]–Weinberger reacted defensively to the problems. He announced reforms for buying spare parts and challenged some major contractors on particular deficiencies. But the only major weapon program he actually killed was the Army's division air defense gun (DIVAD), and then only after a series of failed tests and widespread criticism.[39] And after rejecting the Carter deployment scheme for the MX missile in favor of the much-ridiculed "Dense Pack" plan, Weinberger had to create an outside group, the Scowcroft commission, to find a politically acceptable approach.[40]

After the initial support for a massive military buildup in 1981, Congress showed increasing resistance to the substantial real-growth budgets proposed in subsequent years. The first year, Congress cut the fiscal year 1982 budget by less than 1 percent. The second year it cut the request by 7 percent, the third year by 5.3 percent and the fourth year by 10 percent. Despite these cuts, Weinberger still achieved substantial real growth after inflation: 11.5 percent in FY82, 7.9 percent in FY83, 4.7 percent in FY84 and 7.6 percent in FY85. In 1985, Congress cut the FY86 budget request below the level of inflation, thus starting a decline in defense spending which lasted until 1999. Whatever the Reagan budgets achieved in military capabilities, they soured public and congressional opinion on unrestrained defense spending for years thereafter.

War Planner

The conflict most Pentagon officials planned for, of course, was a nuclear exchange with the Soviet Union. But while previous administrations had worked primarily to deter any such event, the Reagan team sought to fight and prevail in case of nuclear war. It sought nuclear superiority unfettered by past arms control agreements, both through modernization of strategic offensive forces and ultimately through development of effective missile defenses. Along the way, it scared European and American publics by its cavalier approach to nuclear war.

Egged on by his chief adviser on strategic nuclear policy, Richard Perle, Weinberger jumped in front of the rest of the administration with statements saying that arms control would have to be deferred pending the strategic modernization programs and that the neutron bomb would be deployed in Europe, despite widespread opposition from U.S. allies. Weinberger and Reagan each made statements suggesting that a nuclear conflict could be contained to the European continent rather than necessarily involving U.S.–based nuclear systems.[41]

Military planners were told to build in "connectivity" so that U.S. forces could be controlled over a "protracted" nuclear war. A deputy undersecretary of defense, T. K. Jones, provoked anger and disbelief when he said that Americans could survive a nuclear war "if there are enough shovels to go around."[42] Such statements only stimulated a growing public movement calling for a "nuclear freeze" and eroded congressional support for ever-higher defense budgets.

In 1983, when Reagan had been persuaded that an effective missile defense system was feasible, thus making nuclear weapons "impotent and obsolete," the president surprised the world with his call for a Strategic Defense Initiative (SDI). Weinberger had been much more cautious about such programs and was upset to learn the details only shortly before Reagan's announcement, but he rapidly became a stalwart proponent of SDI, so much so that Reagan later called him "the chief evangelist, after me."[43]

Short of nuclear war, Weinberger cautioned against military operations unless several demanding tests could be met. He shared the critique of the Vietnam War made by many military officers who believed that the civilian leaders had interfered too much, imposed too many restraints, and were unwilling to press for victory. He wanted to go public with his views but was blocked by the White House until just after the 1984 elections, when he was allowed to give a major address at the National Press Club setting forth his criteria for military action. The speech came at the end of a year when the secretary of state was arguing for use of force against terrorists and Weinberger had been resisting. Shultz later called Weinberger's approach "the Vietnam syndrome in spades, carried to an absurd level, and a complete abdication of the duties of leadership."[44]

What Weinberger said remains popular among military officers even today, a touchstone for avoiding unpopular wars:

> I believe the postwar period has taught us several lessons, and from them I have developed *six* major tests to be applied when we are weighing the use of U.S. combat forces abroad. Let me now share them with you:
> (1) **First**, the United States should not commit forces to *combat* overseas unless the particular engagement or occasion is deemed vital to our national interest or that of our allies
> (2) **Second**, if we decide it *is* necessary to put *combat* troops into a given situation, we should do so wholeheartedly, and with the clear intention of winning. If we are unwilling to commit the forces or resources necessary to achieve our objectives, we should not commit them at all.
> (3) **Third**, if we *do* decide to commit forces to combat overseas, we should have clearly defined political and military objectives. And we should know precisely how our forces can accomplish those clearly defined objectives. And we should have and send the forces needed to do just that.
> (4) **Fourth**, the relationship between our objectives and the forces we have committed—their size, composition and disposition—must be continually reassessed and adjusted if necessary. Conditions and objectives invariably change during the course of a conflict. When they do change, then so must our combat requirements. We must continuously keep as a beacon light before us the basic questions: "Is this conflict in our national interest?" "Does our national interest require us to fight, to use force of arms?" If the answers are "yes," then we *must* win. If the answers are "no," then we should not be in combat.
> (5) **Fifth**, before the U.S. commits combat forces abroad, there must be some reasonable assurance we will have the support of the American people and their elected representatives in Congress. This sup-

port cannot be achieved unless we are candid in making clear the threats we face; the support cannot be sustained without continuing and close consultation. We cannot fight a battle with the Congress at home while asking our troops to win a war overseas or, as in the case of Vietnam, in effect asking our troops not to win, but just to be there. (6) **Finally**, the commitment of U.S. forces to combat should be a last resort. [45]

Just as Ronald Reagan never irrevocably chose between his two clashing advisers, he also never endorsed the Weinberger tests. Instead, he ordered some military operations in ways and places contrary to his defense secretary's recommendations.

Weinberger successfully opposed Haig's efforts to launch attacks in Cuba or Central America, though he went along with aid to El Salvador, including U.S. military advisers, and aid to the Nicaraguan Contras. When U.S. medical students were endangered in Grenada in 1983, he endorsed a U.S. attack with more than the forces requested by the military. As he noted, "my invariable practice was to double, at least, any Joint Chief recommendations as to the size of a force required."[46]

When intelligence evidence linked Libya to an attack on U.S. personnel in a Berlin disco in 1986, he orchestrated the bombing raids on that North African nation. But he and the Chiefs had resisted pressures for anti-terrorist strikes earlier.[47]

When the Kuwaitis sought protection for their oil tankers in the Persian Gulf in 1987, Weinberger readily agreed, both to respond to a friendly state already threatened by Iran and to prevent the Soviet Union from sending its navy to do the job. Although the State Department and the Navy were reluctant to convoy the Kuwaiti ships, Weinberger went to the president and persuaded him to protect all the tankers. He rejected an argument by his new, hand-picked secretary of the Navy, James Webb, that the mission violated his "tests" by saying the U.S. would "win" each time a ship safely transited the Gulf.[48]

Diplomat

Unlike his predecessors, who generally limited their forays into foreign policy to issues and places involving American defense commitments, Weinberger acted and traveled widely. He had wanted to be secretary of state, and he saw all U.S. foreign policy through the lens of the Cold War struggle against Communism. In his first two years in office, he traveled to thirty-five different countries. By the end of his tour, he had spent more time in countries outside western Europe and more time away from the Pentagon than any of his predecessors.[49] In addition to NATO countries, he also traveled to Asia, Central America, and the Middle East.

In the councils of government, too, Weinberger pressed his own department's viewpoints on foreign policy issues. In the spring of 1981, for example, and despite State Department opposition to such meetings, the defense secretary began a series of meetings with Japanese officials to press them to spend more on defense and too cooperate more closely with the United States on security issues. In 1983, he led a large delegation to China, where he arranged for subsequent meetings of the national leaders but failed to reach agreement on technology transfer issues. He saw value in developing better ties to China, not simply as a counterweight to the USSR. At the same time, he was trying to persuade Reagan not to agree to a summit with Soviet leaders.[50]

In Europe, Weinberger's policies were pointedly anti-Soviet, regardless of other impacts. He pressed for sanctions against U.S. and European firms that participated in building a planned natural gas pipeline from the USSR into the west. When Reagan approved the policy—in part out of anger at Al Haig[51]—the decision generated more hostility toward the United States than punishment on the USSR.

When Argentine forces seized the British-held Falkland Islands in April 1982, Weinberger quickly "passed the word to the department that all existing requests from the United Kingdom for military equipment were to be honored at once."[52] Four weeks would pass before the president finally decided to provide material support to Britain, but Weinberger's action clearly tilted the U.S. position toward London and undercut Haig's attempted negotiations with the parties.

On Middle East policy, Weinberger was viewed as pro-Arab, with some "animus toward Israel."[53] He supported the controversial sale of Airborne Warning and Control System radar warning planes to Saudi Arabia in 1981, despite Israeli opposition. He also signed defense-ministerial agreement with Israel in 1983 declaring a "strategic partnership," but this agreement had been negotiated by the NSC staff.[54] Lebanon was the issue where he fought a steady but losing battle against U.S. military involvement.

NSC Adviser

When Israel invaded Lebanon in the summer of 1982, Weinberger and the Joint Chiefs argued strongly that U.S. forces should not be part of any multinational force (MNF) to separate the Israelis from the Arabs.[55] Reagan's other advisers, however, wanted to support U.S. emissary Philip Habib, who negotiated a plan for an MNF of eight hundred U.S., eight hundred French, and four hundred Italian troops. Its mission was to assure the safe withdrawal of PLO forces but also to help restore the sovereignty and authority of the Lebanese government.[56] The troops deployed and withdrew to ships offshore after barely two weeks.

In mid-September, the newly elected Lebanese president was assassinated and Israeli troops stood by as several hundred Palestinians were massacred in their refugee camps in Beirut. Despite renewed opposition from Weinberger and the JCS, Reagan decided on a new deployment of U.S. forces as an "interposition force."[57] During the subsequent months, the foreign forces became increasingly viewed as participants in the conflict on behalf of one faction, the Lebanese Christians.

By September 1983, the situation had deteriorated and U.S. forces were coming under attack. President Reagan rejected Weinberger's call for withdrawal and approved American fire support for the Lebanese army. A few weeks later, on October 23, 240 Marines were killed by a car bomb attack on their barracks near the Beirut airport. Soon thereafter, Weinberger ordered an evacuation plan, which the president approved in early February 1984.

Weinberger drew from Lebanon further justification for his belief that U.S. forces should not be sent on missions where the objectives were fuzzy or unattainable. Reagan had not accepted his advice on Lebanon because the benefits of achieving peace outweighed the risks of doing nothing. The president withdrew the troops for good when he realized "our policy wasn't working."[58]

While his views on the use of force did not always prevail in NSC discussions, Weinberger was more successful in shaping Reagan's arms control policies. He lost the first round in 1981, however, when Haig, reacting to a statement by Navy Secretary John Lehman that the SALT II treaty should not be adhered to, made a public statement and sent a worldwide cable to embassies declaring that the United States would not "undercut" existing agreements so long as the USSR showed similar restraint.[59] Although Reagan in the campaign had declared SALT II a "fatally flawed" treaty, he and his advisers chose not to countermand Haig's announcement. In fact, the United States did not finally breach the treaty's limits until 1986.

Weinberger and Perle waged a protracted conflict against any negotiations or agreements with the Soviet Union. At first they sought to delay talks by linking them to Moscow's crackdown in Poland. Haig and the State Department wanted to reassure America's European allies that the United States was open to negotiations. Reagan agreed to announce a U.S. willingness to have talks by the end of 1981.[60]

Meanwhile, Perle crafted a clever approach which most analysts considered unacceptable to the USSR—the "zero option," forbidding either the already-deployed Soviet SS-20 missiles or the planned U.S. Pershing missiles. With Weinberger's help, he worked to prevent any "backsliding" or compromise from these proposals. When negotiator Paul Nitze went beyond his instructions in a 1982 "walk in the woods" with his Soviet counterpart, the arms control hardliners orchestrated a reprimand for Nitze and the firing of the arms control agency director. When Nitze and Weinberger argued the issue in front of Reagan in September 1982, the president sided with his defense secretary. "Well, Paul," he said, "you just tell the Soviets that you're working for one tough son of a bitch."[61]

By the following February, Reagan began moving toward compromise, telling one audience "ours is not a take-it-or-leave-it proposal."[62] When the Europeans agreed to the planned deployment of new missiles in November, however, the Soviets walked out of the talks. No serious discussions were held until 1985, when a new Soviet leader, Mikhail Gorbachev, took power. Weinberger remained skeptical and continued to press for U.S. actions to exceed the limits of the unratified SALT II treaty, which occurred in 1986. He also pressed Reagan, with personal interventions and memoranda, to maintain a tough line in any negotiations. Soon after he left office, the United States signed the Intermediate Range Nuclear Forces Treaty (INF) with the USSR and held a summit with breakthroughs in strategic arms reduction talks (START). He and Perle had slowed the process but were ultimately unable to derail it, for arms limits had great political appeal in both the East and the West.

The most vivid example where the president rejected his forcefully-presented advice was in the Iran-Contra affair. Weinberger, like Shultz, repeatedly and consistently argued that selling arms to Iran in the hopes of obtaining the release of Americans held hostage was illegal and unwise. In a December 7, 1985, meeting of the senior advisers, Weinberger took nearly half an hour to go over his extensive brief against the arms sales and transfers. But the president was stubborn, saying, "The American people will never forgive me if I fail to get these hostages out over this legal question." Anyway, he quipped, if people go to jail, "visiting hours are Thursday."[63]

Despite his opposition to the policy, Weinberger was indicted by a federal grand jury in 1992 for obstructing a congressional investigation, making false statements to investigators, and perjury in congressional testimony. Independent counsel Lawrence Walsh was particularly incensed that Weinberger had repeatedly denied knowledge of key events and of taking detailed notes, which were later uncovered in the Library of Congress.[64] Some investigators believed that the defense secretary, having determined that the arms sales to Iran were illegal, tried to protect the president from culpability in an impeachable offense. On Christmas Eve, 1992, outgoing President George H. W. Bush pardoned Weinberger, whose trial had not yet begun, as well as four other officials already convicted of withholding information from Congress.[65] Weinberger himself later called Iran-Contra "the one serious mistake the administration made during the seven years I served as secretary of defense."[66] That mistake, however, tarnished the reputations of those men and many others.

Evaluation

On the wall behind his desk in the Pentagon, Caspar Weinberger displayed a framed copy of a favorite quotation from Winston Churchill: "Never give in, never give in, never, never, never, never; in nothing great or small, large or petty, never give in."[67] That was his motto for dealing with the Soviets, Congress, his bureaucratic rivals—in fact, everybody but the president. Whatever cause he had to defend, he was a forceful advocate, even when his prior positions or personal views might have been different.

Perhaps he stayed in office too long, accumulating too many opponents and weakening the power of his arguments through repetition. But he accomplished a major increase in military spending and he deflected public pressure for reduced Cold War tensions into proposals which sounded reasonable. He earned the admiration of his subordinates and the loyalty of the institution he headed. By all those standards, he was a success.

The Firefighters

Many secretaries of defense have been pulled away from their planned course, diverted from the tasks which they considered most important, in order to deal with immediate problems. These matters were sometimes truly significant, sometimes trivial, but all were in the spotlight of publicity and therefore had to be handled. These officials became what I call firefighters, preoccupied to a major extent by political controversies.

They still had to carry out the primary responsibilities of their office, building budgets, issuing orders, reviewing strategy, sitting in interagency meetings. But their time and attention was often drained by these drive-by issues. They may have had bold visions and grand plans, and did some work on them, but they are judged now by how well they dealt with the headline problems of their time in office.

In addition to the three men discussed here, I would count Louis Johnson and Clark Clifford as firefighters, for they had little time in office and much of it was spent on the biggest wartime controversies of the day. One should note that some of these men handled their jobs quite expertly, and were really the victims of political problems facing their president and his administration. Even so, the Pentagon could not escape the fallout.

Some of the firefighters failed and were sent away from the front lines. Others stayed a full term, doing what they could to douse the flames. Here are their stories.

6

Laird:
The Power of Politics

Of course Laird is devious, but for anyone who has to run the Pentagon and get along with Congress, that is a valuable asset.

–Dwight Eisenhower, 1969[1]

Mel Laird, one of the canniest, most deceptive, toughest in-fighters ever to grace the nation's capital. Laird was a double threat bureaucratically because if he couldn't beat you in the executive branch, he would go to his former colleagues in Congress and nail you there.

–Robert Gates[2]

Melvin Robert Laird wasn't supposed to be secretary of defense. "I got sandbagged into it," he later said.[3] Richard Nixon had offered the Pentagon post, on Laird's recommendation, to Senator Henry M. "Scoop" Jackson (D-Wash.). The president-elect asked Laird to head the Department of Health, Education, and Welfare, but the eight-term representative preferred to stay in Congress, where he was a powerful figure in the Republican leadership. Jackson, after first accepting the appointment, changed his mind to preserve his future Democratic presidential prospects, and backed out the day before Nixon was to introduce his new cabinet on prime-time television.

"You got me into this." Nixon complained to Laird, "you're going to get me out of it."[4] So Laird grudgingly agreed to become secretary of defense. But he insisted, and Nixon agreed in writing, that he would have full freedom over appointments of both military and civilian personnel. From the start, Laird insisted that he would serve only one term. He even booked a Yellow Cab far in advance to take him home after his last day in the Pentagon.

Laird went into the Navy right after graduating from college in 1944. He served in the Pacific and was wounded when his ship was struck by a kamikaze aircraft. Returning home, he decided to run for the Wisconsin state Senate seat left vacant by his father's sudden death. The twenty-three-year old veteran ran and won, becoming the youngest person ever to serve in that body. Six years later, in 1952, he was elected to Congress, where he became knowledgeable and powerful as a member of the House Appropriations Subcommittees on Defense and Health, Education, and Welfare. During his sixteen years in Congress, he visited the major military commands and numerous bases. "I always felt that I knew the defense budget better than anybody in the Congress," he later recalled.[5]

A skilled politician, Laird knew how to deal with other politicians, how to increase his leverage over them, how to protect his own power from their encroachments, and how to manipulate the press and maneuver the bureaucracy to achieve his preferred goals. At the same time, he was indisputably loyal to the president who distrusted him, overruled him, and often tried to keep him ignorant of major policy decisions. He earned the respect of Henry Kissinger, whom he sometimes bested in their frequent bureaucratic warfare. And he retained the admiration of senior military officers even as he imposed painful budget cuts and troop withdrawals from Vietnam which many feared could only guarantee U.S. failure.

Nixon gave Laird no special directions for running the Pentagon. But the new secretary had his own ideas on what he had to do. First, "wind down American involvement in Vietnam, because public support was at the breaking point."[6] Second, end the draft, starting with a lottery and ultimately establishing an All-Volunteer Force (AVF). Third, replenish military hardware and supplies siphoned off for Vietnam. Fourth, improve morale in the Pentagon through what he labeled "participatory management." Fifth, set fiscal guidance so that the services could craft their own budgets. Sixth, put his own people in charge of all defense agencies, guaranteeing their loyalty to him by promising later promotions.[7] Those were his missions, and he largely achieved them, despite the fact that some of them put him in sharp conflict with the White House or the senior military leaders.

Political Relations

Richard Nixon appreciated Laird's political skills and hoped that he would be able to muster a coalition in Congress to defeat the opponents of the Vietnam War. But he distrusted his secretary of defense, as he seemed to distrust many of his closest advisors.[8] Whether from paranoia or experience, Nixon repeatedly blamed his senior national security officials for damaging leaks, self-serving motives, policy sabotage, and insubordination. In return, they tolerated his abuse, were steadfastly loyal—at least in public—and ignored those orders which they, probably correctly, viewed as irrational.[9] Nixon announced that he wanted to run his own foreign policy. To that end, he named Henry Kissinger as his national security adviser and approved the former Harvard professor's plan to centralize information and power in the White House. But the new president went beyond creating a top-down decision process. He established backchannels of communications, cut out some top officials from key meetings and decisions, and bypassed the legal chain of command. He delighted in secrecy and was unusually angry when he could not maintain it.

The system that arose was ultimately self-defeating. Mutual suspicion was—and is—highly corrosive. To maintain secrecy, the Nixon White House had to investigate breaches of secrecy. Wiretaps were placed on key aides following embarrassing disclosures. Instead of revealing disloyalty, however, the taps provided information useful in the bureaucratic battles, so they were maintained. Those officials denied access to sensitive materials sought alternative means to acquire them. Everyone suspected everyone else of improprieties, and they often were right. At one point in time, Laird was receiving cables denied him by Kissinger; the Joint Chiefs of Staff were getting copies of documents stolen from Kissinger's briefcase; the secretary of state was kept in the dark about major foreign policy decisions; and Nixon was briefed on FBI wiretaps of various subordinates and was giving military orders directly to the JCS chairman, bypassing the secretary of defense. This was the atmosphere in which Mel Laird tried to fight a war and carry out other national security policies.

Secretary of State William Rogers was a close friend of Nixon's from the Eisenhower administration. The two men and their wives dined together at the White House. But the president had an overwhelming distrust of the State Department and the career Foreign Service, and he ordered Kissinger to keep Rogers ignorant of and excluded from a broad range of important foreign policy matters. By contrast, Laird had a collegial relationship with the secretary of state, but he was not about to fight Rogers's battles when he had enough of his own.

One action he took helped to reduce tensions between State and Defense. Laird downgraded the office of International Security Affairs, which under McNamara had been an active and effective "little State Department" in the Pentagon. Laird was willing to stay out of State's activities in return for autonomy over defense prerogatives.

Laird's major conflicts came with Kissinger and the White House he represented. They were rarely open battles, however, because Laird fought wars of maneuver, rarely clashing openly or directly, but often winning. He met the young Harvard professor at the 1964 Republican convention and was impressed with Kissinger's work fashioning a foreign policy platform plank acceptable to Rockefeller and Goldwater Republicans.[10] While Kissinger had long and successful experience in academia and foreign policy think tanks, Laird had learned how to build and maintain coalitions of politicians on more consequential issues.

Laird demonstrated his skills in outmaneuvering Kissinger on several issues related to the organization of the National Security Council. When the new national security team met together on December 28, 1968, Nixon presented his ideas for an NSC-centered process and elicited comments. In fact, the president-elect had already decided to proceed without any input from his new cabinet officers. As Henry Kissinger noted, "Like so many meetings in the Nixon administration, the Key Biscayne session had its script determined in advance." Laird responded later with what Kissinger came to see as "his patented technique of bureaucratic warfare: to throw up a smokescreen of major objections in which he was not really interested but which reduced the item that really concerned him to such minor proportions that to refuse him would appear positively indecent."[11]

In addition to smokescreens, Laird practiced endruns, leaks, and winks and nods. Thwarted by the White House, he would solicit allies from his old friends on Capitol Hill. Or he would inspire news articles which supported his positions. Or he would make ritual statements of support for JCS positions in formal meetings, only to indicate privately his contrary personal views. Kissinger acknowledged that even with his cleverest tactics against Laird, "I lost as often as I won."[12] Laird agreed: "Henry was very Machiavellian, but I knew how to beat him at his own game."[13]

For crisis decision making, Kissinger wanted a White House–centered group. After the EC-121 spy plane incident in April 1969, Laird urged the creation of a formal interagency committee instead of the ad hoc group assembled for that crisis. Nixon and Kissinger agreed, and established the Washington Special Action Group (WSAG), chaired by the national security adviser with the deputies from the other departments. While this kept Laird out of the room, it forced the inclusion of the chairman of the Joint Chiefs of Staff to give military advice. Laird considered this an improvement over the previous, less inclusive system.[14]

Later in 1969, Kissinger tried to use the NSC to control the defense budget by creating a Defense Program Review Committee (DPRC) under his chairmanship. Laird believed that cabinet officers had legal responsibility and authority for their departmental budgets and was unwilling to surrender power to a mere White House staffer. "Let Nixon tell me if he wants things done—not Kissinger," Laird argued.[15] He complied in principle with the DPRC system, but in practice managed to delay meetings until he had completed his own budget reviews. In 1970, for example, Laird got a scheduled March meeting postponed until April, then presented materials so confusing that a further meeting was delayed until

July. And then that meeting was delayed another month, by which time Laird had made all his major decisions and the president had been briefed.[16] Many DOD officials, both military and civilian, were especially pleased by the way Laird slow-rolled Kissinger and preserved budgetary autonomy for the Pentagon.

With the military leadership, Laird wanted to be un-McNamara. "I thought there was a lack of communication," he concluded, so he set out to enlist the JCS as allies.[17] At his first meeting with the JCS, in their meeting room known as the "tank," he shook hands around the room, waited for an invitation to speak, and then apologized for taking "time to interrupt your work." He promised cooperation, outlined the new administration's basic policies, and left with another round of handshakes. As Mark Perry concluded, "Laird had accomplished in a few minutes what most officers believed would take years to gain: he had won the trust of a disenchanted high command that was more than willing to a mistrust any defense secretary, regardless of his policies."[18]

Laird knew that he would be cutting the size of the armed forces and the defense budget, and he wanted the trust of the senior military leadership so that he could accomplish that goal. He believed that they would be more willing to go along with his policies if they thought he understood and listened to them. At the same time, he deliberately downgraded the Office of Systems Analysis (SA), which McNamara had used to justify his own decisions contrary to military advice. He eliminated the Senate-confirmable assistant secretary slot for systems analysis and refused to allow SA personnel to testify before Congress. Yet he acknowledged, "I didn't make as many changes as people think."[19] He still relied on their analyses even if he did not as frequently accept their recommendations.

As an example of his determination to listen and try to persuade rather than order compliance, he once spent three days in meetings with the Chiefs over a seven thousand troop withdrawal from Vietnam, where over five hundred thousand troops had been deployed.[20] Laird gave guidance, including budgetary ceilings for each service, but allowed the military departments to allocate those resources. He allowed the JCS to appeal his adverse decisions to the president and Office of Management and Budget, and sometimes was reversed. When he argued with the Chiefs, he tended to point out the political consequences of the pending decision rather than debating the substance of the issue. This was particularly true in his discussions of Vietnam and the All-Volunteer Force.

Congress was Laird's power base, the institution he knew best and to which he turned for advice and support on national security policies. He had been appointed in part to keep Congress in line behind Nixon's policies, but he also derived important political insights from the Hill. For Laird, most defense issues were political issues, to be viewed in terms of their political context and to be resolved in terms of their political impact. Although his bald pate did not seem to require frequent tending, he continued to go each week to the House barber shop, where he chatted with former colleagues and took the political pulse of Congress.[21]

As a former senior member of the Appropriations Committee, he retained close personal ties to the powerful chairman, Rep. George Mahon (D-Tex.), as well as other members. When Nixon gave a direct order to Laird to close a military base in Hawaii so that the land could be turned over for civilian uses, the defense secretary alerted chairman Mahon and then delayed action until Congress prohibited the closure. Although he did not win every battle on the Hill, which ended cutting the Pentagon budget substantially each year, he managed to preserve key weapons programs and personnel reforms.

Laird believed that officers and civilians in the Pentagon "have a certain disdain and contempt for Congress." One of the most important lessons he wanted his subordinates to learn was "that Congress is just as important as the presidency as far as defense policy is concerned."[22]

Operating Style

Laird was open to discussion and solicitous of advice, but he acted stealthily, often confusing even those closest to him. "He always operated behind the scenes—we never knew what he was really doing," a close aide told Richard Stubbing.[23] He considered Robert McNamara "strong and smart," but hampered because he didn't get along well with Congress.[24] He knew he had to be unlike McNamara in very symbolic ways, particularly showing greater deference both to military views than to the systems analysts and toward Congress and its peculiarities and prerogatives.

He labeled his approach "participatory management," and that meant to him inclusion of the military in the decision process, decentralization of programmatic and budget decisions, and delegation of authority with only broad guidance.[25] Both the military leaders and the civilian service secretaries appreciated their enhanced roles.

To gain the loyalty of his key subordinates, he made clear that they knew he was personally responsible for their appointments and promotions. He had the signed agreement from the president giving him authority over DOD appointments, free from White House interference. He interceded on the Hill to get JCS Chairman General Wheeler's term extended for a year and to permit David Packard to become deputy secretary despite his financial holdings in the computer firm he founded. He picked new officers to head the Defense Intelligence Agency (DIA) and the NSA and promised them subsequent four-star appointments from what had previously been terminal three-star positions. In addition to carefully vetting service chiefs, he also interviewed candidates for the director of the joint staff and even the watch officers in the Pentagon's command and control center. "I wanted those officers . . . to know that their appointments didn't come from the chairman, or from the Joint Chiefs, but from the secretary of defense."[26]

His rewards were loyalty and support—and, often, information. White House officials suspected that he got reports of presidential communications that were channeled through the Army Signal Corps, a suspicion fed by the master wiretapper, FBI director J. Edgar Hoover.[27] Various members of the Joint Chiefs told Laird of presidential orders that Nixon deliberately tried to keep secret from his defense secretary, and when the JCS liaison office in the White House purloined documents from Kissinger's briefcase and other files, Laird was also kept informed.

Laird used the information, of course, in planning his own counter-strategies, whether within the executive branch or on Capitol Hill. He was dubious of White House efforts to keep major activities, especially in the Vietnam War, secret from Congress and the American people. He believed that public support required open discussion. At times, though, Laird lived up to his reputation for deviousness. He kept his personal views and some activities secret. Sometimes he argued for one position in NSC meetings but then quietly revealed an acceptable alternative. He either leaked information to the press or told people who might be likely to pass the word on, and then was one of the first to cover his tracks by calling the White House to complain about the leak.

Just as Henry Kissinger practiced "linkage" of foreign policy issues so that the desire for major agreements would provide leverage to solve minor problems, Laird had his own style of linkage. With the White House and Congress, for example, he used his support for arms control agreements with the Soviet Union as leverage to sustain his strategic weapons programs against "peace dividend" cuts. In fact, he demanded that Congress pass the 1973 defense budget before voting on the SALT I agreements. Similarly, he linked U.S. troop withdrawals from Vietnam to military modernization programs strongly favored by the JCS and thereby gained military support for his Vietnam policy, creation of the AVF, and Nixon's arms control agreements with the USSR.

Manager of the Pentagon

Laird delegated to Deputy Secretary Packard the regular oversight of the DOD, while he retained the public role as newsmaker and witness before Congress. He told Packard, "Dave, you've got to run the store day-to-day, and I want you to be chief operating officer. I'll try to be the chief executive officer."[28] He met with Packard each morning and tried to have at least one meal with his deputy each workday.

Unlike many of his predecessors and successors, he showed little interest in nuclear strategy or favorite weapons programs. He was content to issue budgetary guidance to the services and let them choose priorities and structure their programs accordingly. As Richard Stubbing observed,

"Laird's interest often lay not in the rational planning or cost effectiveness of the defense program, but in supporting the interests of the military services and cementing his relations with the Chiefs."[29]

He changed the McNamara budget process in significant ways. Instead of letting systems analysts draft the memoranda to which the services had to respond and justify their programs, he set budgetary guidelines and then let the services develop Program Objectives Memoranda (POMs) and the JCS produce a Joint Force Memorandum (JFM). He welcomed comments from the systems analysts on the POMs and JFM, but wound up cutting the service requests far less than in the McNamara years. Then, the secretary imposed cuts of usually more than 20 percent; under Laird, the figure was only about 4 percent.[30]

In keeping with a Nixon campaign promise, Laird established the Fitzhugh Commission to study Pentagon management. That action allowed him to concentrate on his major objectives by deferring fights over reforms until the commission produced its commonsense recommendations. One of the most important innovations, begun even before being blessed by the commission, was the use of competitive prototypes in new programs, so that expensive new systems would "fly before buy."

Ending the draft was another Nixon campaign pledge, but Laird was a late convert to the cause. He had long favored universal military training, although he recognized the political attractiveness of ending a system which had sent so many thousands of young men to Vietnam. He also was personally bothered by the two-track military pay system that paid draftees far less than career people. To buy time with the public and to allow time to win military support, he supported creation of the Gates Commission to study the AVF. He then worked to persuade the JCS of the benefits of moving away from conscription. One tactic was to oppose a White House-generated proposal for a new, less generous military retirement system. Instead, Laird favored pay comparability with the private sector, a standard which promised high pay raises across the board for military personnel. This helped to win over the Chiefs.[31]

War Planner

The Nixon administration's first acute military crisis came on April 14, 1969, when a North Korean aircraft shot down an EC-121 electronic espionage plane, killing all thirty-one people on board. The incident also set in motion the administration's sometimes dysfunctional approach to decision making. Nixon and Kissinger viewed the attack as a deliberate test and favored immediate retaliation. Laird opposed an air strike because he thought it might lead to a second front war in Korea and could undermine the Vietnam policy. He also sensed no congressional support for retaliation. Secretary Rogers and the U.S. ambassador to Seoul also counseled against military attacks. Faced with such strong opposition, Nixon decided against retaliatory strikes.[32]

During the crisis, Kissinger energized his staff to probe the Joint Staff for military options, up to and including the possible use of tactical nuclear weapons. Laird knew of these efforts to bypass the chain of command through him and advised General Wheeler to support action but insist on time to array the necessary forces. Meanwhile, he cancelled all similar reconnaissance flights worldwide without informing the White House. When the president told a news conference that his response would be to provide armed escorts for the spy planes, Laird delayed resuming the missions for three weeks. While these steps prevented the president from taking the more forceful actions of which Laird disapproved, they also prompted Kissinger and Nixon to disparage the defense secretary and seek to bypass him on future sensitive issues. The crisis also reinforced Nixon's preference for deciding issues in advance of NSC meetings.[33]

Laird's highest priority was to wind down American participation in the Vietnam War, not to win the war, not necessarily to negotiate an honorable settlement, as Nixon and Kissinger wanted, but to turn the fighting over to the South Vietnamese. As a congressman, he had called for a formal declaration of war and had criticized the Johnson administration for deceiving the American people about the war. But once in office, he was convinced that continued public support for any combat required U.S. troop withdrawals.[34]

In March 1969, with U.S. troop strength peaking at 543,000, he traveled to Vietnam and returned brimming with confidence in the ability of the South Vietnamese to assume a greater combat role. Instead of "de-Americanizing" the conflict, he coined the term "Vietnamization." At the same time, Nixon ordered secret bombing raids on suspected enemy positions in Cambodia. While Laird was not enthusiastic about the raids, and certainly not about trying to keep them secret, he used his support for the JCS-favored action to persuade the Chiefs to support his proposals for initial troop withdrawals.[35]

Laird proposed various options for withdrawals during the first year, ranging from a low of fifty thousand to a high of one hundred thousand. He envisioned continuing withdrawals over eighteen to forty-two months, with a residual U.S. force of two hundred and sixty thousand to just over three hundred thousand troops. Kissinger says that Laird "officially supported the lowest figure (fifty thousand) but indicated privately that he would not mind being overruled."[36] Nixon hoped to negotiate mutual withdrawals of American and North Vietnamese forces, but the prospects of bringing American troops home took on its own momentum.

Laird also engineered a formal change in the mission of the U.S. armed forces in Vietnam. In mid-August 1969, he announced that their objective was no longer to defeat North Vietnamese forces and force their withdrawal, but rather to provide "maximum assistance" to strengthen South Vietnamese forces, support pacification efforts, and reduce the flow of supplies to enemy forces. Laird had notified the White House of his planned change of mission, but the president was on vacation in California and Kissinger somehow never saw the note. Nixon tried to countermand the new orders, but Laird had already made them public.[37] This mission change was particularly significant because it relieved the military of the need to seek offensive operations for victory and of the blame for any outcome short of that.

To maintain the momentum for Vietnamization, Laird worked tirelessly to convince the Chiefs that withdrawals were necessary to preserve public support for continuing the war—and to allow funds for weapons modernization programs. He also resorted to leaks about withdrawal plans to prevent any backsliding by the White House. At the same time, he generally supported military and White House proposals for expanded military operations to signal or pressure the North Vietnamese to negotiate. And when antiwar protesters invaded Washington for major marches in October and November of 1969, Laird was able to announce that troop cuts of sixty thousand already permitted cancellation of draft calls in November and December.[38]

With fewer men being drafted, and with a new lottery further lowering the risks of induction, the antiwar movement became more quiescent, only to be revived by the May 1970 invasion of Cambodia and two years later by massive attacks on Hanoi and the mining of Haiphong harbor. Laird supported a cross-border attack by South Vietnamese forces but not U.S. troops and cautioned against the president's declaration that the Cambodian operations were aimed at seizing the elusive command center for the Vietnamese communists. In 1972, Laird argued against the mining and bombing, urging instead more equipment for the South. But in each case he dutifully defended the decisions Nixon made.[39]

While Laird was preoccupied with the ongoing war in Vietnam, he did develop and promulgate a major revision in strategic planning. Instead of the existing "two and a half war" criterion, by which the Pentagon sized its forces for possible wars in Europe and Asia and perhaps a smaller contingency elsewhere, Nixon in 1969 declared a new "one and a half war" strategy, which permitted somewhat lower manpower levels. Laird also fought for the development of a new generation of military weaponry: new tanks, fighters, bombers, and strategic missile systems.

Diplomat

While the Nixon administration's major foreign policy initiatives were toward China and the Soviet Union, Laird himself took a special interest in NATO and Japan. He became the first U.S. secretary of defense to make a formal visit to Japan, staying for a full week. He also attended regular NATO ministerial meetings, where he pressed the allies to increase their own defense spending, despite the fact that the United States was reducing its expenditures. His argument for greater burden sharing played well in America but was less impressive abroad.

A stalwart supporter of NATO, Laird nevertheless employed a risky strategy to gain presidential and congressional support for higher defense budgets, and he again outmaneuvered Henry Kissinger in the process. In September 1969, Laird announced substantial cuts in naval forces committed to NATO and reduced readiness levels for Army divisions slated for rapid deployment to Europe in the event of war. He correctly anticipated that the severity of the cuts would reduce pressures for further cuts either by Congress or OMB. But when Kissinger tried to forbid further public discussion of the matter until the president could set broad policy, Laird preempted him by writing to Nixon and telling him, in effect, that he would have to approve higher defense spending or risk breaking his commitments to European leaders. Nixon acquiesced, but agreed with Kissinger's counterploy to establish an NSC-run group to oversee the Pentagon's budget, the Defense Program Review Committee (DPRC). As pointed out earlier, Laird managed to slow-roll the DPRC so that it never achieved the influence which Kissinger desired.[40]

NSC Adviser

There is less to say about Laird's role as a member of the National Security Council because of Nixon's and Kissinger's efforts to centralize their control over foreign policy and to bypass both of the cabinet officers who were statutory members. As the foregoing examples demonstrate, Laird was frequently left in the dark as the White House maneuvered.

The advice he gave in meetings and memos, however, was usually more on the politics of proposed policies rather than on the substance of the issue. Laird's comparative advantage was in his ability to maintain public support for the administration. He took a skeptical view of the Soviet Union and used arguments of the growing Soviet strategic threat as a justification for new U.S. programs. He supported Nixon's decision to restructure but proceed with an ABM system. He named Paul Nitze as his representative on the Kissinger-run delegation in the SALT negotiations, but rarely got directly involved in the details of the diplomacy.[41] When the SALT agreements were sent to the Hill, he testified in favor, along with the JCS, but insisted that the nuclear weapons limitations required full speed ahead on military modernization of both strategic and conventional weaponry.

Nixon and Kissinger tried to exclude Laird from several major policy issues, perhaps anticipating his opposition but certainly to maximize their own flexibility and secrecy. "Cutting out Mel Laird is what we did for a living," said Laurence Lynn of the NSC staff.[42] From the earliest days, the White House sought to communicate directly with military commanders, even issuing orders for military operations. Perhaps the civilians there did not realize that by law and by careful Pentagon practice, the secretary of defense must personally sign all overseas deployment orders.

On two notable occasions—during the India-Pakistan war of December 1971 and a year later when major bombing raids were launched against Hanoi—the White House bypassed the defense secretary and went directly to the chairman of the JCS, then Adm. Thomas Moorer. But the chairman kept the secretary fully informed.[43] Moorer also told Laird what he learned from the documents purloined by a young Navy yeoman assigned to the JCS liaison office at the NSC.[44]

Laird played the good soldier as an NSC member, offering advice and loyally defending decisions made. But he also maneuvered within and outside that system to support actions which he particularly favored. The process did not work as well as the president and national security adviser might have wished, however, because of their own obsession with secrecy and the corrosive effects of the distrust they felt toward their own senior colleagues.

Melvin Laird and Adm. Thomas Moorer. *Department of Defense*

Evaluation

By all accounts, Melvin Laird was a popular and successful secretary of defense. He accomplished his primary objectives in difficult circumstances. He persuaded the military commanders to undertake risky withdrawals from Vietnam and to reduce manpower levels in order to fund a new generation of weapons. He maneuvered to prevent deeper spending cuts by either OMB or Congress. And he was one of the few secretaries of defense to defeat a strong national security adviser in bureaucratic warfare. As a measure of the respect he felt toward Laird, Nixon brought him back into the White House in the spring of 1973 as the Watergate scandal began to engulf his presidency.

Laird was not a revolutionary, seeking to change the Pentagon in fundamental ways. Nor was he merely a manager, fulfilling his legal responsibilities and leading the Defense Department. Instead, Laird was the quintessential firefighter, preoccupied with the crises and controversies of his tenure. Yet he attacked the fires in his in-basket with a long-term vision and a clear sense of priorities. Withdrawing from Vietnam made all else possible: military modernization to negotiate from strength with the Soviet Union; an All-Volunteer Force to reduce political pressures from draftees and their families; and the restoration of military esteem and self-confidence, along with less chafing at civilian control. He pursued his goals with adroit bureaucratic maneuvering, yet without making long-term enemies or losing the confidence of the president. Few of his successors were as skilled or as successful.

7

Aspin:
The Politics of Failure

He was a bright, gregarious, immensely likable figure, but the appointment was in many ways to be a disaster, unacceptable for the country and the administration, and literally and figuratively for Aspin.

–David Halberstam[1]

Leslie Aspin Jr. wanted to be secretary of defense, dreamed of it, studied for it, got crucial experience to prepare for it, positioned himself to be selected, and then embraced the job enthusiastically. But he never outgrew his intellectual habits or his personality quirks, nor did he build the political alliances that could have protected him when he got in trouble. His is the story of great promise and poor performance, a Washington tragedy.

Born in Milwaukee in 1938, Aspin was the son of an accountant and a mother who dropped out of law school during the Depression. His father had emigrated from England to Canada, fought in France with Canadian forces in World War I, then moved to Wisconsin. Young Les went to Yale, Oxford, and MIT, where he obtained his PhD with a dissertation on the National Labor Relations Board. He had been in the Army ROTC program at Yale, where he was even given the Distinguished Military Student Award—not for his military bearing, but rather for his Phi Beta Kappa academic work. Commissioned in the Army, he performed his military service as one of McNamara's "Whiz Kids."[2]

Aspin won a seat in Congress in 1970 and joined the House Armed Services Committee, where he frequently made news with press releases exposing mini-scandals in Pentagon spending. In 1985, he led a revolt in the Democratic caucus to topple the ailing octogenarian chairman of the committee. He angered enough of his colleagues with his centrist positions on defense, such as support for some MX missiles, that in 1987 he was temporarily dethroned by that same caucus. After two weeks of soul-searching, contrition, and new promises, he regained the chairmanship. Thereafter, while in the House, he never lost touch with his political base—a lesson he failed to follow once in the Pentagon.

Aspin and his Senate counterpart, Armed Services Chairman Sam Nunn (D-Ga.), had different responses to the G. H. W. Bush administration. Nunn demanded that Colin Powell and Dick Cheney "fill in the blanks," the unanswered questions about their Base Force, their 25 percent cut in force structure and 10 percent cut in defense spending. Aspin had his staff develop its own set of alternatives and gave speeches supporting his Option C, a deeper cut than Cheney and Powell proposed that still provided a force strong enough to fight and win another Iraq war. Option C later became the Clinton proposal, both in the campaign and in the early months of the administration.

Nunn also led the fight against authorizing military force to drive Iraq from Kuwait in 1991, which passed the Senate on a narrow, mostly party-line vote. Aspin supported the Gulf War and brought a sizable number of Democrats along with him. By 1992, with the hindsight of history, he was vindicated while Nunn and his colleagues (except for Al Gore and a few others) were seen as weak in responding to military threats. That stance by Aspin, along with his help during the campaign, made him the leading Democratic candidate for secretary of defense and largely ruled Nunn out.

The other person being actively considered shot himself in the foot. Congressman Dave McCurdy (D-Okla.) tried to undercut Aspin by spreading the word that the chairman's selection would turn Armed Services Committee leadership over to the liberal, African-American Ron Dellums (D-Calif.). The blowback knocked McCurdy off the list.[3]

Bill Clinton had also come to like and respect Aspin. Warren Christopher, head of the president-elect's cabinet search, felt the same way after interviewing him. "I found him a lively conversationalist and understood why the president had said he preferred discussing theoretical defense concepts with Aspin more than anyone else he knew."[4]

Typical of the Clinton style, the president-elect had pleasant conversations with Aspin but never closed the deal or gave clear directives. "I was never actually asked to be secretary of defense," Aspin told Bob Woodward. "It was the usual kind of interview. We talked about the politics of the thing." But he wasn't offered the job. After a weekend of background checks, Clinton summoned Aspin to Little Rock for a news conference to announce his selection, telling him he was wanted for the job, but still without asking him to take it.[5]

He already had role models to emulate. He admired McNamara because he had been the first defense secretary to grasp the reins of power in the Pentagon and force rational, step-by-step planning on the services. He shared McNamara's devotion to number-crunching: "I do have a very strong faith in the ability of analysis to answer certain types of questions." But he thought McNamara failed by too much "top-down management." His second model was James Schlesinger, who in his view created incentives and got cooperation from the services for the innovations he sought. Aspin wanted to take the best of both approaches. "Sometimes an incentive system is the best, and sometimes a direct order is the best."[6]

In his confirmation hearing, Aspin echoed Clinton campaign themes when describing his own priorities for the Department of Defense. "Our first foreign priority and our first domestic priority are one and the same, reviving the economy." He said the president "wants the United States firmly on the side of the global movements toward democracy and market economies," which couples "our strategic interests and our moral values." The Pentagon, he argued, faced the challenge of maintaining the quality of the force and its high-tech advantages while responding to four dangers: the "new nuclear threat"; "regional ethnic religious conflicts;" "failure of reform in the former Soviet Union"; and "economic" dangers—meaning that economic well-being is vital to national security. He promised to reduce force levels "in a way that maintains their effectiveness," while cutting $60 billion more from defense than the Bush budget called for over the next five years.[7] He was quickly confirmed by voice vote.

His private agenda was more personal. He wanted to create a policy team with a cadre of "wonk practitioners" who could dominate the interagency process, imposing their views and their method of analysis on their inchoate colleagues. He recruited a group of friends and informal advisers from academia and think tanks and sought to install them as assistant secretaries for policy development. The service secretaries, by contrast, were named by the White House.[8]

As things worked out, he was only partially successful. Congress resisted some of his nominees and some of the redrawing of the portfolios. More significantly, delays in nomination paperwork by the White House and in review by the Senate left Aspin dependent on the small inner circle of aides from the Armed Services Committee. These people played important and valuable roles, but they lacked the authority of line officers confirmed by the Senate. No assistant secretaries were nominated before the end of April, and of the ten people named to those positions during 1993, only four were confirmed and in their positions by early July.[9]

Political Relations

Aspin got off on the wrong foot with his most important constituencies—the president, the congress, and the military—by the way he handled the controversy over gays in uniform. During the presidential campaign, Clinton endorsed the notion of "an immediate repeal of the ban on gays and lesbians serving in the U.S. armed forces." A few days after the election, when a reporter asked if he would fulfill his campaign pledge, Clinton responded, "Yes, I want to." Soon he discovered that there would be a heavy price to pay. Senator Sam Nunn had warned him, "The military isn't ready for it." Colin Powell, in his first meeting with the president-elect, also warned, "The chiefs and the CINCs don't want [the ban] lifted." He suggested asking his new secretary of defense to study the matter for six months or so, to keep the issue from being the first one between the new president and the armed forces.[10]

Clinton asked one of his transition aides, John Holum, to try to work out some way to lift the ban within the first month of the administration, but Holum encountered fierce resistance on Capitol Hill and among the senior military as well as anger from gay activists when they learned of possible compromises. Aspin took over the issue and tried to sell the idea of a six month study. When he went on "Face the Nation" soon after the inauguration to defend the policy, however, the new defense secretary gave answers that were intellectually honest and politically quite damaging. He noted that Congress and the senior military had the power "to derail this thing," which of course was true. He added, "if we can't work it out, we will disagree, and the thing won't happen." That comment seemed to invite the opponents to gang up and fight, which they did. The senior military went on record strongly opposing any change in the policy, and Senator Nunn held the administration's first legislative priority–the Family and Medical Leave Act–hostage to an agreement on what became known as the "Don't Ask, Don't Tell" policy. Clinton and Aspin tried to add "Don't Pursue," but in July agreed to the slight modification in existing practice, permitting closeted homosexuals to stay in the military.[11]

The issue weakened both Aspin and Clinton in their relations with the military and emboldened congressional critics to team up with the senior military in later disputes. It also sowed doubts about Aspin among Clinton's political advisers.

Clinton's enthusiasm for Aspin also waned as the new president met civilian and military opposition in the Pentagon to a more forceful Bosnia policy, as Somalia turned into a briar patch, and as a mob of Haitians made the U.S. Navy look impotent. Aspin's biggest political failing was that he couldn't solve the problems that arose in his department, or couldn't at least keep them from becoming problems for the White House. Clinton told a friend that Aspin wasn't taking care of national security issues–in particular, wasn't keeping them off his desk.[12]

Aspin had cordial relations with the other members of Clinton's national security team. Warren Christopher had helped choose him and

Tony Lake, the national security adviser, was an old friend. The three met for lunch every Wednesday and exchanged phone calls frequently.[13] Nevertheless, each seemed more concerned in handling his own direct responsibilities and preserving his own relationship with the president than with working together to resolve disagreements. They also took differing policy positions, starting with Bosnia, which pulled them apart.

Aspin also had strained relations with the senior military, at least at the start. He had clashed with Powell in hearings on the Base Force. The chairman of the Joint Chiefs of Staff had a low opinion of Aspin's organizational skills, which later experience reinforced. When the president-elect asked Powell for his views on different potential secretaries, he said of Aspin, "Les might not bring quite the management style you're looking for."[14] Aspin also had the burden of representing the views and authority of Bill Clinton, whose draft avoidance and anti-military comments decades before still poisoned the relationship between the administration and the senior military. The bitter and visceral disagreements over gays in uniform were followed by anecdotal reports of anti-military comments by junior White House staffers. The whole Clinton entourage was suspect.

As time went on, Aspin tried to improve his relationship with military leaders. He consulted with them in the "tank"; he took policy positions on Bosnia and Haiti which were similar to their own views favoring restraint; he even tried to build better personal ties. When the Navy secretary recommended firing the chief of naval operations, Adm. Frank Kelso, for failing to curb sexual misconduct at the 1991 Tailhook convention, Aspin overruled him on that as well as on punishing several other high-ranking officers. On the other hand, Aspin countermanded a policy directive by the commandant of the U.S. Marine Corps, Gen. Carl Mundy, which would have forbidden the enlistment of married recruits in the future because of the high incidence of marital problems among young Marines.[15] In these cases, Aspin tried to walk the narrow line between political correctness and good order and discipline.

When the time came, in the summer of 1993, to replace the retiring Colin Powell, Aspin recommended and the president eagerly approved Gen. John Shalikashvili, uniformly called "Shali," as the new chairman of the JCS. Unlike Powell, Shali was less dogmatic on the use of force and more willing to "do windows," meaning the peacekeeping operations that Powell had resisted.[16]

By the end of the year, however, after months of frustration with Aspin and his unorthodox operating style, the military were as eager for his departure as the White House politicos.

Even in Congress, Aspin had only mediocre relationships. His former committee remained cooperative, but Sam Nunn remained a friendly rival, always ready to press his own views regardless of the president's position. Congress won the first round, over gays in uniform, by preventing Clinton from going beyond the "Don't Ask, Don't Tell" policy and then by writing that position into permanent law, so that neither Clinton nor any future president could change policy by a stroke of the pen. Congress went along with Aspin's "bottom-up review" and the modest additional cuts it sought in defense spending. But Congress also pressured the administration to pull out of Somalia and undercut its flexibility by writing into law the president's timetable for withdrawal after the October 3 firefight in which eighteen U.S. soldiers were killed.

Operating Style

Pentagon officials could tolerate Aspin's non-military bearing, his rumpled suits, askew ties, and leg-over-the-arm-of-the-chair posture. They could salute and follow his orders, even for deeper cuts in their forces and programs. But what drove them crazy, disrupting their own schedules while still leaving them hanging in uncertainty, was his operating style, his non-decision-making.

Les Aspin never stopped being a professor, an intellectual, more eager to ask questions than to answer them. He enjoyed ruminating while his subordinates waited for decisions and orders. His morning staff meetings often lasted an hour or longer, with wide-ranging but inconclusive discussions. He could see every side of an issue, wanted to examine every side, and only rarely was he willing to choose a single approach. Some of these criticisms surfaced while he was secretary; they gushed forth after his forced resignation.

Colin Powell called Aspin's style "disjointed," with "marathon gabfests." But he found the same proclivity for "wandering deliberations" and unstructured meetings with the president at the White House.[17] An unnamed "senior national security official" told the *New York Times* right after the resignation announcement, "His inability to distinguish between discussion and decision led to a combination of problems. His inability to make choices drove the uniformed guys crazy."[18] A close and admiring associate called him "smart but miscast" for secretary of defense. A senior military officer offered broader criticism. "The new administration," he said, "didn't have a clue how to do national security policy."[19]

It did not help that Aspin tried to install his own small circle over the sprawling Pentagon. Many of his assistant secretaries disagreed and competed with each other, and few were truly plugged in to the bureaucracies beneath them. They were so dysfunctional they often could not produce even the briefing memos needed for high level meetings. Bill Perry openly criticized the policy shop and reorganized it once he became secretary. Aspin also wanted, but never really achieved, a competing military staff in his own office to provide information and options that never seemed to be coming from the Joint Staff.[20]

Although he played squash vigorously and often, he also grabbed for snacks set out for official meetings. Less than a month in office he suffered chest pains and shortness of breath and was diagnosed with heart disease. When a second episode occurred a few weeks later, doctors installed a pacemaker. But aides report that he never fully recovered the energy level he had previously.[21] He was weakened physically and then proceeded to be weakened politically by nasty leaks and back-stabbing comments.

Manager of the Pentagon

Like others, Aspin delegated daily management of the department to his deputy, Bill Perry. In fact, he had little interest in routine issues, according to aides. He was more interested in his interagency roles. Nevertheless, he presided over the bottom-up review (BUR), which justified his old Option C for slightly smaller force structures and spending than the Bush plan. Compared to the Cold War levels, Aspin recommended a 33 percent cut in force levels and a 40 percent cut in spending.

The new strategy still called for fighting and winning two wars, called "Major Regional Conflicts." But instead of sequential operations–"win-hold-win"–Aspin claimed that U.S. forces could win in both even if they occurred "nearly simultaneously." The BUR called for cutting active Army divisions to ten, compared with Cheney's twelve; cutting the Navy to eleven carrier battle groups, compared to Cheney's twelve; and cutting the Air Force to thirteen active and seven reserve fighter wings, compared to Cheney's fourteen and ten. On the other hand, Aspin decided to keep fifteen thousand more Marines than Cheney had planned.[22]

Responding to congressional concern about the growing costs and increasing delays in the major C-17 cargo aircraft program, he acted decisively to fire the program manager and three other officials, while bringing in someone both to regain congressional support and to run things in a more cost-conscious manner.[23]

In keeping with the administration's diversity goals, Aspin decided in April to allow women aviators to fly combat aircraft–fighters, bombers, and armed helicopters. He also sought and obtained repeal of the law banning women from the crews of combat ships. Women already had access to non-combat positions on other ships and to unarmed aircraft.[24]

War Planner

The new administration inherited one conflict in Somalia that it mishandled and could not gain military support for the one it wanted to pursue in Bosnia. Indeed, many observers believe that U.S. military leaders, after months of resistance, endorsed intervention in Somalia in the final weeks of the Bush presidency precisely in order to make it more difficult and unlikely that the new administration would intervene in Bosnia.

Clinton and Gore had both strongly criticized Bush for failing to act more decisively in the Balkans. When the new team met to discuss policy options, Aspin sided with Colin Powell, who had gone public with his opposition to intervention in Bosnia during the 1992 campaign. Aspin considered the situation "a loser from the start" and Powell opposed just "doing something," arguing that only troops on the ground could make a difference. While the other civilians were willing to consider a force of five thousand, the Chiefs demanded at least fifty thousand—a figure all recognized as politically unacceptable. As the administration moved toward "Lift and Strike"—ending U.S. enforcement of the UN ban on arming the contending forces so that Bosnian Muslims could be helped and conducting air strikes at Serb forces—Aspin continued to push for a ceasefire with only limited protection of Muslim enclaves. Clinton approved "Lift and Strike," provided NATO allies would support it, so Warren Christopher was sent to win allied agreement.[25]

In fact, Clinton himself seemed to have second thoughts about the Bosnia policy even while Christopher was still in Europe. He told Aspin and Powell of a book he was reading, Robert Kaplan's *Balkan Ghosts,* which detailed the long history of ethnic troubles in the region. As soon as Aspin returned to the Pentagon, he called Tony Lake and a top official at State to warn, "He's going south on this policy. His heart isn't in it."[26] Nor were the NATO allies willing to risk wider conflict, so Christopher returned empty-handed. Serb atrocities continued at a level just below the threshold for international outrage during the rest of Aspin's time in the Pentagon.

Although Aspin had grown up intellectually when McNamara and the game theorists were developing—and applying in Vietnam—notions of escalation ladders and graduated responses to threats and other symbolic uses of force, as secretary he stood with Powell in resisting military operations until clear and plausible objectives could be established. The administration's first use of deadly force was at the end of June, against Iraq, when twenty-three Tomahawk cruise missiles struck the Iraqi intelligence headquarters in response to an assassination attempt against the former president Bush when he was visiting Kuwait. The president approved the Aspin-Powell force package but changed the timing to avoid the Muslim Sabbath and to strike at night to minimize civilian casualties.[27]

By contrast, the administration did not really recognize that it was sliding into a more vicious conflict in Somalia. There were no meetings on Somalia by the "principals," the cabinet-level officers who participated in the National Security Council, until after the deadly October 3 firefight. Throughout the spring and summer, there were few meetings of lower level officials and virtually no real coordination of the interagency players. The president welcomed returning troops to the south lawn of the White House and thought he had turned the problem over to the United Nations. There were still a few thousand U.S. troops offshore, as emergency backup for the UN peacekeeping forces, but they were not in danger.[28]

When twenty-four Pakistani troops were ambushed and killed on June 5, there was no dissent when Washington was asked about supporting a UN Security Council resolution calling for the arrest and punishment of those responsible for the deaths. In fact, that haphazardly considered measure (it is unclear who was consulted on the language and vote) marked the turning point in the conflict, the point at which the U.S. military mission shifted from defense to offense against the militia headed by Mohamed Farah Aideed. Aspin and Powell then came under pressure from the field to send combat units, starting with helicopter gunships and AC-130 attack planes. Onshore deployment led to casualties, which led to requests for additional troops and additional firepower. When four soldiers were killed by a remote-controlled mine on August 8, Aspin and Powell reluctantly agreed to send Rangers and the elite Delta Force to Somalia to try to capture Aideed. They were the units caught in the October 3 attacks which killed eighteen and wounded seventy-three.[29]

Sensing growing opposition in Congress to the Somalia policy, Aspin gave a speech in late August to reassure skeptics that progress was being made in feeding the people and that the American troops still had a limited mission; specifically, restoring security in Mogadishu and not rebuilding the country's shattered economy and political system. He promised that the recently dispatched troops could be withdrawn as soon as three conditions were met: restoration of calm conditions in Mogadishu; "real progress towards taking the heavy weapons out of the hands of the warlords"; and the development of credible police forces in the major populations centers.[30]

It was that determination to limit U.S. involvement that led Aspin to reject requests from field commanders for tanks to bolster their capabilities. He didn't want to open a credibility gap with the press and public by dramatically increasing U.S. combat power just after he promised to keep the mission limited.

When the firefight occurred, Clinton was livid. "How could this happen?" he demanded of his advisers. "No one told me about the downside." He sent Christopher and Aspin to Capitol Hill to consult, despite Aspin's warning that the time was not right. Powell had retired on September 30 and Shalikashvili was unable to take over until October 25, so no senior military officer was there to explain and defend the policy. The meeting was a disaster. The members of Congress expected a briefing on the incident and administration policy. Aspin said, "I'm up here to get your ideas about what we should do." The members were so accustomed to being told what policy had been decided, without being consulted, they responded angrily at Aspin, and the word got back to the president.[31]

Clinton met with his advisers and eventually decided on beefing up the force already in Somalia while trying to negotiate with Aideed. He also promised to withdraw all U.S. troops within six months—a promise the Congress quickly wrote into law. Aspin's handling of Somalia, coupled with what happened in Haiti a few days later, weakened Clinton's confidence in Aspin and led to his search for a replacement in mid-November.

In Haiti, the administration again thought it had succeeded because it negotiated a July 1993 agreement between Aristide and Haiti's military rulers calling for Aristide's return to power on October 30. One of the preliminary steps was to be the dispatch of two hundred U.S. military trainers and engineers to help train the police and build some roads. When intelligence reports warned that the Haitian leaders didn't intend to live up to the agreement, Aspin argued against sending troops, saying their mission was unclear and fearing that they would get caught in a local civil war. He was overruled by Lake, Berger, and Christopher, who felt that the United States had to live up to its part of the bargain. The matter was not referred to the president for decision. When the *USS Harlan County* arrived at Port-au-Prince on October 11, a crowd of demonstrators, some armed, were on the dock, while local police and military personnel stood by. Since the Seabees on board were only lightly armed, the ship backed off and awaited instructions. Officials in Washington dithered, uncertain whether it looked worse to wait and be expected to fight their way in, or turn tail and withdraw. While Lake, Christopher, and even Gore argued for military action, Aspin warned, "Be careful. Look at the last time we invaded Haiti." On October 12, the *Harlan County* sailed away.[32]

Once again, Aspin was blamed by Clinton and his advisers for the outcome of an action he had warned against. One close associate, citing the parallel to a British movie from the 1940s, commented, "He was convicted of the one murder he didn't commit."[33] Aspin's talent as a war planner did not extend to recovering from setbacks.

Diplomat

In his year in office, Aspin made eight overseas trips. He was not as engaged in diplomacy as many of his predecessors and successors. Indeed, Powell even complained of his reluctance to meet foreign leaders.[34]

Aspin took a special interest in Korea. He made a careful review of the standing war plan for the defense of South Korea and traveled there for consultations. He also set up a special policy team on the issue, hoping to wrest control from the State Department. While he agreed with Christopher on the basic approach of "stick and carrot"—sanctions plus efforts to negotiate—he and his staff advanced ideas and remained active in the interagency deliberations over particular actions.[35]

He also took a special interest in Europe, but was at odds with his colleagues, for he opposed the expansion of NATO which they favored. He believed the end of the Cold War allowed a reduction in the U.S.

military commitment to Europe, and that adding members to NATO would push in the other direction. Aspin also shared the concerns of the uniformed military that the prospective new members were burdened with old and incompatible weapons and doctrine that would make it difficult to keep NATO a strong fighting force. Instead of immediate membership in the alliance, Aspin and his staff developed a creative alternative, the Partnership for Peace (PfP), that promised only military exchanges and cooperation, not necessarily NATO membership. It also fit the interagency requirement of giving both supporters and opponents of NATO expansion a first step on which they could all agree.[36]

NSC Adviser

As is evident, Aspin was an active participant in NSC-level discussions, but his advice, especially on critical use of force questions, was often not accepted. Sometimes his advice was unclear because of his tendency to explore options rather than offer conclusions. As one reporter noted after Aspin's resignation, "The president once described Aspin to an associate as 'a man with one thousand brilliant questions' but few answers and no plan of action."[37]

Despite his weekly lunches with Lake and Christopher, the top three policymakers fell into polite disagreement over many issues, and no one pushed the matters to resolution. Early on, the secretary of defense tried to dominate the interagency process with a group of smart subordinates, people with the "talent and temperament to team," as one close associate described them. But that team never jelled, never got confirmed in time to play their assigned roles or never settled their own turf fights over particular issues.[38] The result was mixed success—and in Washington, failure is self-reinforcing.

In the weeks after Mogadishu and the *Harlan County*, Aspin sensed that he was in trouble. The president gave only a lukewarm defense of his secretaries of state and defense in a television interview, saying that "some of the attacks" on them were unfair. Close aides urged a makeover for Aspin—new suits, tied ties and buttoned shirts, greater punctuality. He tried, for a while, but it was too late. Superficial improvements could not overcome his bigger failures.[39]

Once in trouble, every misstep got widely reported in the press—when he spent five nights with his girlfriend at a $400 per night hotel in Venice, paying for himself but letting the government pay for his accompanying aides, and when he crossed a picket line to take a vacation flight and thus save the taxpayers money. He couldn't win.

In early November, Clinton started the search for a successor. At a lengthy White House session on November 8, "Everyone in the meeting had friends in the Pentagon who had called them to complain about Les." They quickly settled on retired Adm. Bobby Inman, who started his own cat-and-mouse game about taking the post. On December 13, Tony Lake told Aspin that the president wanted to make a change. The next day, Aspin met with Clinton, argued that he had accomplished a lot and that the president should give him more time to demonstrate his leadership. That gave Clinton second thoughts, and he went back to his aides, asking whether he was doing the right thing. Finally, after a two-day reconsideration, he called Aspin to the White House to announce his resignation.[40]

Aspin never matched the expectations of the president or of his colleagues. His advice never allowed breakthroughs between dilemmas or bridges over clashing opinions. When he got in trouble, no one rushed to his defense.

Evaluation

Aspin entered office well-prepared intellectually, but still deficient managerially. He couldn't manage his own time, much less the huge

Les Aspin with President Clinton. *Department of Defense*

department that he headed. He understood the power game, how to gain and maintain power, how to build alliances, how to be influential in interagency deliberations. But he failed in applying that knowledge once in the Pentagon.

Les Aspin had vision, a broad view of the challenges the United States faced, but he got distracted fighting the inevitable fires that burn in a SecDef's "in" basket. He had many friends and admirers, but many, notably the president, lost confidence in his capabilities. As a result, his time in office was short, his accomplishments few, and his departure painful. Nevertheless, his tenure is instructive, for it illustrates the extreme case where a bright and well-motivated official makes small but consequential mistakes that ultimately accumulate and outweigh his other strengths. Ironically, Aspin had the flaws of his heroes, McNamara and Schlesinger. His hyper-rationality blinded him to the importance of personal relationships, and his attempted deal-making fell short of the big goals he sought to pursue.

8

Cohen:
The Politics of Defense

Bill Cohen's independence is as rigid as his backbone.

–Senator John Warner (R-Va.)[1]

*He was a Republican moderate from Maine, something
of a maverick centrist.*

–David Halberstam[2]

William Sebastian Cohen lacked the typical qualifications for secretary of defense. He never served in uniform. He never managed a large company. He never held a policy-making position in the executive branch. He never conducted scientific research on defense technologies. He was a career politician, but not in the president's party. He had even criticized many of the president's national security policies, strongly and publicly. And he was a poet and novelist who majored in Latin in college.

Despite those apparent shortcomings, Cohen was offered and gladly accepted Bill Clinton's nomination to run the Pentagon. He had spent a good part of his eighteen years in the Senate working actively on defense issues as a member of the Armed Services Committee. He had acquired an excellent outsider's view of how the Department of Defense operated and the big issues it faced. Retiring from the Senate in part because of his unhappiness with the strident partisanship of recent years, he welcomed the chance to bridge the political divide between the White House and the Republican-controlled Congress and to make national security policy more bipartisan.

As a Republican in a Democratic president's cabinet and as a moderate in an increasingly conservative party, Cohen continued his lifelong tendency to be different, to be ostentatiously independent. He was the son of an Irish Protestant mother and a Russian Jewish father. "To most Gentiles I was a Jew. To Jews I was always a Gentile. On either side I was the outsider, the outcast," he said. Although he studied Hebrew for six years, he finally rebelled and refused to go through with his bar mitzvah, angrily tossing his mezuzah into the river. "That was my turning point," he later wrote. "Now I knew I was in this alone, and I didn't have to be part of anything that I didn't want to be."[3]

Born in a tenement in Bangor, Maine, a floor below where homeless men slept on cots, Cohen early on began helping his father, a baker who worked sixteen hours a day, six days a week, for nearly seventy years, until he died while mixing dough in October 1995. His father's death was a major factor in Cohen's decision not to run for another term in the Senate. "Tomorrow is not promised to any of us," he concluded. "I really asked myself, is this what I want to do for the next six years?"[4]

He went from college directly to law school, and at age twenty-five set up his own law practice in Bangor. He received draft deferments during the Vietnam War, first for being married and then for becoming a father. He served in local offices, then was elected to Congress in 1972 and to the Senate in 1978. He gained national notoriety as an independent-minded politician when he was one of the Republicans on the House Judiciary Committee who voted to impeach Richard Nixon.

Cohen showed a willingness to cooperate with the Clinton administration early in 1993 and was even considered as a possible replacement for Les Aspin before Bill Perry was chosen a year later. Those gestures did not prevent him from being a sharp critic of some Clinton policies, however, notably intervention in Bosnia and the administration's opposition to a national missile defense program. But with Republicans in control of Congress, the president saw political advantages in naming a Republican to a top cabinet post. Soon after his own reelection, he began a courtship of Bill Cohen, calling him to the White House several times and engaging in long discussions. Cohen thought he was being considered as head of CIA, and was asked to take over Defense only the day before the formal announcement in December.

On that occasion, Clinton noted that he had worked "to find common ground on difficult issues" and praised him for his "discipline, intellect, creative independence, and deeply held principles." He also expressed the hope that Cohen would "secure the bipartisan support" the armed forces deserve. When a reporter asked whether Cohen might go "against the grain" of the administration, Clinton responded that he had talked with Cohen about that issue a lot, and that he wanted to encourage his officials "to be independent, to speak their mind, to argue for new ideas, to break new ground."[5]

The president gave Cohen no particular mandate on defense issues. His only guidance was to try to avoid interagency fights. He also gave his new secretary broad freedom over his Pentagon appointments, knowing that Cohen would bring many people from his Senate staff and would likely also seek to appoint some Republicans to DOD posts.

Cohen articulated his own priorities in his confirmation hearing. His first declared priority was "to continue to attract and retain the high quality of personnel necessary to preserve U.S. military superiority." "Ensuring high levels of readiness" was second. And "modernization of the force" was third. These were no different from Bill Perry's goals. But Cohen went on to indicate his interest in foreign policy issues, stressing his intention to pursue a "pragmatic partnership with Russia" and a "new focus" on Asia-Pacific relations. He acknowledged past disagreement with Clinton policies, but declared, "I am convinced that President Clinton is determined to transcend party lines and labels in formulating his national security policies and that he recognizes the importance hearing the voices of those who might differ with him."[6]

Political Relations

Bill Clinton liked Bill Cohen, admiring his intelligence and political skills. He knew from his first term that Cohen was a moderate who was willing to work with the administration some of the time. He wanted the symbolism of a noted Republican in his cabinet and also hoped that Cohen could keep national security policies from being caught up in the already vicious partisanship that clouded his second term.

In practice, Cohen was a buffer for Clinton, valuable for liaison to Capitol Hill and as a defender of administration policy when congressional Republicans attacked. Most notably, he stood in the well of the House of Representatives for almost two hours in December 1998, explaining and defending the administration's "Desert Fox" air attacks on Iraq to irate Republicans who believed and argued that the raids were only an attempt to divert attention from the president's impeachment. He was also helpful in building support for the Kosovo war in the spring of 1999. Even when Cohen disagreed with administration policy, he does not appear guilty of leaking his complaints to the press.

Cohen was also close to Vice President Al Gore, who directly and through his expanded staff played an active role in defense and foreign policy issues. The two men had worked together on arms control and strategic weapons issues since the 1980s and had mutual respect. During the search for Perry's successor, Gore had urged Clinton to pick Cohen.

With Secretary of State Madeleine Albright, however, Cohen had a rougher relationship. People who saw the two up close use similar words to describe it—"prickly" or "testy." Cohen viewed his cabinet colleague as a grandstander, too outspoken on policy matters and too eager to use military force. In her memoir, Albright notes that she had been critical of Cohen in earlier years but that the two worked collegially in the Clinton administration. "Although I did not always agree with the secretary of defense, we were usually able to work through problems caused by the differing perspectives of our two departments." She found Cohen "honest in his approach and resolute in implementing policies once they had agreed upon." She also says that the members of the Clinton foreign policy team "actually liked one another and often got together socially."[7]

Albright, like national security advisers Tony Lake and Sandy Berger, remembered the bitter, public, and quite damaging fights between Cyrus Vance and Zbigniew Brzezinski in the Carter administration, and all worked assiduously to avoid similar internecine feuds under Clinton. They largely succeeded both at the personal level and at the working levels between State and Defense, unlike the open clashes between cabinet members and their top subordinates in the Reagan and G. W. Bush administrations. Cohen and Albright both tended to include officials from the other department on their foreign travels, thus building camaraderie and smoothing coordination. The two did have differing personalities—she was assertive and sometime strident, while he was more soft-spoken and restrained—as well as conflicting perspectives derived from their respective institutions. The secretary of state wanted to back her diplomacy with the threat, and occasionally the use, of force, while the secretary of defense wanted to avoid empty threats or military action as mere gestures.[8]

With Berger and the NSC staff, Cohen had a good working relationship. "He was so gentlemanly, he got along with everybody," one senior staffer said. Cohen also respected the fair, inclusive, and well-organized way that Berger ran the NSC process. In addition to formal NSC or Principals Committee meetings at least twice a week, the top officials met informally twice a week, for breakfast and for lunch, to discuss and resolve matters without staff or interagency paperwork. Their deputies also had a weekly lunch. These venues helped to minimize surprises or open disagreements.[9]

Cohen worked hard to develop and maintain close relations with the senior military. "He didn't want to get out in front of them," one NSC official observed. "Indeed, he tended to line up *behind* them." A Pentagon official said, "He had close to an ideal relation with the CINCs and the Joint Staff," calling on them for information and advice while he promised to handle the questions of political feasibility. "He worked to be sure there was no daylight between himself and the Chiefs," this official noted. While Perry's meetings with the JCS in their "tank" were more formal, Cohen's were more frequent, sometimes twice weekly, and more substantive, with wide-ranging discussions. Cohen used these to get "buy in" from the Chiefs for administration policies and to learn in advance the positions the Chiefs wanted to take. "It's foolish not to use our two votes" in interagency meetings, he argued. "We shouldn't cancel each other out."[10]

He also met twice a week for breakfast with people, mostly three and four-star officers, visiting Washington from field assignments. He used these sessions both to gather "ground truth" and to identify candidates for future promotions. On occasion, he even had several prospects for a roundtable discussion as part of a "runoff" for a top command. A few months after taking office, he recommended the vice chairman of the JCS, Air Force Gen. Joe Ralston, as successor to the retiring General Shalikashvili, but Ralston ran afoul of opposition because of an adulterous affair in the 1980s and asked to have his name withdrawn. Cohen remained close to Ralston and frequently worked through him as continuing vice chairman, even after Gen. Hugh Shelton became chairman in September 1997. Later, Cohen got Ralston named NATO commander and subsequently hired him in his post-government consulting group.[11]

Cohen handled the toughest civil-military controversies of his tenure with self-confidence and ultimate success. After nineteen U.S. Air Force personnel died in a terrorist car bomb attack on their Khobar Towers residence in Saudi Arabia, the subsequent internal investigations exonerated the local commander, Col. Terryl Schwalier. Cohen rejected the recommendation from USAF Chief of Staff Ron Fogleman that Schwalier be promoted to brigadier general and instead insisted that a commander must be held accountable for the welfare of his subordinate personnel. Fogleman then retired early, arguing that such punishment would drive commanders to put force protection ahead of accomplishing their military missions. Cohen stood his ground.[12]

Sexual harassment abuses in the Army and the sexual misconduct of military officers sparked added controversy, but Cohen worked to keep the issues confined to the individual services and away from the White House. He failed to secure the promotion of General Ralston, but he succeeded in avoiding punitive actions by Congress.

With Congress, Cohen had the generally close and cooperative relationship that the president had anticipated. As his deputy secretary from 1997 to 2000, John Hamre, who also served on Capitol Hill as a staffer for the Senate Armed Services Committee, observed, "You have battles, but you are in the brotherhood."[13] Cohen also tried to avoid the mistakes he had witnessed by some of his predecessors. He believed that Weinberger's rigidity and unwillingness to compromise with Congress had been a mistake. "I don't think Cap particularly has the time, the patience, the inclination to want to sit down and try to take into account congressional concerns or proposals," he told a reporter at the time. "He has a mindset which precludes, for the most part, taking into account diversity of opinion or at least recognizing the legitimacy of diverse opinion."[14] He also believed that Les Aspin had needlessly angered his former colleagues, both in the way he tried to organize the OSD and in his mishandling of Somalia.

Cohen was a valuable conduit for Republican views and a good judge of the prospects for administration programs. He made a point of adding Republicans to his big name advisory group, the Defense Policy Board. His tenure did not include the usual legislative-executive clashes over defense spending because ceilings on Pentagon and domestic spending had been written into the 1997 budget balancing law, so they were no longer subject to annual disputes, and Clinton was willing to accept supplemental funds, particularly for military operations in the Balkans, despite the use of budget gimmicks.

Operating Style

Cohen organized his office like his Senate staff, relying on a few key aides. Even Deputy Secretary Hamre frequently worked through the staff. "He didn't want to be bothered with a lot of trivia. And he didn't really want to have to interact with a lot of people. He wanted, basically, maximum flexibility in his day," Hamre recalled. "I also felt that [his chief of staff] Bob Tyrer was absolutely his trusted agent, and when I talked to him it was as if I was talking to the secretary. I spent a lot more of my time talking to Bob than to the secretary," Hamre said.[15]

His preference for dealing with only a few people caused some problems, however, with the military. He named a longtime friend and former Marine Corps liaison officer to the Senate, Lt. Gen. Jim Jones, as his senior military assistant, a job that normally went to a two-star officer. "Secretary Cohen in many ways would have liked not to talk to anybody in uniform other than Jim Jones, but Jim made sure that he reached out beyond that," Hamre noted. "Jim's real battle was how not to supplant the chairman of the Joint Chiefs as the primary military adviser to the secretary," Hamre said. "It was very hard for Jim not to become the only military man that Cohen would talk to."[16]

Cohen followed a rigorous, workaholic schedule: up at 4:30 a.m. for an hour of exercise, at work by 7, not home until 9 p.m., where he continued paperwork until close to midnight. He was well-organized and meticulous: every book in his library was indexed and numbered using the Library of Congress system. He had daily meetings with his deputy and the chairman and vice chairman of the JCS–just those four, with no staff– followed by much larger and longer meetings, with various officials, including the service secretaries.[17]

Like most of his predecessors, Cohen delegated day-to-day management to his deputy secretary, reserving for himself those matters he alone could do–media relations, major budget issues, congressional relations and NSC-level policymaking. He also set aside substantial time for foreign travel and hosting foreign dignitaries. With the "ABC" (Albright-Berger-Cohen) breakfasts and lunches and two or more NSC member meetings every week, not to mention frequent Hill testimony, he had to spend a substantial portion of his time away from the Pentagon.

Manager of the Pentagon

Although Cohen delegated many management tasks, he knew that he would be held responsible. He also knew that many members of Congress and their beavering staffs would be looking for those television-worthy examples of Pentagon misspending, just as he had as a member of the Armed Services Committee. In fact, Cohen had gained notoriety a dozen years before when he confronted Caspar Weinberger with a report that the DOD had paid $600 for a toilet seat for the P-3 aircraft. This, Cohen said, "gives new meaning to the word 'throne.'"[18] He did not want anything similar to occur while he was secretary.

Cohen entered the Pentagon with a record of concerns and actions from his eighteen years on the Senate Armed Services Committee. Besides defending parochial interests, like shipbuilding programs for Bath Iron Works, he had taken the lead on legislation forcing modern business practices on the DOD. He was involved in the think-tank study group that developed ideas and public support for the defense reforms that became the Goldwater-Nichols Act in 1986. Most significantly, he and Sam Nunn (D-Ga.) authored the provision in that law that created a separate Pentagon office for special operations activities and gave the Special Operations Command (Socom) its own protected budget line. He tried to give even greater status to these forces by naming the former Socom commander, General Hugh Shelton, as JCS chairman after Ralston's nomination was withdrawn.

Congress saddled the secretary with the requirement to conduct by mid-1997 a major strategic and budgetary reassessment, much like Aspin's bottom-up review, but called the quadrennial defense review (QDR). As a sign of its reluctance to believe what the Clinton administration might produce, Congress also mandated a second opinion from a group of outsiders, including many retired senior officers, on a national defense panel (NDP). Perry had begun the process months before he left office, and the Joint Staff was ready for the new secretary with briefings and option papers.

To the dismay of many outside the Pentagon, Cohen rejected radical changes and approved a steady-state QDR. It retained the strategic goal of being able to fight two major wars nearly simultaneously while adding the Clinton administration's policy of global engagement. It proposed modest cuts in personnel levels (4 percent of active military, 6 percent of guard and reserves, 11 percent of civilians) and urged a faster ramp up of the procurement budget for force modernization. But it did not recommend canceling any of the big ticket weapons programs that were soon coming into production. The NDP, by contrast, urged greater attention to nontraditional threats, including terrorist strikes at home and abroad, and more resources for revolutionary new technologies. Both groups anticipated major savings from base closures which Cohen recommended but which Congress rejected, in part because of GOP anger over Clinton's political tinkering with the 1995 closure list.[19]

Instead of drastic cuts or the rapid embrace of new technologies (as George W. Bush suggested in the 2000 campaign when he called for skipping a generation of weapons), Cohen opted for more moderate management efforts. He announced what he called the Defense Reform Initiative, which he foresaw as "igniting a revolution in business affairs within DOD." Nearly half of the projected $6 billion annual savings came from planned base closures, and most of the rest from internal streamlining that did not require new legislation, but that ran into a buzz saw on Capitol Hill because it would require outsourcing of Pentagon jobs to civilian contractors.[20]

The net results were modest savings and a gradual—much too gradual for the Chiefs and outside critics—increase in procurement spending. Congress added somewhat to proposed budgets, both to cover unforeseen peacekeeping costs and to reduce readiness shortfalls that provoked sharp exchanges in congressional hearings. The administration accepted these additions and slowed the GOP push for early deployment of a nationwide missile defense system. Cohen in the Senate had supported a full-scale ABM system, but worked as secretary to fashion compromises between the reluctant White House and the adamant Congress, leaving both sides feeling that they had preserved their basic positions. Cohen's skill as a manager was like his skill as a legislator—the ability to bridge differences in creative and pragmatic ways.

War Planner

Cohen also bridged the gap between the Clinton administration's humanitarian interventionists and Colin Powell's doctrine of military restraint. He had argued for sanctions against Saddam Hussein by evoking lessons from the 1930s appeasement of Hitler, yet he had questioned the need for U.S. action in Bosnia and the durability of any U.S. commitment. "And the hearts that beat so loudly and enthusiastically to do something, to intervene in areas where there is not an immediate threat to our vital interests," he told the Senate, "when those hearts that had beaten so loudly see the coffins, then they switch, and they say, 'What are we doing there?'"[21]

He modified his position on the use of force to mirror the administration's announced strategy of selective engagement, with general conditions that had to be met, questions that had to be asked and satisfactorily answered, especially for actions where "less than vital" interests were at stake. He still deemed Bosnia "not in our vital national security interest," but conceded that America had an "important interest" there. He told his confirmation hearing, "I am very reluctant to see us engaged in too many areas."[22]

As secretary, he was deeply engaged in operational planning. He reviewed several of the standing war plans, including for conflicts involving China, Iran, Iraq, and North Korea, accepting some as proposed and ordering changes in others. He also pushed his staff to engage actively in developing the contingency planning guidance for potential crises. In the case of North Korea, he forced a re-write with numerous changes to deal with both the possible collapse of the North Korean government and its possible use of chemical weapons and other weapons of mass destruction.[23] In short, he took full advantage of the civilian oversight powers established by Goldwater-Nichols.

Cohen imposed some restraints on the military operations that occurred during his tenure. When Gen. Wesley Clark sought to root out hard-line Serb opponents of the Dayton Accords in 1997, Cohen told him he was "just barely" within the secretary's intent for the mission. In 1999, he canceled at the last minute U.S. participation in a long-planned raid to disrupt illegal funding for radical Croat politicians because of his concerns over possible American casualties.[24]

These disputes were part of an escalating series of conflicts between Cohen and Clark, which became open and sharp during the seventy-eight-day Kosovo war in 1999 and led to Clark's forced early retirement a few weeks later. Cohen, with the support of the JCS, disagreed with many aspects of Clark's strategy and recommended against several of his requests for U.S. actions. Clark told friends that his relationship with Cohen was one of the worst in his professional life. Cohen told his aides, "I rue the day I made him Supreme Allied Commander Europe."[25]

Cohen faced several cross-pressures. Like his predecessors, he believed that the regional commander, the man on the battlefront, deserved support. He said as much to the press in early April. "Whatever General Clark feels he needs to carry out this operation successfully, he will receive."[26] He also had to deal with the advice from the members of the JCS, some of whom, especially Army Chief of Staff Reimer, were reluctant to get deeply involved in Kosovo. The Chiefs also disliked the incremental nature of the fighting, since it was counter to the Powell doctrine of overwhelming initial force and since any expansion of target lists required NATO concurrence. The Chiefs went even further to demonstrate their opposition to Clark and the military strategy by leaks to the press criticizing the military plans and warning against the use of ground troops. Cohen had also opposed the possible use of U.S. ground troops from the start, fearing that that would undermine public and congressional support for the war.[27]

Clark's behavior throughout the crisis also bothered Cohen. The NATO commander was pressing him to move farther and faster than he was willing, often with statements to the press or other governments that added to the pressure. Several times, in response to Cohen's obvious displeasure, General Shelton or General Ralston had to call Clark and relay sharp criticism. He inserted himself into meetings, including the fiftieth anniversary NATO summit, from which his superiors wanted to exclude him. Clark also consulted frequently with Secretary of State Albright, who was widely and correctly viewed as the most stalwart advocate of force against Milosevic, so much so that the conflict was usually labeled "Madeleine's War."[28]

With regard to Iraq, however, Cohen was much more hawkish. He had supported the 1991 Gulf War and favored strong UN sanctions and inspections to forestall Iraqi acquisition of weapons of mass destruction. The Clinton administration had a robust series of measures, including: enforcement of northern and southern no-fly zones and a southern no-drive zone; nearly continuous deployment of U.S. ground forces to Kuwait; maritime interdiction operations; regular air strikes against air defenses and command and control facilities; and other enhancements of U.S. facilities and capabilities in the region.[29]

In December 1998, Cohen strongly supported and defended U.S. air strikes to punish Iraq for failing to comply with UN Security Council resolutions on inspections. The president had approved a bombing campaign on November 14, but the four-day operation did not begin until December 16–the day before the House of Representatives was scheduled to begin debating, for only the second time in history, the impeachment of a president. When irate Republicans accused the administration of using combat to counter the impeachment charges, Cohen went to the well of the House and defended the attacks, totally denying any political motivation to them.[30]

Cohen later claimed, with some justification, "During my tenure at DOD, no matter had a higher priority than countering the threat posed to America, our people, and our interests by international terrorism."[31] In fact, terrorism had been the first item on the president's list of challenges when introducing his second term foreign policy team. And Cohen included counterterrorism measures as part of his QDR. He also recognized and warned of the dangers of bioterrorism and chemical warfare long before many other officials. As early at October 1997, he went on national television with a five pound bag of sugar and warned that that amount of anthrax, if dispensed in the air, could destroy at least half the population of Washington. Meanwhile, the DOD went ahead with programs strengthening National Guard capabilities for dealing with possible attacks, training local first responders, organizing and conducting numerous interagency exercises, and, in October 1999, creating the Joint

Task Force–Civil Support (JTF–CS) to prepare for and respond to attacks within the United States.[32]

Although he had a strong record of support for special operations, Cohen also shared General Shelton's skepticism about its effectiveness against some overseas terrorist targets. Too often, he later argued, there was no "actionable intelligence" to justify high risk operations. An exception was the August 1998 attacks on an al Qaeda training camp in Afghanistan and a purported chemical weapons facility in the Sudan. But the blowback from that operation led him and Shelton to conclude that future actions should be targeted on the terrorist leadership, not their primitive facilities.[33]

His remaining time in office involved fending off pressures to "do something" when he and Shelton viewed the options unfavorably. When the U.S. military is reluctant to get involved in a situation, the senior officers and planners create options which they expect the civilians to find unacceptable. "A typical Army answer," a senior officer says, "is that it would take $2 billion, two divisions, and six months." For operations

William Cohen with Gen. Hugh Shelton. *Department of Defense*

against al Qaeda and bin Laden, Under Secretary of State Thomas Pickering said, "the standard military position [was], 'give us forty-eight months and five divisions.'"[34] After a terrorist attack on the USS *Cole* in October 2000, General Shelton developed a paper listing thirteen military options which were admittedly designed to "educate" Sandy Berger about the "extraordinary complexity" of adopting any of them.[35]

Diplomat

Cohen signaled his interest in working on relations with Russia and the Asia-Pacific region in his confirmation hearing. He told his staff to set aside ten days per month for foreign travel. He went to Korea, Japan, and Southeast Asia each year; to NATO meetings four times a year; and to the Persian Gulf area twice a year. And he added other travel as different crises demanded. One official estimated that Cohen had four hundred diplomatic meetings each year, mostly but not entirely with defense officials.[36]

He was drawn to Europe by longstanding interest as well as the current issues of NATO expansion and pacifying the Balkans. He saw China's growing power, economic and military, and was eager to use contacts elsewhere in Asia to bolster support for U.S. policies toward Beijing. He was traveling in Southeast Asia during the 1998 financial crisis and was used as the U.S. government's emissary to warn the Indonesian military against using force in breakaway East Timor. He later worked, unsuccessfully, to persuade congressional human rights supporters to permit renewed military-to-military ties with Indonesia.[37]

Like Perry, Cohen believed in cultivating foreign military officials in advance of actual crises. He foresaw renewed troubles in the Middle East over Iraq and Iran and made a special point of visiting Gulf leaders systematically. It is significant, however, that when General Musharraf seized power in Pakistan in 1999 and the United States protested, he insisted on calling CENTCOM commander General Zinni, who was with Cohen at the time. Take the call, Cohen said, "Just don't commit to anything."[38] This incident shows that the CINCs played even more important diplomatic roles than the secretary of defense.

NSC Adviser

Cohen took his NSC role very seriously. He had been one of the most active members of the joint congressional committee investigating the Iran-Contra scandal in the Reagan years, and he believed in following the regular order of the NSC process rather than letting rogue staffers act as they saw fit. His perspective was still that of a senator, asking how a given action would be seen by others. He was most interested in how to build and sustain public and congressional support for administration policies. "He was thoughtful, cooperative, a very good team member," one senior staffer recounted. "He was very good at synthesizing views, looked for ways to get things done. He was a problem solver." Sandy Berger declared, "I would say there has been nobody more of a team player in this administration than Bill Cohen."[39]

While he worked collegially, he often spoke as an outsider. David Halberstam says that "when he spoke in White House meetings, he often seemed to be speaking on behalf of the Congress (and the Republican party), not the administration (and the Democratic party)." His warnings about congressional opposition were often seen as if he were himself opposed to the policy. Eventually Sandy Berger took him aside and said, "I will regard this administration as a success when you refer to the administration as *we*, and not *you*."[40]

By the end of Clinton's term, Cohen had solidified his standing within the administration. He had supported the president's policies through the ordeal of impeachment; he had been outspoken in warning the nation of the dangers of terrorism; and he had been a stalwart leader during the Kosovo war. He had also probably burned his bridges to Republicans in the successor administration.

Evaluation

While his colleagues called Cohen a team player—and he was that—he can more usefully be viewed as a firefighter, someone who related to the Pentagon as a problem solver. He was inevitably drawn into the controversies of the period and forced to try to keep them from tarnishing the administration. He took the responsibility for decisions on punishing Air Force officers deemed negligent in the Khobar Towers attacks and General Fogleman's subsequent early retirement. He kept the pressure on the services to manage their sexual misbehavior scandals in politically sensitive ways. He succeeded in winning support, from the president and Congress, for increases in defense spending and especially in military procurement and even for a national missile defense system. He broadened military cooperation with nations of Eastern Europe and Central Asia, which later proved invaluable in going to war in Afghanistan. He kept defense policy disagreements with Congress from damaging the president. And with the fires successfully extinguished or contained, he left the Pentagon in the wake of praise and satisfaction.[41]

The Team Players

Most secretaries of defense have been diligent and supportive members of an administration, helpful in how they handled their jobs and in how they worked with their colleagues. They picked their battles carefully, within the Pentagon and within the administration, neither pushing too far nor too fast. They got along with the president, with Congress, and with the senior military. What waves they made were non-threatening to the other boats.

These men were usually well-regarded during their tenure and afterward. I would count most of the defense secretaries during the 1950s as team players, as well as those discussed here and two short-service secretaries, Elliot Richardson and Frank Carlucci. They earned those plaudits by quiet competence. They knew how the Pentagon worked, for sure, and often how Washington works—the power game.

This is not meant to be faint praise. Many of these men were ideal cabinet officers, both in managing their departments and in working to advise and support the administration in which they served. While all faced problems, like the firefighters, they did not become distracted by them. While some had innovative ideas, they did not overload the system with their reforms.

Here are three stories of successful team players.

9

Brown:
The Technology of Power

He's a very intelligent man. He's not a politician.
He's a scientist and an administrator.

–House Appropriations Committee Chairman George Mahon[1]

Harold Brown had more high-level prior experience inside the Pentagon than any other secretary of defense. A McNamara "Whiz Kid," he became director of defense research and engineering, the key research and development post, at the age of thirty-three and secretary of the Air Force at 38. He was an adept problem-solver of technical issues who faced as secretary of defense an even greater array of political challenges.

A child prodigy who at four removed a refrigerator panel to study its motor in operation and who earned his PhD in physics by the age of twenty-one, Brown worked on nuclear weapon design during the 1950s and became director of the Lawrence Livermore Laboratory in 1960. As head of defense research and development under McNamara, he played major roles in canceling the nuclear airplane, the Skybolt missile, and the B-70 bomber, but in promoting the Minuteman II ICBM and the F-111 fighter/bomber. He was viewed as smart, but also impatient and abrasive.[2]

He remained active and involved in defense policy matters during the Nixon and Ford administrations, when he was president of Caltech. He was part of the delegation negotiating the 1972 Strategic Arms Limitation agreements known as SALT I. He was active in the group of US-Japanese-European notables called the Trilateral Commission, where he got to know the ambitious governor of Georgia, Jimmy Carter, as well as several other future colleagues. He was one of several defense policy advisers to the Carter presidential campaign, and an obvious choice for secretary of defense.

During the campaign, Jimmy Carter criticized excessive Pentagon spending and pledged to cancel the B-1 bomber and cut $5 to $7 billion from the defense budget. He wanted a secretary who understood the technical issues and who could ride herd over the conflicting interests within the DOD. He decided on a team of Brown as secretary and Charles Duncan, the president of Coca-Cola, as deputy.

As Carter later wrote in his memoirs:

> I was determined to eliminate as much waste in defense spending as possible. . . . The Pentagon needed some discipline, and I wanted both a scientist with a thorough knowledge of the most advanced technology and a competent business manager, strong-willed enough to prevail in the internecine struggles among the different military services.[3]

Brown's own priorities were to maintain a strong defense even while achieving the 5 percent spending cut and to shape the force structure vital to U.S. foreign policy interests and commitments.[4] From the start, he believed that he had an important role to play in the broad spectrum of national security policies, not simply the management of the Pentagon. He also believed that the various service programs had to be woven into a coherent whole. He initiated defense management reforms and encouraged the JCS to seek greater technical and policy jointness, but these efforts were inadequate without the legislative changes that culminated in the Goldwater-Nichols Act of 1986.

From the start, he recognized the challenge facing anyone in his position. He hung in his office a portrait of the ultimately frustrated and failed first secretary of defense, James Forrestal. And he reminded a reporter of the mixed record of his predecessors. "There have been thirteen secretaries before me, and some have gotten at cross purposes with Congress, with their president, with the military. Not all of those are equal mistakes, but they limit effectiveness."[5]

One of Brown's highest priorities was to gain firm control over the Pentagon, but in a way obviously different from the image of McNamara's tenure. "To assert clear civilian control over the military, to convince the Congress and the people that these questions are being looked at in a rational way, without being decided by computers, that they're being decided in a way responsive to national needs–these are personal goals."[6]

Political Relations

Throughout his tenure as secretary, Brown remained unquestionably loyal to his president, always defending Carter's decisions even when his own advice had been rejected. Nor did he join his colleagues in writing a memoir to give his side of administration controversies. His only post-Pentagon book was prospective and analytical, with the modest title *Thinking about National Security*.[7]

Carter reciprocated with admiration, noting in his memoirs that "there were certainly no others who were better than he in my administration."[8] Despite that confidence in Brown's intelligence and judgment, Carter's own operating style weakened his defense secretary on numerous occasions and in many ways.

Like most defense secretaries, Brown had direct and regular access to the president. He came to the White House several times a week for meetings, though Carter usually asked for an NSC staffer to sit in on his meetings with Brown. To get privacy, Brown often would call the president at 7 a.m., when both first got to their offices. Although initially only National Security Adviser Zbigniew Brzezinski, Secretary of State Cyrus Vance, and Vice President Walter Mondale were invited to the regular foreign affairs breakfast on Fridays, Carter soon included Brown.[9]

But Carter went beyond these routine senior leadership meetings and scheduled large formal sessions where he could preside and decide. He often reviewed and made decisions that his predecessors had left to others. Barely a week in the White House, Carter called a meeting of his senior advisers to examine each of forty-five defense budget issues which had been worked out by Brown and the head of OMB, Bert Lance, in order to fulfill the campaign pledge of spending cuts. The meeting lasted seven hours. While Carter eventually supported most of the positions reached by his subordinates, this act of detailed personal oversight undercut Brown's effectiveness. Carter persisted with such micromanagement, even of small budget items, in later years. Only eleven months later, when preparing the budget for fiscal year 1979, the president reconsidered twenty-five major defense budget issues and held several meetings before making further cuts, some of which overruled Brown's recommendations.[10]

Brown reacted to Carter's style by restraining himself, expressing his views less forcefully in front of the president and sometimes giving advice without clear recommendations. Carter expressed some annoyance at Brown's "ambiguity."[11] In his final options paper for the president on the B-1 bomber, for example, Brown did not include a specific recommendation, despite his awareness of Carter's campaign promise to cancel the program. Many close to him believed he favored continuation, but Carter wrote in his diary on June 24, 1977, "Harold Brown has been very courageous to recommend that the B-1 not be built."[12]

Perhaps Brown's ambiguity was to protect the president by avoiding leakable pieces of paper showing that he had rejected Pentagon advice. Perhaps it was to minimize his own embarrassment at being clearly overruled. Perhaps it was his way of giving grudging support to the president's inclinations while reserving the right to argue for different decisions when the circumstances became more persuasive. Perhaps it was the consequence of his brilliance, for he was always testing arguments and weighing new information. Whatever the cause, the result was something Brown definitely wanted–that "he should not publicly acknowledge any distance between his own views and those of his president."[13]

To Zbigniew Brzezinski, Carter's national security adviser, Brown was often "the man in the middle, siding first with me, then with Vance, and sometimes (and he could do so quite effectively with his agile mind) with both of us at the same time." In the last two years of Carter's term, however, Brown became Brzezinski's "closest partner" as he supported normalization of relations with China and toughness toward the USSR.[14]

The defense secretary resisted the NSC staff's efforts to inquire into and interfere with DOD activities. In November 1977, for example, Brzezinski noted in his journal, "I have finally worked out an arrangement with Harold Brown for earlier intrusion of NSC personnel into the work of DOD. It was like negotiating with a foreign state."[15]

Brown also opposed efforts by other outsiders to violate DOD prerogatives and the chain of command. When he learned that an assistant secretary of state had called military commanders to request the dispatch of an aircraft carrier to the coast of Africa, both as a show of force and to prepare for the possible evacuation of U.S. nationals, Brown reminded all concerned that the chain of command ran through him.

With the secretary of state, Brown had a cordial, cooperative relationship. They had known each other since the McNamara days, and Brown considered his colleague a man of great integrity and trustworthiness. They agreed on some issues, disagreed on others, but never let their differences spill into the open, as did the policy conflicts between Vance and Brzezinski. Their differences reflected their departments: Vance favored diplomacy and agreements with the Soviet Union, while Brown was more hawkish and skeptical. Vance and the president stressed human rights while Brown was more concerned about a country's attitude toward the United States.

Vance accepted the legitimacy of DOD involvement in a broad range of foreign policy issues, though he pressed for State Department leadership of interagency groups. For his part, Brown saw enormous overlap between his responsibilities and Vance's. As he later wrote, "But foreign and military policy are closely connected, so the secretary of defense and, under his direction, the Joint Chiefs of Staff (JCS) influence foreign policy, and the secretary of state influences military strategy and programs." Brown saw no problem in letting the secretary of state make recommendations on deployment of weapon systems or even carrier fleets, but he also insisted that the secretary of defense could comment on the security consequences of technology transfers and trade as well as the risks of distancing the United States from a nation whose internal policies are distasteful.[16]

With the Joint Chiefs of Staff, Brown sought a close, supportive relationship. He met daily with the chairman and weekly with the full JCS. He tried to bring them along with some controversial policies and decisions of the president, succeeding on most of the foreign policy issues but not on defense budgets and programs. He also consulted in advance so that the Defense Department could speak with a single voice at interagency meetings.

This was at a time—before the Goldwater-Nichols Act strengthened the role of the chairman—when the Chiefs still operated through consensus and logrolling, when their advice was a compilation of their wish lists. Brown disregarded their collective views but paid close attention to their personal comments. He worked especially hard, sometimes with multiple meetings, to secure JCS approval of several key Carter policies, notably the Panama Canal treaties, the SALT II arms control treaty with the USSR, the Camp David agreements between Israel and Egypt, and the normalization of relations with China.[17]

On other issues, particularly defense spending and several iconic weapons programs, Brown had the difficult task of enforcing presidential decisions about which he felt less than enthusiastic. Jimmy Carter provoked anger and hostility among many senior officers by his style and policies. Although he had served in the Navy as a nuclear submarine officer, he had sharply criticized the Pentagon during his campaign and viewed nuclear weapons as immoral. He also had a demeanor toward his subordinates that many viewed as condescending and sanctimonious.

At his first meeting with the Chiefs, even before his inauguration, he was met with "an air of suspicion." Although he made ritual comments about wanting good civil-military relations, he shocked the Chiefs by asking how long it would take to reduce the numbers of nuclear weapons in the U.S. arsenal. He even asked, "What would it take to get it down to a few hundred?"[18] Since the U.S. strategic arsenal at the time was 2,400 warheads, and there were more than twenty-three thousand so-called tactical nuclear weapons with U.S. forces, the prospect of cuts to only "a few hundred" sparked fears of unilateral disarmament and dangerous weakness vis-à-vis growing Soviet power. The substantive disagreements between the new president and his military commanders were so profound that no social amenities could bridge them.

The Politics of Defense

While Brown was a consummate team player, he did have to fight several fires of political controversy. Some were ignited by Carter's decisions, such as canceling several weapons programs deemed vital to the various services. Others flared up because conservative members of Congress wanted to deter, defeat, or deflect Carter and some of his proposals, particularly arms control with the Soviet Union and improved relations with China. Nor did it help that Carter's landmark achievement of treaties to turn control of the Panama Canal over to Panama while reserving rights to defend it triggered massive domestic opposition and ultimately led to the defeat of many administration supporters in subsequent elections.

Although Democrats controlled both houses of Congress by comfortable majorities in 1977, many members were newly emboldened to stand up to the president, even one from their own party. The abuses of presidential power in the Watergate scandals brought many of them to Washington, where they eagerly asserted congressional prerogatives against the executive branch. Party discipline was weak in Congress, and the senior chairmen had been forced to give perks and power to their juniors.

Brown knew the necessity of cultivating the senior leaders on defense issues, and did so, but he could do only so much. As he told a reporter in 1978, "Various styles can be successful, but you can't be something you're not and get away with it. I have never pretended to be terribly gregarious or politic, and I guess it's too late for me to start now."[19] Many in the Congress agreed. They praised his intellect but viewed him as distant. As House Appropriations Chairman George Mahon (D-Tex.) commented, "He's a very intelligent man. He's not a politician. He's a scientist and an administrator."[20]

Policy toward the Soviet Union was the sharpest controversy. Henry Kissinger's efforts at détente had been derailed by conservatives, including Gerald Ford's defense secretary, Donald Rumsfeld, in order to counter Reagan's challenge to Ford in the 1976 GOP primaries. Many Republicans, and some Democrats like Senator Henry M. "Scoop" Jackson (D-Wash.), believed that the USSR could not be contained by treaties, but instead needed to be countered by an increase in U.S. capabilities. Although Carter's human rights policy had an anti-Soviet component, his congressional foes still tried to block his arms control initiatives and defeat his defense cuts.

Defense spending was linked by conservatives to the Soviet issue, but by others to the needs of the services. By 1977 there was already evidence of serious deficiencies in military readiness, and each service had long-delayed procurement programs for a new generation of weaponry. These arguments for defense increases ran counter to Carter and Brown's effort to achieve significant cuts. Since the defense budget had just topped $100 billion, a $5 to $7 billion cut was significant in percentage terms.

Brown tried to win congressional support by convincing Carter to endorse a policy of "3 percent real growth" in defense—after the promised cuts had been made. Carter agreed in 1977, but later undercut the political impact of his decision by limiting the increase to the presumed NATO share of two-thirds of overall defense spending and then allowing only a 2 percent increase in requested spending while claiming that the 3 percent promise was met by counting outlays from previous years' budgets.[21]

As Carter made specific decisions canceling major programs in each service, Brown discovered that fewer and fewer people on Capitol Hill were willing to support the administration. The angry services and internal policy dissenters opened back channels to administration foes, feeding them facts and documents to highlight the dangers of the Carter policies. Brown loyally defended the policies, but he found fewer allies in Congress.

His greatest achievement politically was keeping the Chiefs in support of key policies. By 1980, however, he was pushing for defense spending increases that the president partially adopted but resented. As he angrily told a White House aide, "Harold's been a horse's ass on defense budgets. He's caused me more work and took a hard line and never yielded."[22]

Operating Style

Brown ran the Pentagon with the usual routine meetings—a daily session with the chairman of the JCS to discuss operational issues, an 8 a.m. legislative and public affairs staff meeting to discuss the agenda for the day and big topics for the week, and formal sessions with the other Chiefs, the service secretaries, and policy councils. But he often seemed uncomfortable and distant in these meetings. Like the president he served, he preferred to read the relevant materials, ponder them, and then decide in private. One rising young colonel, Colin Powell, observed that Brown "preferred paper to people. I always had the impression that Brown would be just as happy if we slipped his paperwork under the door and left him alone to pore over it or to work out theorems."[23]

He was up early, usually at his desk by 7 a.m., careful about setting aside time for his daily swim. He found that he could more easily avoid intervening staff and reach the president, another early riser, by calling at that early hour. The president had given him freedom to pick his own subordinates, and he hired an array of talented people who formed part of the stable of defense experts who later staffed the Clinton administration, including William Perry, John White, Walt Slocombe, Jim Woolsey, and Lynn Davis. Brown usually accepted service recommendations for key military slots, but he pushed for Gen. David Jones to replace the ailing George Brown as JCS chairman and for Gen. Lew Allen, a scientist and missile expert he had known since the McNamara days, as Air Force chief of staff.[24] He also followed precedent in delegating much of the day-to-day oversight of the department to his deputy.

Drawing on his experience under McNamara, he reinstituted systems analysis and a more centralized management style, along with more detailed and formal budget guidance. His technology background made him especially animated when reviewing research and development budget items.[25] He applied his keen intellect more to the trees than to the shape of the forest. He did not try to articulate grand strategies or overarching visions, but rather spent his energies mediating between the president who wanted restraint and efficiency and the defense community in Congress and the Pentagon who wanted added resources.

Manager of the Pentagon

Despite his prior experience and self-confidence, Brown was ultimately disappointed in what he was able to achieve as DOD boss. Two months after he left office, he gave a speech at the University of Michigan titled, "Managing the Defense Department—Why It Can't Be Done." He listed the many political and economic factors that hindered efficiency.[26] Later, he mused that the secretary of defense had one of the most difficult tasks in government because of the need to understand the ideas and interests of the various components of the defense community and then build a consensus on policy.[27] Nevertheless, he worked hard at those tasks.

Like McNamara, Brown controlled the defense department primarily through the budget process. When he announced his first full budget in 1978, he bragged that "three hundred different defense programs were brought to me and about two thousand decision elements. I looked at every one myself."[28] Despite Carter's pledge to cut $5 to $7 billion from defense, Brown believed that, for political and strategic reasons, the United States had to increase military spending, not only to offset inflation but also to guarantee real growth.

The outgoing Ford administration fired a parting shot in the defense spending fight by issuing a budget plan that called for five years of annual real growth at 4 to 5 percent. The plan also embraced highly optimistic assumptions about economic growth so that it could forecast a balanced budget by 1980. Among the proposals were a doubling in the rate of ship construction and huge increases in all military procurement. In the following years, Brown repeatedly faced comparisons between his own budgets and the politically appealing but unrealistic plans left behind by Ford and Rumsfeld.[29] In one sense he returned the favor in 1981, when the departing Carter administration issued a defense budget which already contained the real growth that Ronald Reagan promised in his campaign. Without blushing, however, Reagan and Weinberger just added more real growth on top of the Carter plan.

Initially Brown and OMB Director Bert Lance worked out $3 billion in immediate defense cuts, most largely cosmetic, which the president accepted after his own detailed review. The defense secretary then orchestrated a change in administration policy by persuading the president to accept the target of 3 percent real growth in defense spending.[30]

He did this by getting Carter to push for NATO-wide defense increases, starting at the NATO summit in May 1977. A week later, Brown obtained the support of alliance defense ministers on the 3 percent goal. This was also formalized in August 1977 as part of the administration's comprehensive strategic review which led to Presidential Directive (PD) 18. While Carter later reneged on the goal by arguing that it applied only to NATO-related U.S. defense costs and that 3 percent real growth in outlays was as good as a smaller increase in new budget authority, the principle allowed Brown to avoid greater and difficult cuts.[31]

Nevertheless, Brown and Carter did feel compelled to trim the programs and spending plans left by the Ford Administration. In doing so, they managed to alienate each of the services by cutting back high visibility items. The most significant and symbolic action was Carter's June 30, 1977, decision to cancel the B-1 bomber, the Air Force's latest attempt—after McNamara cancelled the B-70—to replace the B-52s first built in the 1950s. Congress had denied production funds for the bomber in 1976, preferring to let the new president decide.

As a former secretary of the Air Force under McNamara who saw the need for an eventual B-52 replacement, Brown was predisposed to favor the B-1. During the 1976 debate over the bomber, he wrote that the Pentagon "had the best of the argument." But he pressed his subordinates for a thorough and balanced analysis of the aircraft and alternatives. While listing all of the arguments, the final version of the DOD study recommended a smaller force of B-1s as a hedge against uncertainties. Brown had several meetings with Carter to discuss options, though his own preference was for keeping the B-1 option open, perhaps by pausing for a year but then slowly starting production. He did not push his views strongly, however, because "from the outset he had let Carter know he would not force the president to overrule his own secretary of defense."[32]

Carter decided to keep his campaign promise, but also argued that U.S. security could be maintained by shifting from penetrating manned bombers to stand-off cruise missile carriers. Although highly secret stealth technology was already under development, it was only later, toward the end of the Carter term, that Brown was convinced that the nearly-invisible-to-radar B-2 bomber would be an even better alternative to the B-1.

The Navy was upset that Brown rejected its proposal for another nuclear-powered aircraft carrier and cut back shipbuilding to a more realistic rate, but one that would not allow a "six hundred-ship Navy" to replace the force which had shrunk to 484 as World War II–era ships had been retired. With Carter's support, he also rejected a proposed nuclear cruiser and procurement of submarine-launched cruise missiles.[33] When Congress added money for a new nuclear carrier in 1978, Carter vetoed the defense authorization bill, forcing deletion of the funds.

Brown favored shifting money to the Army in order to help redress the unfavorable balance of ground forces in Europe. But the administration did try to cancel the Bradley fighting vehicle, only to have Congress restore funds.[34] The net result was that Carter and Brown were held responsible, and faced continuing political assaults, for reducing the funds and programs proposed in the final Ford budget.

War Planner

As someone who had designed and tested nuclear weapons, Brown took special interest in strategic forces and sought to achieve coherence and modernization. Although the B-1 was canceled, he pushed an airborne cruise missile carrier, a new nuclear-powered Trident submarine and more accurate strategic missile, and a new ICBM, the MX. He also accelerated development of stealth technology.

While Jimmy Carter, in his inaugural address, had promised to begin moving toward the goal of "the elimination of all nuclear weapons from this earth,"[35] Brown was more interested in achieving a stable strategic balance through a combination of treaty limitations and force modernization. As the administration developed its first proposals to the Soviet Union in March 1977, he recommended a ban on new ICBMs, a missile flight test limit, and deep cuts in existing forces. This put him on the side of the NSC staff, against the State Department, and closer to the proposals of Scoop Jackson and his aide Richard Perle, who later were in the forefront of opponents of the SALT II agreement which Carter eventually signed in June 1979. The new president preferred bold, far-reaching proposals to merely codifying and extending the Ford-Brezhnev understanding at Vladivostok. But he undercut his negotiator, Vance, by telling a news conference, "If we're disappointed—which is a possibility—then we'll try to modify our stance."[36]

Soviet leaders accepted the invitation to reject Vance's proposals and return to the older frameworks. For the next two years, with Brown's active participation, the administration inched toward what became SALT II. In June 1979, Carter and Soviet leader Brezhnev signed a treaty capping strategic nuclear delivery vehicles (missiles and bombers) at 2,400 and imposing sublimits on land-based multiple-warhead carrying ICBMs. It did permit each side to build a new ICBM—for the United States, the MX. The treaty faced stiff opposition in the Senate from Jackson and many Republicans, but before the agreement came to a vote the Soviet invasion of Afghanistan prompted Carter to withdraw the treaty and impose various sanctions on the USSR. Meanwhile, Brown was proceeding with strategic force modernization, including plans for a survivable land-based ICBM. After considering some thirty-four different basing modes, the administration finally adopted the multiple protective shelter (MPS) shell game system, whereby each group of one hundred missiles would be moved randomly among twenty-three different revetments to guard against a Soviet knockout blow. This scheme was ridiculed by many Republicans, including Ronald Reagan, who rejected MPS but never came up with a survivable basing mode of his own.

In the months before the 1980 elections, Brown secured Carter's endorsement of a new nuclear strategy and weapons employment policy. Called PD-59, its NSC document number, the directive called for continued deterrence but added measures for "flexibility, enduring survivability, and adequate performance" in case deterrence failed. In what it labeled "an era of strategic nuclear equivalence," it declared an "evolving countervailing strategy" so that the United States could "preserve the possibility of bargaining effectively to terminate the war on acceptable terms."[37] The Reagan administration built on these concepts in developing its strategy for protracted nuclear war.

The only war Brown actually had to fight, indeed the only use of combat forces during the Carter administration, was in the failed attempt to rescue hostages held in the U.S. embassy in Tehran. Immediately after the embassy seizure on November 4, 1979, Carter convened his national security team and ordered the development of plans for punitive action against Iran as well as emergency rescue of hostages if some were killed. The president indicated, however, that he was not inclined to use either approach except as a last resort.[38] To prepare the requested plans, Brown deferred to JCS Chairman David Jones, who used the Joint Staff to de-

Harold Brown in his office. *AP photo*

velop them. Jones used an untried and inexperienced system to prepare and train for this unprecedented mission. After the fact, it became clear that the need to maintain operational security, to prevent either the prior movement of hostages or other actions to defeat the rescue force, caused the planners to fail to coordinate and rehearse the mission adequately.

Initially, Jones told the president that a rescue mission was "nearly impossible." But as the planning progressed and apparent solutions were devised for the many operational challenges, he became more optimistic. By the time the force was ready to be deployed, Jones and Brown believed that the mission had a 60 to 70 percent chance of success. When Brown sensed that Carter still had serious doubts, he arranged for a secret face-to-face meeting and briefing by the Delta Force commander.[39]

In the final days before the operation, Brown argued for its approval. "Neither the naval blockade or mining the harbors will bring the hostages home," he said. "The rescue mission is the best of a lousy set of options."[40] When the on-scene commander recommended aborting the mission after too few helicopters reached the Iranian desert launch site, Brown concurred and Carter agreed. Eight servicemen died a few minutes later when a helicopter collided with a C-130 aircraft. The fallout from the failure doomed Carter's presidency and led to a military-led reform movement which sought to improve inter-service jointness and strength—the power of the JCS chairman.

Diplomat

As mentioned above, Brown believed that his responsibilities included advice and action in a broad range of foreign policy matters. His military programs were profoundly affected by the outcomes of U.S.-Soviet and U.S.-European relations, as well as changes in the Middle East and East Asia. Consequently, he was a key player in the development and implementation of Carter administration policies toward these areas. He and JCS Chairman George Brown also were instrumental in developing the provisions which allowed the United States to secure the Panama Canal even after control was transferred to the Panamanians.

Early on Brown pressed for a stronger NATO, both by improving U.S. capabilities and by persuading the allies to set and meet the 3 percent real growth target. Later, he helped obtain support in Germany for the deployment of enhanced radiation weapons (ERW), the "neutron bomb" designed to kill Soviet soldiers without devastating European cities. When Carter, after months of silence that was taken as consent, suddenly decided that he could not support these new nuclear weapons, Brown had to try to repair the damage to U.S.-NATO relations. In 1979, he was a major proponent of the two-track policy of planning to deploy new intermediate range missiles in NATO while seeking agreement with the Soviet-led Warsaw Pact on force reductions and weapons limitations.

He took a personal interest in Japan, which he saw as a potential military power. He sought to improve each side's ability to conduct operations together in defense of Japan. Since no other senior American leader paid special attention to Japan, he had a freer rein, which he exploited with annual visits to Tokyo.

Brown was dispatched by the president on diplomatic missions several times. He traveled throughout the Middle East in February 1979, soon after the shah fled Iran, to reassure local leaders that the United States remained determined to keep the region free from Soviet domination. He also sought to get agreement for prepositioned stockpiles so that America could have a rapid deployment force for the region. In January 1980, soon after the Soviet invasion of Afghanistan, he was sent to China to explore the possibility of military-to-military relations and possible arms sales. A year earlier, when Carter normalized relations with Beijing, Brown spent several sessions with the JCS to convince them that improved U.S.-Chinese relations would pin down many Soviet divisions and would otherwise be helpful to U.S. security.

In these diplomatic activities, he was fully in league with the administration, not freelancing with his own agenda, as some other defense secretaries did. He recognized the DOD's equities in many foreign policy questions and was forthright with his advice and support.

NSC Adviser

As a member of the National Security Council and in his weekly senior leaders meeting with the president, Brown was a solid team player and active participant. He helped the administration as it negotiated arms control agreements and the Panama Canal treaties and as it shaped policy toward Europe and Asia.

He also had to dampen the controversy when Carter pursued policies he had counseled against, such as the neutron bomb cancellation and the withdrawal of troops from Korea. In that latter case, Carter had suggested during his campaign that the time had come to withdraw remaining U.S. forces from South Korea, both to save money and because of authoritarian and repressive nature of the Seoul government. He ratified that decision in May 1977 with PD-13, but immediately encountered a firestorm of opposition from his own military commanders and the South Koreans. Brown had to relieve one army officer, Maj. Gen. John Singlaub, for his outspoken criticism, but the negative views were more widespread. Brown defended the policy in public but worked in private to delay its implementation. In the meantime, new analyses concluded that the North Korean threat was greater than previously believed, and growing. That helped Brown to secure presidential agreement to cancel further withdrawals in 1978.[41]

Brown seemed to believe that he should offer his views forcefully, but then accept presidential decisions and defend them loyally. Unlike many other senior officials in his own and other administrations, he did not play the leak game to counter his colleagues. But he was subjected to the leaks from within the Pentagon, which allowed critics in Congress and the press to challenge his defense programs.

Evaluation

Harold Brown was an assertive and successful head of the Pentagon, a steady team player trying to balance pressures from his White House and State Department colleagues. Although he had to battle the brush-fires sparked by external events or Carter's impulsive decisions, he took a broader view of his responsibilities than many of his predecessors and played important roles in the Carter administration's foreign policy. His strengths were his scientific expertise and incisive intellect, which enhanced his influence with his colleagues and others. He was collegial in a cabinet which had an unfortunate share of highly publicized disagreements.

Brown was undercut, however, by Jimmy Carter's operating style. The president made decisions, such as Korean troop withdrawals, contrary to Brown's advice, but which the secretary loyally defended. Carter's line-item review of defense budget items also weakened Brown's leverage over the DOD because his own decisions could be appealed directly to the White House.

10

Cheney:
The Power of Decisiveness

Cheney was very impressive. He was a team player and, while he presented his views forcefully and consistently, when he lost he didn't leak or try to play games behind people's backs.

−Robert M. Gates[1]

Richard Bruce Cheney was an accidental secretary of defense. Although he held many important jobs in Washington prior to 1989−and would later become vice president−he never aspired to be put in charge of the Pentagon. He had served on the House Intelligence Committee, but never on the panels with direct oversight of the Defense Department. Newly chosen as minority whip, the second-highest Republican position in the House of Representatives, he might have looked forward to moving up to be GOP leader, and perhaps some day even Speaker.

But President George H. W. Bush was in trouble in March 1989. His nominee as secretary of defense, Texas Senator John Tower, former chairman of the Armed Services Committee, had been rejected by his former colleagues after several weeks of painful and embarrassing hearings regarding his personal behavior. Bush considered nominating his national security adviser, retired Air Force Lt. Gen. Brent Scowcroft, but decided that he needed Scowcroft close at hand in the White House. He searched for someone who was in good standing with Congress and thus would likely be easily confirmed.[2]

Bush called Dick Cheney to the White House and offered him the job. The president considered the Wyoming congressman knowledgeable about defense matters from his intelligence committee work, effective at working with others in Congress, and experienced in policy making from

135

his time as Gerald Ford's chief of staff. Moreover, the president observed, "He had a reputation for integrity and for standing up for principles and, at the same time, for getting along with people."[3]

Cheney was a proven team player joining a proven team. The president, the national security adviser, the secretary of state (James Baker), and Cheney had all worked together, and collegially, in the Ford administration. Three of them had been promoted together when Ford reorganized his cabinet: Bush became CIA director; Scowcroft replaced Henry Kissinger as head of the NSC staff; and Cheney became White House chief of staff as his boss, Don Rumsfeld, was sent to the Pentagon. Cheney picked Baker to head the Ford's delegate operation in 1976 and later made him campaign manager.

The new national security team avoided the public disputes and damaging leaks that plagued its predecessors and successors. As Cheney observed, "The three of us [Baker, Scowcroft, and Cheney], when we had breakfast together, had some knock-down, drag-out battles, but it never went outside that and I never had to worry about my backside. I was never going to see anything I said in those conversations used against me in the press. It started from that foundation of trust, which was crucial."[4]

Cheney succeeded in Washington as the bright and promotable deputy. He was first hired by Don Rumsfeld, then director of Nixon's Office of Economic Opportunity. He became deputy to Rumsfeld in the Ford White House, then moved to become chief of staff. After Ford's defeat, Cheney returned to his home state of Wyoming and was elected its only congressman. In 1988, he became deputy to House Minority Leader Robert Michel (R-Ill.), just before being named secretary of defense. In each position he impressed his superiors and won the admiration of his colleagues. He was smart but self-effacing, tough but not mean, hard-line in his views but not hard-edged in his relationships. "Cheney was an egalitarian man with little time for pomp and circumstance," David Halberstam writes. "He was judged by those who worked with him as not particularly likable but adept at making a bureaucracy work. He did not schmooze, he did not socialize."[5]

He approached his new job strategically. To succeed, he believed he needed to maintain good relations with the president, Congress, the press, and the NSC apparatus. Within the Pentagon, his highest priorities were picking good people, both civilians and senior military officers; mastering the budget; setting grand strategy while delegating lesser matters to his subordinates; and improving the operational command of the armed forces for wartime.[6] He pursued those goals with determination, rarely being distracted.

Political Relations

Cheney had known George Bush since 1969, when Cheney first came to Washington on a congressional fellowship and met the congressman from Houston. He believed that keeping the president informed and supportive was necessary to his success as secretary. He had regular access to Bush, usually meeting with him every other week in addition to group meetings. "I could pick up the telephone and call the president whenever I wanted to," Cheney says. "I tried not to abuse the process. I never had any problems getting access to him."[7] In group meetings, however, Cheney frequently dozed off, thereby earning from the president his second annual award for "soundness of sleep."[8]

Scowcroft had known and liked him from the Ford Administration. "Dick and I worked closely together. He was solid, no-nonsense, and practical, with no ego to get in the way of business at hand. His approach encouraged cooperation from everyone."[9] When Cheney later came to Congress, Scowcroft made a point of inviting him to participate in a study group on arms control and other strategic issues, thus broadening his knowledge of defense matters.

Secretary of State James Baker was also close to Cheney, personally and professionally. "We had fished together and had pack trips in the Wyoming wilderness," Cheney recalled. "Both in 1989 and '90 we went out in the fall for late fall fishing and elk hunting."[10] Baker echoes the closeness of the two men, saying they had "a strong friendship, mutual respect, and close working relationship."[11] In the Bush cabinet, they spoke frequently by phone and had regular Wednesday breakfasts. They had their policy disagreements, but largely kept them out of the press. Baker also trusted Cheney to stay off State Department turf.[12]

Cheney had authority from Bush to name his own subordinates, and he used it to cultivate several officials who would later return with him to high office. He took special care in naming senior military officers, starting with a new chairman of the JCS. He had first met Colin Powell in 1986 when he traveled with a congressional delegation to Germany. He came to know and appreciate the rising officer's talents even more when Powell was Reagan's national security adviser. In early August 1989, he summoned Powell for a job interview. He favored Powell as chairman, he said, because the general knew his way around the White House and Washington, understood arms control, and had the required military background. The president was uneasy, however, because Powell was the most junior of fifteen officers legally eligible for the position, having earned his fourth star only a few months earlier. Bush wondered if the appointment would cause problems with other senior officers. Knowing of strong support from the Army Chief of Staff, Powell assured Cheney, "I'm not worried about that." He got the job.[13]

Departing Adm. Bill Crowe had presided over the transition from the collegial JCS established in 1949 to the powerful chairman created by the 1986 Goldwater-Nichols Act. Not wanting to bruise egos or provoke unnecessary friction, Crowe took pains to preserve the Chiefs' sense of importance. Powell took full advantage of the chairman's new authority as the principal military adviser to his superiors and as boss of the joint staff. He also admired Cheney as "incisive, smart, no small talk, never showing any more surface than necessary. And tough."[14]

While Cheney voluntarily included Powell in the chain of communication of commands, he also insisted that the Pentagon speak with one voice in interagency meetings. "One of the things that I wanted to end when I arrived at the Pentagon was a practice in the Reagan years of oftentimes differences between OSD and JCS on these issues. I didn't want that to be the typical way we did business. So General Powell and I worked fairly hard to stay hitched together," Cheney said. "I wanted all that stuff resolved before we ever went over to the White House."[15] He also worked with and through Powell to deal with the other Chiefs and the regional commanders, then called CINCs (commanders-in-chief).

On Capitol Hill, Cheney was a seasoned politician who knew how to stroke his former colleagues. As Admiral Crowe noted, "Cheney's style was particularly engaging. He was not combative, he never lost his temper, he never condescended."[16] In time, however, he came into conflict with key members of Congress, especially with the majority Democrats. He was skeptical about the decline and eventual dissolution of the Soviet Union, arguing longer than others that the United States should be concerned about a resurgent Russia. He sharply cut back the production of new weapons and the defense budget overall, but far less than Hill budgeters wanted. And while he tried to cancel two major aircraft programs, the A-12 and V-22, he failed to overcome pro-Marine support for the latter and wound up ultimately losing a lawsuit on the former.

Operating Style

Although his only managerial experience before 1989 was his fourteen months as White House chief of staff, Cheney knew how to wield power almost instinctively. As Powell had observed, he was businesslike, self-contained, decisive, not the effusive, glad-handing personality usually associated with successful politicians. In his first week on the job, the new secretary publicly rebuked the Air Force chief of staff, Gen. Larry Welch, for talking to people in Congress about options for the controversial MX missile program. Welch had permission from Scowcroft and the acting secretary, a temporary holdover from the Reagan administration, but Cheney still called the discussions "inappropriate for a uniformed officer." He made the warning clear by saying, "Everybody's entitled to one mistake."[17] His actions sent a loud message throughout the Pentagon that Cheney was in charge and planned to stay that way.

His willingness to fire subordinates without doubt or hesitation was unusual—and highly effective. A few months later he relieved the commander of U.S. forces in Latin America for inadequate preparations for war in Panama. And a year after that he ousted the new Air Force chief of staff for indiscreet comments to reporters about U.S. Gulf War planning.

In his management of the Pentagon, Cheney followed the usual model of delegating day-to-day operations to his deputy. But he took personal charge of personnel selection. "I felt very strongly that it was very important to get the best people I could up front and I spent a lot of personal time doing that," he said.[18] He busied himself not only with the forty-four presidentially confirmed slots in DOD but also with the senior military officers. He interviewed many and personally signed off on all three- and four-star appointees. He also asked the service chiefs and department secretaries what they were doing to cultivate the best younger officers. "Who are their top one-stars? What kind of plan do they have laid out to move them into the key billets so that down the road the chief of staff of the Army will have the requisite training to have that option? That kind of thing I thought was crucial."[19]

Beyond personnel, Cheney's next highest priority was budget development, especially his first year. He wanted to immerse himself in the details so that he could be an effective defender on the Hill. He also took special personal interest in grand strategy and the wartime system for military command and control.[20] These issues became particularly important in his later years as secretary.

He held the meetings required by the system to resolve budget and policy issues and to make senior officials feel comfortable with their access, including periodic lunches and other private sessions. But he felt no need to reach out informally to those in the Pentagon. Cheney did insist, however, on getting information unfiltered and from outside the chain of command. As he told Powell early on, "[Y]ou tend to funnel all the information coming to me. That's not the way I want it."[21]

Manager of the Pentagon

The Bush defense budget outline had been decided even before Cheney took office. Despite the outgoing Reagan administration proposal for 3 percent growth, the new president had agreed to four years of zero real growth in defense until Admiral Crowe fought back and demanded a meeting with the president. He and the other chiefs were granted the meeting and used it to persuade Bush to relent to real growth levels of zero, one percent, one percent, and two percent.[22] Cheney inherited those bottom lines and worked to reshape the content to fit his sense of military priorities.

When Powell took office in October 1989, he moved quickly to develop what he considered a defensible minimum force structure, which he labeled the Base Force. He knew of congressional pressure for deep cuts, for a "peace dividend" to celebrate the end of the Cold War symbolized by the opening of the Berlin Wall on November 9. Five days later, Powell briefed Cheney on his ideas for a 25 percent manpower cut by 1994.

The chairman and secretary disagreed fundamentally on the nature of the evolving Soviet threat. Powell had been arguing for more than a year that the geopolitical situation had significantly changed and that Soviet leader Mikhail Gorbachev was struggling to prevent the collapse of his system, not cleverly trying to lull the West into premature disarmament. Cheney, by contrast, remained skeptical of Soviet reforms and concerned that America and its allies would embrace dangerous reductions in defense capabilities. As he told his confirmation hearing, "I am frankly skeptical about the likelihood of [Gorbachev's] success in terms of his reform drive." He added, "I think there's a real danger that in the West the perception of change in the Soviet Union will exceed the reality of change in the Soviet Union." Barely a month in office, Cheney stirred up a diplomatic controversy—and caused problems for Secretary of State James Baker—by predicting in a broadcast interview that Gorbachev would "ultimately fail."[23]

Despite his concerns, Cheney heard Powell's briefing on November 14 and asked him to brief the president the next day. In that session, Powell stressed strategic reasons to shift focus, not budgetary reasons. Bush was noncommittal but intrigued. While Powell returned to the Pentagon to begin briefing the service chiefs, whom he had left in the dark prior to his meeting with the president, Cheney launched a parallel civilian strategic review by Under Secretary for Policy Paul Wolfowitz, who shared the secretary's pessimism about the Soviet Union. Cheney foresaw the coming clash with Congress and wanted to be sure that the Pentagon controlled the expected build-down in forces. "I wanted to get on top of the debate that was about to begin on future U.S. defense needs. I had decided with Colin and the Chiefs that we need to lead on the debate with Congress."[24]

When the new budget was presented in January 1990, Cheney presented only a 2 percent real reduction in defense spending over FY1991-96, to be achieved by terminating twenty weapons programs and forbidding new starts as well as by closing sixty-seven bases and streamlining management practices. Congressional Democrats challenged the administration's lack of responsiveness to the dramatic events in Europe and pressed for deeper cuts. They were aided by a budgetary dilemma forced by the Gramm-Rudman-Hollings amendment, which required automatic across-the-board spending cuts to meet each year's deficit targets. The sluggish economy and unexpected high costs of the savings and loan industry bailout confronted the president with unpalatable choices: either break his "read my lips, no new taxes" campaign pledge, or let the automatic cuts slash 25 percent from defense spending and 38 percent from domestic programs. Bush chose to negotiate with Congress for a budget deal, including the possibility of some "revenue enhancements" (also known as taxes).[25]

Concerned that Cheney and Wolfowitz would fight even moderate cuts and that the Congress would seize the initiative and impose much deeper cuts, Powell went public with his views, first with a public speech defending his Base Force and later with an interview with reporters from the *New York Times* and *Washington Post*. Pressed for specifics, Powell volunteered cuts "[s]omewhere in the neighborhood maybe of twenty to twenty-five percent." Cheney called Powell to his office after the story ran and demanded, "I have to know if you support the president. I need to be sure you're on the team." Powell said he was, and regretted causing a problem.[26]

Forced to give something to the budget negotiators, Cheney picked elements from the studies by Powell and Wolfowitz. He adopted the 25 percent cut in manpower and force structure from the Base Force, but insisted on planning for the possible "reconstitution" of larger forces as a hedge against backsliding in Soviet reforms. His "illustrative plan," presented on June 19 after approval by the president, fell far short of congressional expectations. Budget negotiators questioned how a 25 percent cut in forces would lead to only a 10 percent cut in spending. Cheney made arguments trying to explain the differences, but House Armed Ser-

Richard Cheney testifying with Gen. Colin Powell. *Department of Defense*

vices Committee Chairman Les Aspin (D-Wis.) released a Congressional Budget Office study that said a 25 percent cut in combat forces should have led to a spending cut of 17 to 27 percent. The final agreement in September contained some tax increases, modest defense cuts (6 percent, or $19 billion) with specific dollar ceilings for the next three years, and also protection against future amendments shifting money from defense into domestic programs. The drastic cuts which otherwise would have been required by Gramm-Rudman-Hollings were avoided, but Republican criticism and defections presaged Bush's difficult fight for reelection in 1992.[27]

Cheney tried to shape and slow the defense cutbacks urged by Congress by terminating production of several current generation weapon systems, cutting back on troubled programs, and shifting funds into follow-on weapons. He also proposed a reduction in the size of the Navy and a reduced and reoriented missile defense program. He earned some goodwill with Congress by these actions, except for his repeated and ultimately unsuccessful efforts to kill the Marine Corps' new troop carrier, the V-22 Osprey, a hybrid airplane/helicopter. He surprised everyone in 1991 by abruptly canceling the Navy's new carrier-based bomber, the A-12.[28] Overall, he managed the force reductions so as to keep defense spending within the budget deal targets.

War Planner

Cheney presided over two major military operations, in Panama and Kuwait. In each case, he carefully reviewed the plans proposed by the military commanders, sought alternative views from outsiders, accepted arguments for massive force deployments, and avoided interference once the operations were launched. Military officers greatly appreciated the lack of micromanaging, which they considered a major flaw in the Vietnam War.

George H. W. Bush had publicly disagreed with President Reagan on how to deal with Panamanian dictator Manuel Noriega during the 1988 campaign. Reagan was willing to drop drug indictments in Florida against Noriega in return for his resignation from power. Bush opposed the deal, as did large majorities in Congress. Having denounced dealing with the dictator, Bush as president looked for another way of removing him from power.[29]

Under Reagan, State Department officials pressed for the removal of Noriega at all costs, while Pentagon officials argued that the threat he posed was not worth the risks and costs of taking him down.[30] Under Bush, the two civilian leaders of the departments were agreed on tougher action. As Secretary of State Baker later acknowledged, "In truth, we were doing our best to foment a coup."[31]

Cheney discovered, however, that his regional commander was opposed to military actions. Gen. Frederick Woerner, head of the Southern Command (Southcom), found fault and great risks with the suggestions coming out of Washington. Woerner also angered his civilian superiors—and demonstrated his lack of understanding of Washington politics—by declaring that there was a policy vacuum regarding Panama and by angering a group of visiting congressmen with condescending remarks. The defense secretary concluded that Woerner had "gone native" and couldn't come up with a timely solution to the Noriega problem.[32]

Acting with his customary decisiveness and with the president's strong support, Cheney relieved Woerner of command and named Gen. Max Thurman, who was just days away from retirement. Although he had not commanded forces in the field for fourteen years, Thurman was a talented, aggressive soldier. "Where many senior officers saw obstacles or made excuses," Bob Woodward notes, "Thurman saw possibilities."[33]

In October 1989, there was an attempted coup in Panama, which Noriega smashed even before U.S. officials could decide precisely how to react. The Bush team learned the lesson that they needed contingency plans, and Thurman prepared them. They then waited for a provocation that would trigger their use. Cheney raised detailed questions about the operations, seemingly down to the squad level. He also was dubious about the use of F-117A stealth fighters and vetoed at least one recommended target. When one U.S. officer was killed and an American couple beaten in mid-December, Cheney asked Powell to query the service chiefs on both the military and political aspects of the planned intervention. All four endorsed the action. On the night of the first attacks, Cheney had gone to his office and slept for several hours, wanting to be rested and alert once decisions might be required.[34]

When Iraq invaded Kuwait in August 1990, Cheney was dissatisfied with the limited military options that were being presented to him. "I need some options I can show the president," he told Powell.[35] His civilian aides had prepared a paper proposing a declaration of vital U.S. interest to oppose the invasion of Kuwait and advocating military action against Iraq, but Powell dismissed the approach as "Carteresque." As Cheney continued to press for military ideas and Powell dodged the issue by insisting that political goals be defined first, the secretary grew increasingly frustrated. Finally, he tersely demanded, "I want some options, General."[36]

Meanwhile, Cheney began "pulsing the system," as he called it, for creative ideas, including a possible quick, "surgical" strike on Saddam Hussein. Later, he established a small group of retired and active duty officers to devise plans that avoided some of the risks Cheney saw in the plans being developed by the regional commander, General Norman Schwarzkopf. This group came up with what came to be called the "Western Excursion"—an extended flanking movement. These measures angered Powell but were consistent with Cheney's ideas of civilian control in wartime. He told Wolfowitz he didn't want to micromanage the planning, "But I intend to own [the war plan] when it's finished."[37]

As the war plans were developed, Cheney reviewed them closely. He personally was involved in picking categories of targets and in some cases particular targets, just as he had done in Panama. At one point in early September, he even raised the possibility of using nuclear weapons. "Let's not even think about nukes," Powell pleaded. But Cheney insisted that the military "take a look to be thorough and just out of curiosity." He pressed Powell further: "Let's see an offensive plan with a little imagination this time."[38]

When the new Air Force chief of staff, Gen. Michael Dugan, traveled to the Middle East in September, he took along some journalists. He felt he was only proselytizing for air power when he told them "air power is the only answer that's available to our country" to avoid a bloody land war that would probably devastate Kuwait. But he also suggested specifically targeting Saddam Hussein and his family. And he gave a status report on U.S. deployments with details the administration had tried to keep from the media. Cheney was furious. He called Camp David and asked the president if he would have a problem if it were necessary to fire Dugan. Bush was not as upset, but he agreed to back his defense secretary. Cheney summoned Dugan to his office the next day and read from three pages he had written on a yellow legal pad, including nine reasons to dismiss Dugan, starting with "egregious judgment."[39] Dugan was fired, but his preference for massive air strikes before any ground invasion remained the essence of the war plan.

Diplomat

Cheney played key diplomatic roles in obtaining Saudi support for military actions and U.S. basing rights and in other ways in building the coalition of forces to fight the Gulf War. Secretary Baker worked on the diplomatic coalition, as demonstrated in UN Security Council votes and financial contributions, with an active, persuasive president also phoning around the globe.

In addition to ministerial conferences in NATO, Cheney took personal interest in the former Warsaw Pact countries and became the first defense secretary to visit Poland. Otherwise, his travel was mainly to Europe, particularly the regular NATO events. He did not seek a personal role in diplomacy except where his presence was needed for security-related purposes. He was content to let Jim Baker handle foreign policy.

NSC Adviser

As a member of the National Security Council, Cheney regularly met to discuss pending policy questions and crisis responses. He was ideologically predisposed to look with disfavor on arms control deals with the

Soviet Union, so he frequently weighed in with words of caution. He was critical of a suggested proposal to reduce U.S. troops in Europe as part of the Conventional Forces in Europe (CFE) negotiations and so strongly opposed to additional strategic reduction deals with the USSR that NSC staffers referred to him as the "defensive secretary."[40]

When the Soviet Union began to disintegrate, however, Cheney moved to the forefront urging U.S. actions to accelerate that process, such as early recognition of the new government of Ukraine. Bush chose a slower course toward that goal so as not to cause greater problems with Gorbachev.[41]

On use of force questions, he usually sided with Powell in raising objections and concerns. He accepted Powell's advice that it might be easy to get into Haiti and overthrow the government that had ousted the elected president, but very difficult to get out. He also shared Powell's view that even shows of force offshore of Bosnia could start America down a slippery slope to futile and costly intervention.[42]

Where Cheney excelled was on strategic vision. In Congress he had been the leading cosponsor, with Senator John Warner (R-Va.), of an amendment to the Goldwater-Nichols Defense Reorganization Act which requires the president to submit an annual national security strategy report, setting forth the administration's overall goals and priorities. The amendment was designed—and to a limited but useful extent has served—as a means of coordinating the broad strategies of the State and Defense Departments, and to make them consistent with White House plans.

In his first Defense Planning Guidance (DPG), issued annually to guide budget and force structure development, he specifically overruled Admiral Crowe and ordered an increase in the relative priority of Southwest Asia, ranking it above South America and Africa in terms of global wartime priorities. He wanted to prepare against both a Soviet attack on oil supplies or a "robust regional threat," presumably Iraq.[43]

By 1992, he was working actively to fashion a post–Cold War strategy to preserve U.S. hegemony in a unipolar world. The draft Defense Planning Guidance leaked to the press in March declared that the first objective of U.S. strategy was "to prevent the re-emergence of a new rival" and "to prevent any hostile power from dominating a region whose resources" made it a global power. While the draft DPG seemed focused on a resurgent Russia or an assertive China, it also called for planning for the possibility of using force to prevent the spread of weapons of mass destruction (WMD) into North Korea or Iraq. The draft said that the United States could consider preemptive attacks to respond to such threats. When public outcry greeted the Administration's "illustrative scenarios" for future wars—in Poland and Lithuania, Iraq and North Korea, Panama and the Philippines—officials tried to back away from their planning documents.[44]

While Cheney did not hold office long enough to enshrine that strategy in Pentagon planning, he had a later opportunity when he became vice president. The declared strategy of George W. Bush echoed these earlier ideas to a remarkable extent–and Cheney and his then-deputy Paul Wolfowitz held key posts to press for their adoption.

Evaluation

Dick Cheney was skilled in the use of power and eager to employ it for his chosen goals. He achieved dominant civilian control over the Defense Department, in part through his willingness to punish anyone who fell out of step with his close-order drill. Yet to the president and his national security colleagues he was a dependable team player, keeping within his domain and supporting others, without resorting to typical Washington backstabbing. He remained popular with his peers and his subordinates through numerous challenges. In short, he was a very successful secretary of defense.

11

Perry:
The Power of Decency

Perry was the rarest of public figures who had operated at that level at the Pentagon—a man much respected and fair-minded, with almost no enemies. His confirmation by the Senate was unanimous. He had a low profile outside the building, but was greatly admired within it.

—David Halberstam[1]

Perry, a scientist and opera buff, was soft-spoken, patient, confident, systematic and cerebral.

—Strobe Talbott[2]

William James Perry was not Bill Clinton's first choice to succeed Les Aspin, nor his second, third, or fourth.[3] But he proved to be a superb choice—an effective manager of the Pentagon and a cooperative team player on national security issues.

Growing up in a grocer's family in a small town north of Pittsburgh, Perry developed a love of mathematics and music. He served as an Army enlisted man in the occupation of Okinawa just after World War II, then went to Stanford, where he studied mathematics and joined ROTC, later becoming a reserve artillery officer. He gained a PhD in mathematics and went to work in defense industry, starting with GTE/Sylvania and then founding his own electronics firm, ESL, Inc. During the Carter administration, he served as the under secretary for research and engineering, where he guided the development of the post-Vietnam generation of weapons and spurred advances in stealth technology and computer systems.

In 1981, he returned to Stanford and worked with venture capital firms specializing in high technology, but he remained active in national security issues both as codirector of Stanford's Center for International Security and Arms Control and as a member of presidential commissions studying defense reforms and strategic weapons modernization. He was the logical choice for deputy secretary, the insider job, when Les Aspin was picked to be Bill Clinton's first secretary of defense.

While Aspin sought to increase OSD's capabilities and influence in the full range of national security issues, Perry dutifully worked on the budget and procurement policy. He was ready with a series of far-reaching acquisition reforms just six days after taking the oath as secretary in February 1994. After having been passed over for the top slot when the president chose retired Vice Adm. Bobby Inman, Perry needed strong persuasion from Vice President Gore to take the job.[4] Clinton praised him for "the right skills and management experience" and "the right vision for the job." He also acknowledged Perry's stellar reputation. "Time and again, we heard about him what I have come to know personally: Bill Perry is a real pro. You can depend on him."[5]

Political Relations

Despite his rocky start, Perry had the president's confidence as Pentagon leader, though he was still considered too diffident to be the strong public defender of administration policies. He proved himself by his strong management, careful advice, and loyal support even for presidential decisions contrary to his own recommendations—most notably on NATO expansion. Unlike Aspin's handling of the gays in uniform controversy and the ill-fated Somalia missions, Perry kept Pentagon problems from troubling or tarnishing the president.

Perry's relations with other senior administration officials were amazingly cordial. He had worked closely with Gore on arms control issues in the 1980s. He had known and worked with Secretary of State Warren Christopher in California and in the Carter administration. Both were from Stanford, and both were old-school gentlemen. He knew Tony Lake from the Carter days and the first year of the Clinton administration. From his prior government service, he had learned the painful lesson that interagency disputes weakened public support for the president. He was therefore determined not to get into open fights with the State Department or NSC, and to be sure he and the military leaders spoke with one voice.

He grew especially close to General Shalikashvili and worked mainly through him to deal with the other Joint Chiefs of Staff, seeing that arrangement strengthen the chairman as envisioned by the Goldwater-Nichols reforms. He had regular sessions with the Chiefs in their "tank," but these were formal consultations rather than wide-ranging discussions. He also made a point of trying to see every one of the regional combatant commanders, the CINCs, so that they would have a personal relationship to him in advance of any crisis. One trait that endeared him to the military was his deep and sincere concern about quality of life issues for military personnel. "He really focused only on two things," one subordinate says, "use of force questions and taking care of people and their dependents." He was proud of having been an enlisted man, and he took a special interest in the senior NCOs. His support for personnel improvements dovetailed with a key lesson he derived from the Carter years: maintain high levels of readiness or risk major political embarrassment.

Everyone who worked with him–peer and subordinate, in the DOD and elsewhere–liked him and praised him in similar ways: for his intelligence, his openness and fairness, his quiet competence. One official said he was "more studied, thoughtful. He sought to solve problems and was very productive." Another said, "His personal authority was so great that he had a big impact."

Perry spelled out his agenda for the DOD in his confirmation hearing. He listed as his "first priority to reviewing and assessing war plans and deployment orders." Second was "to ensure readiness." Third, interestingly, was to "be a key member of our national security team." Fourth was to maintain "strong relations with and respect for the military leadership." Fifth was to prepare the budget, making tough choices as necessary. Finally, he promised "to institute innovative management techniques."[6]

Congress embraced these goals and gave strong support to Perry's leadership. The Senate vote for his confirmation was unanimous. He was the kind of witness who listened to his questioners and pondered his responses before speaking with care and precision. He was forthright in explaining his conclusions without being disputatious. He buttressed his answers with solid analysis and technical expertise.

When the Republicans took control of Congress after the 1994 elections, they challenged many Clinton policies. Newt Gingrich's "Contract with America" called for higher defense spending, a national missile defense system, and reduced U.S. support for or involvement in UN-led peacekeeping operations. Perry fought these proposals on policy and budgetary grounds, especially since the added funds tended to go for programs that the administration opposed. In 1995, he secured a rare presidential veto of the defense authorization bill, primarily because of a provision accelerating development of a nationwide missile defense system. When this was dropped, the president signed the revised bill. In 1996, Perry held defense appropriations to a slight ($1.4 billion) increase above the presidential request and persuaded Congress to drop several controversial provisions on social policies.

Soon after Clinton's reelection in November 1996, Perry announced his retirement. He had grown increasingly frustrated with the partisanship in Congress and the negative impact that was having on the military establishment. He was still highly regarded on Capitol Hill, but he was less enamored of the legislative branch and the demands it made.

Operating Style

Perry was a skilled manager, starting each day with a small-group, fifteen-minute meeting to scope out the forthcoming day, in contrast to Aspin's larger, rambling sessions. He knew the Pentagon, how it worked, and how to make it work for him. He knew more, especially about technical issues, than many of his subordinates, but he never flaunted his knowledge. They knew he could not be fooled. He also wanted to know concrete details; for example, he demanded pictures of the perimeter of the Mogadishu airport during the U.S. deployment to Somalia.[7]

Like his predecessors, he delegated substantial work to his deputies, first John Deutch and later John White, while he concentrated on strategic issues, White House meetings, and foreign travel. He placed a high value on personal relationships, both with senior military commanders and foreign officials. He visited numerous places overseas so that others would know him better before he might have to come back and ask something of them. Yet he also took an agenda to each of these personal meetings, specific goals to accomplish in addition to the get-acquainted aspects. He was always pragmatic and programmatic, for he had been a businessman, not just a scientist.[8]

He was unhappy with the policy apparatus within OSD, calling it an "ineffective organization" in his confirmation hearing. He had little confidence in some of Aspin's selectees and proceeded to replace and reshuffle several of the key personnel.[9]

Manager of the Pentagon

Perry had already had five years' experience managing the Defense Department when he became secretary, so he knew what to do and how he wanted to do it. At the top of his list were the management reforms announced just a few days after he took office. These measures drew upon his work for the Packard Commission, the defense reform group set up during the Reagan administration, whose ideas were publicly welcomed and then ignored in practice. The heart of his recommendations, then and later as secretary, was "to change from milspecs to commercial industrial standards, and from buying practices unique to defense procurement to those used in traditional commerce."[10] The former businessman wanted the Pentagon to be businesslike.

He also took a long-range view of defense industry. In the spring of 1993, he persuaded Secretary Aspin to convene a dinner meeting of top defense executives, later dubbed the "last supper." At that meeting, he warned the company leaders that the post-Cold War reductions in defense spending were significant and continuing. They should not expect them to be cyclical or temporary. "I suggested that they should prepare for a long dry spell, and that this would certainly entail a consolidation of the defense industry, because the Defense Department would not support the excess overhead entailed by unused and unneeded facilities."[11] A wave of defense mergers followed Perry's warning.

During 1993, Aspin and Perry conducted their bottom-up review (BUR) of defense programs, which concluded that key military missions could be accomplished even if forces were reduced 33 percent and budgets cut by 40 percent, compared with the peak levels of the mid-1980s. This was deeper than the Bush-Cheney-Powell "Base Force," which endorsed a 25 percent cut in forces and 10 percent cut in budgets. The key goal in both cases was to be able to fight two major regional conflicts, notably Korea and Iraq, nearly simultaneously.[12]

The BUR cut the previous administration's baseline spending by $104 billion, or nearly 8 percent. Nearly three-fourths of the projected savings came from anticipated base closures and personnel cuts plus reductions in the missile defense programs.[13] In 1994, the Democratic-controlled Congress cut the Clinton defense budget requests by less than one percent. The Republican-controlled 107th Congress tried to increase defense spending and to accelerate missile defense programs, but ran into a presidential veto of the DOD authorization bill in 1995. When appropriators added $6.9 billion (2.8 percent) to the administration's budget, the president let the bill become law without his signature. Instead, the White House argued that the extra funds would go for the deployment of forces to Bosnia in support of the just-concluded Dayton agreement. In 1996, Perry's last full year as secretary, Congress added $9.7 billion (4 percent) to the proposed budget, with extra funds for missile defense and weapons procurement. In the presidential election year atmosphere, Clinton decided to sign the bill.[14]

While many in Congress fought to add funds for favored programs and amendments dealing with social issues, they accepted Perry's management reforms. In March 1996 he promulgated a new acquisition policy that cancelled more than thirty existing policy memoranda and reporting formats and replaced them with ones that were 90 percent shorter.[15] He also continued to stress quality of life enhancements for military personnel in order to maintain high levels of readiness and retention, despite the frequent overseas deployments during the Clinton years.

War Planner

Perry seemed to view use of force questions as practical, not ideological, issues. He had put reviewing and assessing war plans as his first priority as secretary, and he went about that task in a businesslike manner. He pressed his revamped policy staff to review the major contingency plans, especially for Iraq and Korea, and took a close, personal interest in them. He asked numerous questions and sought specific details to help him understand the way the plan would be executed. On more than one occasion he rejected the plans proposed by regional commanders and sent them back to make revisions. He was particularly concerned about avoiding rigidity and providing greater flexibility of choice for the civilian leaders.[16]

While any secretary of defense tends to resist military operations that are tentative or symbolic, Perry did not embrace the "hardly ever" criteria enunciated by Weinberger. Like many other post-Vietnam officials, he preferred the use of air power instead of ground combat troops, but he accepted Powell's logic of using an abundance of force. When discussing the capabilities of the NATO force planned for Bosnia in October 1995, for example, he said it would be "the biggest and the toughest and the meanest dog in town."[17] A year earlier, he used more measured language in NATO discussions on Bosnia. "When we go in, I want to go in with compelling force. Force not necessarily just proportionate to the act at stake, but enough to make it clear that there is a heavy price to pay for violating the rules that NATO has established."[18]

General Shalikashvili was also much more willing to consider military operations than his predecessor, General Powell. Indeed, the new chairman of the JCS openly told military audiences that "we can't say: we only do the big ones."[19] After a childhood in war-torn Europe, he was more attuned to the problems of that continent and sympathetic to the plight of refugees. Together, Perry and Shalikashvili ultimately accommodated the president's willingness to use force for humanitarian interventions.

At first, however, they were gun-shy. Although their predecessors had made the key decisions on Somalia, they concluded that public and congressional reactions to that operation precluded action in Rwanda during the mass killings in the spring of 1994. DOD officials were strongly opposed to U.S. military intervention to halt the genocide, and also reluctant to engage in "soft intervention" like jamming the broadcasts of the local hate radio station.[20]

In the summer of 1994, Pentagon officials raised numerous concerns about military intervention in Haiti to restore the democratically elected president who had been ousted in a coup in 1991. They thought it would be easy to overthrow the existing government, but were uncertain how well things would go in the aftermath. Marine Lt. Gen. Jack Sheehan was dispatched to Haiti several times to pressure the military government to turn over power peacefully. In a meeting of senior advisers in early August 1994, Perry reportedly argued strongly against setting a deadline for an invasion if Haitian military leaders refused to leave the country. Perry believed that a deadline would put the U.S. in a box, limiting its ability to maneuver.[21]

At the last minute before the planned invasion, Jimmy Carter, along with Colin Powell and Sam Nunn, obtained an agreement by Haiti's military leadership to step down and go into exile. The en route U.S. forces cancelled the "forcible entry" aspects of their mission and went unchallenged to their assigned areas. The operation was a political and military success for the administration, and did much to dispel its reluctance to use force for humanitarian purposes. Perry himself called it "a textbook example of coercive diplomacy."[22]

Throughout his early months in office, Perry was deeply involved in military planning for a much more challenging conflict on the Korean peninsula. He was a key ally of the administration's point man on the issue, Ambassador Robert Galluci. "North Korea was at the top of [Perry's] list. He alone among top officials in the Clinton administration was prepared to take responsibility for the issue."[23] He traveled to Seoul in April 1994, and again in October to consult with South Koreans and U.S. commanders. He asked for updating of the longstanding contingency plan for defending South Korea, OPLAN 5027, and also sought a new contingency plan to destroy key components at the site of the North's nuclear reactor. Perry and Shalikashvili concluded, however, that an attack on the reactor would likely unleash a massive and deadly North Korean attack on the South, with "hundreds of thousands, perhaps millions, of casualties" before the North was defeated. These dismaying prospects led Perry to endorse a policy of economic and political sanctions on the North, as recommended by Secretary Christopher.[24]

On June 14, 1994, Perry summoned the regional commander, General Luck, back for consultations on OPLAN 5027 and discussions of what might be done to prepare for possible execution of that plan if diplomatic measures failed. After two days of meetings and some modifications of the plan to deal with possible chemical as well as nuclear weapons, Perry briefed the president. He noted, "We had to choose between an 'unpalatable' option and a 'disastrous' option." Before the briefing ended, however, Clinton took a call from Jimmy Carter, who reported North Korean willingness to begin negotiations. This led to the October 21 Agreed Framework by which the North Koreans agreed to freeze certain of their nuclear activities and submit to international inspections. Once again, Perry traveled to Seoul to help convince the South Koreans to support the agreement. Perry concluded that the careful planning for the possible use of force had helped bolster the peaceful diplomacy that led to an agreement. In 1998, he was recalled by the Clinton administration to serve as a special policy adviser and coordinator for North Korea to try to limit North Korean nuclear activities.[25]

Diplomacy also averted U.S. ground combat operations in Bosnia, but only after a series of embarrassing setbacks for the Clinton administration and some efforts at coercive bombing raids. Although the president campaigned for office criticizing the Bush administration for insufficient help to the Bosnian Muslims, he soon became persuaded by the military arguments against U.S. intervention. In 1994, Perry endorsed the new U.S. initiative calling for negotiations but threatening air strikes, but he still warned against any U.S. ground combat role. In March 1995, he was explicit in warning that even limited U.S. involvement in Bosnia would send the United States "headlong down a slippery slope. At the bottom of that slope will be American troops in ground combat."[26]

The turning point for Perry was the fall of Srebrenica in July 1995 and the mass executions inflicted by the victorious Serbian forces. He and Shalikashvili flew to a NATO meeting and won support for a new policy promising to defend the designated "safe area" at Gorazde with significant air strikes if Serb forces even massed for an attack. The first such strikes followed in August after the shelling of the Sarajevo market place.[27]

By then, however, the administration faced a domestic political dilemma. Congress had passed, by veto-proof margins, a law requiring the United States to end compliance with the UN-ordered arms embargo to the former Yugoslavia and to arm the Bosnian Muslims. When Clinton felt compelled to veto the measure, the Senate delayed voting on the veto override in order to give diplomacy one last chance. Richard Holbrooke took advantage of that opening, and pressured the Serbs and their allies

William Perry speaking to U.S. troops. *Department of Defense*

to end their conflict under the terms of the agreement negotiated at Dayton in October 1995.

With Gen. Wesley Clark representing the Joint Staff, the Holbrooke team negotiated new political arrangements and a lengthy military protocol that limited what U.S. forces would have to do as part of peacekeeping. These provisions satisfied Perry and Shalikashvili that Bosnia would not become the feared slippery slope into broader combat.

In 1996, when China conducted provocative missile tests near Taiwan, Perry joined other administration officials in warning a visiting Chinese official against such actions. He also worked with General Shalikashvili to develop military options. They recommended, and received presidential approval for, sending two carrier battle groups into the Taiwan Strait. It was what Perry called "a message of capability and firmness, without undue provocation."[28]

Diplomat

Perry embraced and enjoyed the diplomatic aspects of his job. Indeed, he traveled abroad more frequently than any of his predecessors and to a broader range of countries on all continents. *The Economist* headlined an article on his travels "Perrypatetic" and suggested that he seemed to be overshadowing the secretary of state. Perry enjoyed traveling. He told his staff, "I need to visit every CINC." And he met with most commanders twice a year. He also wanted to develop working relationships with foreign leaders, on their own turf, before he had to ask them for help in a crisis.[29]

He took the lead among cabinet-level officials in working on North Korea issues, traveling to the area several times both before and after the Agreed Framework was concluded. He knew that the peninsula had the potential for serious conflict and that he had the credibility to build support for diplomatic measures.

Perry also took a special personal interest in U.S. relations with China. He had led the first U.S. military delegation to Beijing after Jimmy Carter extended diplomatic recognition and he traveled there a half-dozen times in later years. "As a result of these contacts, when I became secretary of defense I believed that I could play a leading role in the administration's efforts to reestablish a constructive engagement with the Chinese government," he wrote.[30] He believed in closer ties, built not only through trade but also through "mil-to-mil" contacts and exchanges. In China and in the countries emerging from the collapsed Soviet empire, Perry believed that frequent contact with the U.S. military at all levels would knit ties that would strengthen security cooperation for years to come. As he wrote with regard to Europe but practiced globally, "Military-to-military links are the key to preventing new divisions and new wars."[31]

The true measure of Perry's foreign policy activity is that, while he had four high-level meetings with the Chinese while secretary, he had fourteen with Russian leaders. He had worked on nuclear arms control issues for decades and worried about the dangerous consequences of the proliferation of nuclear weapons and technology. Once back in the Pentagon, he pushed for practical plans to implement the Nunn-Lugar legislation that sought to give scientists and governments incentives to move away from nuclear weapons programs.

Perry also took great satisfaction in helping to get Ukraine, Kazakhstan, and Belarus to give up their nuclear weapons, which had been stationed on their territory in the days of the Soviet Union. He also traveled to the region to observe the destruction of former missile sites, and to use such occasions as opportunities for strengthening ties with the United States. His long history of involvement with Eastern Europe and nuclear issues made him the ideal emissary when problems arose and reassurances needed to be given.

NSC Adviser

At NSC and Principals Committee meetings, Perry represented the Pentagon, but was willing to go beyond his agency position in order to resolve problems. An NSC staffer remembers when Perry displayed the book of point papers prepared for a particular meeting and announced, "This is what my staff wants me to say." He then dropped the book on the table and left it unopened. "He was studied, thoughtful, very productive," an NSC official commented. Another recalled that he could bring discussion to a halt by uttering a few soft-spoken sentences indicating that his limits had been reached.[32]

He was careful, however, not to draw lines in the sand, not to cement his concerns into hard opposition. As his under secretary for policy, Walt Slocombe, observed, "My sense of all the cabinet officers I've worked with has been that they are very reluctant—and this may be partly because it's the Defense Department—to put the president of the United States in a position where he potentially will have to overrule the secretary of defense." He also observed that "all three secretaries of defense that I worked for in [the Clinton] administration . . . were very conscious that you don't want—if there is a way to avoid it—to force the president to decide important issues by picking between the secretary of state and the secretary of defense."[33]

With his broad interests and travel, Perry was an active participant in foreign policy discussions, whether or not military assets might be involved. He gave his cautionary advice on Bosnia and Haiti, China and Taiwan, North Korea, and especially Europe. The one issue where he fought the longest and hardest against the position of his colleagues and the president was NATO expansion. Strobe Talbott commented, "He would have preferred to postpone enlargement for a decade, or perhaps forever."[34]

Like many others who had worked long and hard with the Soviet Union on nuclear weapons issues, Perry was concerned that NATO expansion would be unnecessarily provocative to Russia, risking setbacks or delays in counter-proliferation matters. During 1993 the Pentagon had been instrumental in crafting the Partnership for Peace (PfP) program in order to have cooperative military relationships with the nations of Eastern Europe. To Perry and other DOD officials, PfP was an alternative to NATO membership. In fact, it became the first stepping stone toward that goal.

Other administration leaders believed that the president had essentially decided in favor of NATO expansion in October 1993. He signaled as much in January 1994, when he declared in Prague that "the question is no longer whether NATO will take on new members but when and how." Defense officials continued to raise concerns in interagency meetings as they refused to accept the finality of the president's apparent decision. Finally, on December 21, 1994, Perry sought a special meeting with the president to argue for further delay in seeking alliance agreement on expansion. Top officials from State and NSC joined the meeting, where Perry argued that early expansion was a mistake, that it would provoke distrust and dismay in Russia. The president listened, but told the secretary that the die was cast, that it was not feasible to defer the admission of new states any longer and that the Russians could be convinced the expansion was not directed at them.[35]

Despite the president's rejection of his firmly held advice, Perry then acted in a way unusual in Washington: he accepted the decision and loyally supported the president, speaking forcefully in public and not engaging in the typical backstabbing leaks. He became an even more pronounced advocate after a September 1995 trip to several Eastern European capitals, where he gained a more favorable impression of the readiness of a number of the candidate countries. He also helped to craft the criteria for NATO to use in assessing the applicants. These "Perry principles" were: economic reforms, commitment to democracy and human rights, civilian control of the military, and the ability to contribute militarily to NATO.[36]

Evaluation

Perry's conduct on the NATO expansion issue demonstrates his commitment to action as a team member, a collaborative partner on national security matters, who was willing to subordinate his personal preferences to presidential policy. He was a practical problem solver who kept his disagreements within the walls.

To outsiders, Perry was a reasonable, thoughtful, decent person. He was more a manager than a policy innovator, but he was quite successful at that task. He ran the Pentagon deftly, by listening to his subordinates and then making clear decisions. Members of Congress who disagreed with some of his budget and program decisions nevertheless believed that he had made his choices rationally, with little regard to extraneous political pressures. He made few, if any, enemies and garnered many friends in Washington.

Perry tackled only a handful of high priority concerns, but he made a difference on those issues—especially nuclear weapons policies, relations with Eastern Europe, and quality of life concerns of military personnel and their families.

12
The Rumsfeld Transformation

Donald Rumsfeld does not lose.

–former Congressman and DOD Deputy Secretary Robert Ellsworth[1]

Don has some class. He was ruthless within rules.

–Ford speechwriter Robert Hartmann[2]

Rumsfeld afforded me a close-up look at a special Washington phenomenon: the skilled full-time politician-bureaucrat in whom ambition, ability, and substance fuse seamlessly.

–Henry Kissinger[3]

The Constitution calls for civilian control of this department. And I'm a civilian.

–Donald Rumsfeld[4]

Donald Henry Rumsfeld was the youngest and oldest person to hold the job of secretary of defense. He first took the oath of office at age forty-three, with scant experience in national security policy, though he had served three years as a naval aviator in the mid-1950s. He returned to the Pentagon at age sixty-eight, seasoned with unusually broad experience in business, foreign policy, and threat analysis. He bookended a period of relative peace, serving just after the United States withdrew from one war in Vietnam and then again as America began a long daylight struggle in Afghanistan, in Iraq, and in what he called the "global war on terrorism."

His first tour of Pentagon duty lasted only fourteen months–the tail end of the Ford administration. In that brief time, however, he learned lessons of leadership which, coupled with his other, wide-ranging activities, well prepared him to be the bold and dominating secretary of defense of recent years.

Rumsfeld was born in Chicago on July 9, 1932, the son of a real estate salesman and a part-time teacher. He learned patriotism early from his father, who forced himself to gain weight so that he could enlist in the Navy at the start of World War II, when he was 38. He learned familial devotion and strength of character from his mother, who moved young Don and his sister Joan four times in three years, from Illinois, to North Carolina, to Washington state, to Oregon, and then to California, to be near his father during his wartime service. Young Don also learned perseverance, as encapsulated in one of the first of the ever-growing list of "Rumsfeld's Rules." "If it doesn't go easy, force it," was his father's assessment of his son's operating principle at age ten.[5]

Rumsfeld excelled as a wrestler in high school, in college, and during his time in the Navy. Wrestling suited his shorter stature and abundant self-discipline; its individual nature and binary outcomes–win or lose, pin or be pinned–matched his personality. "Wrestling is pretty much you're operating alone out on the mat," he says.[6] He brought his longtime obsessions with fitness, fast maneuver, and domination of opponents to the E-Ring of the Pentagon.

Except for the wartime disruptions, Rumsfeld lived a near-idyllic life in residential communities north of Chicago. He was an athlete, Eagle Scout, and class officer; he attended summer camp in New Mexico; he earned an academic scholarship to Princeton; and he had an "understanding" with his high school sweetheart that led to marriage after they both finished college far apart: the American dream. In the Navy, he became a flight instructor and later an instructor of instructors. Afterward, he spent three years as a congressional aide, learning the ropes on Capitol Hill and whetting his appetite for elective office. Returning to Illinois, his big chance came when an eight-term Republican congresswoman announced her retirement. Rumsfeld jumped into the race to represent the 13th congressional district, campaigned tirelessly, and easily won the primary and the general election in 1962. In the House, he was assigned to the Science and Astronautics Committee, the Government Operations Committee, and the Joint Economic Committee.

As a junior congressman from the minority party, Rumsfeld joined with other Young Turks to challenge the GOP leadership to be more aggressive in fighting the Democrats. In his first term, he helped line up votes for then Rep. Gerald Ford (R-Mich.) to oust the current Republican Conference chairman. In 1965, he organized the effort to help Ford defeat the long-serving minority leader, Charles Halleck (R-Ind.). But when he tried and failed four years later to dump the GOP whip, Leslie Arends, who happened to be the dean of the Illinois delegation, Rumsfeld was denied a seat on the Appropriations Committee. Feeling "cramped" in Congress, he resigned and took the first of many jobs in the new Nixon administration. Then, as later in his life, Rumsfeld was impatient to change things.[7]

Nixon asked Rumsfeld to head the Office of Economic Opportunity (OEO), the centerpiece of Lyndon Johnson's war on poverty. Rumsfeld demurred, noting that he had opposed creating OEO. "That is exactly why we want you," Nixon said.[8] Rumsfeld took the job after Nixon sweetened the pot with an additional job with cabinet rank, assistant to the president.[9] Rumsfeld brought into OEO a group of eager, bright, young people who later rose to other positions of notable public service, including Frank Carlucci, Dick Cheney, Ken Adelman, Christie Todd, and Bill Bradley.

Rumsfeld did not try to strangle OEO, but he did work to de-fang and shrink it. He cut off funds for cities where radical activists took control of the community action programs. He devolved the successful Head Start program to the Department of Health, Education, and Welfare. He wanted to make OEO an experimental laboratory that quickly turned successful projects over to other agencies to run. In short, he sought a radical transformation of the organization.[10]

After a year and a half at OEO, Nixon gave him another unwanted task: head of the Cost of Living Council set up to impose wage and price controls. Rumsfeld told Labor Secretary George Shultz, "But I don't agree with that stuff." Shultz replied, "That's why we're appointing you."[11] He took the job in part because it came with another White House promotion, this time to counselor to the president. In that position, Rumsfeld had several conversations with Nixon, who advised him to get foreign policy experience if he wanted to run for the Senate from Illinois. The president warned him away from a second tier job at defense. "The service secretaries, well, they're just warts," he said. He also dangled the prospect of a cabinet post whenever one opened up.[12]

With the Watergate scandal unraveling in 1973, Rumsfeld got himself appointed ambassador to NATO, an overseas job with nice perks and much more family time. He was in Brussels when Gerald Ford recalled him in August 1974 to help organize the White House staff. Although Ford wanted a more open presidency, with no formal chief of staff, his fumbles in his first weeks in office led him to ask Rumsfeld to take on that job. Once again, Rumsfeld resisted an important job offer, telling Ford he wouldn't do it unless he had complete authority and control over access to the Oval Office. Rumsfeld agreed that Ford's office organization "projects the openness you want. In practice, however, it won't work." Reluctantly, Ford agreed.[13]

Rumsfeld brought Cheney in as his deputy, and later his successor as chief of staff. Ford's first year was a series of struggles—primarily to gain presidential stature and approval with the public so that he might win reelection in 1976 and to deal with mounting economic problems, including inflation rates above 10 percent, unemployment rising above 9 percent, and industrial production plunging to post-World War II record lows. He was successful, however, in taming the heavily Democratic Congress with a string of vetoes.[14]

Rumsfeld challenged the appointed vice president, Nelson Rockefeller, over control of domestic policy and used his position to point out even minor problems caused by Kissinger. By October 1975, Ford was convinced of the need to reorganize his administration, which he did dramatically by dropping Rockefeller and firing his defense secretary and intelligence chief. He also kicked Kissinger out of his NSC post, letting him keep only his State Department hat. Rumsfeld denied orchestrating this plot, but he clearly benefited from the changes.[15]

First Tour

Ford offered him the Defense Department, but at first Rumsfeld was reluctant to leave the White House. Cheney had to help convince him to make the move. As secretary, he demonstrated his political and bureaucratic skills. His closeness to the White House gave him leverage inside the Pentagon and throughout the interagency system. He was well regarded in Congress, thus helping him win support for larger defense budgets. Although he had the opportunity to name only one new member of the Joint Chiefs, Gen. Bernard Rogers for the Army, he made clear that he was boss. When Gen. George Brown made highly controversial remarks criticizing Israel, Britain, and the shah's Iran, Rumsfeld kept him as JCS chairman, but forced him to read a two-page statement of apology and clarification at a news conference.[16] His only real rival was Henry Kissinger, but Rumsfeld had the advantage of representing a point of view increasingly popular among Republicans.

In his confirmation hearing before the Senate Armed Services Committee, he faced a barrage of skeptical questions regarding the Kissinger policy of improved relations and arms control agreements with the Soviet Union, usually labeled "détente." Despite press speculation that the firing of Schlesinger marked a defeat for the foreign policy hard line and a victory for Kissinger, Rumsfeld declared that he was in basic agreement with the ousted defense secretary on Soviet policy. He went even further after his hearing by sending the transcript to the president, along with a note pointing out senatorial concerns about Kissinger's power.[17]

Détente was under attack by some Democrats, including presidential hopeful Sen. Henry Jackson (D-Wash.), and many conservative Republicans who supported the challenge to Ford mounted by California Governor Ronald Reagan. Whether Rumsfeld believed that the policy was flawed or simply saw its political downsides, he was effective at blocking progress toward formal agreements with the USSR. At one point in January 1976, with Kissinger in Moscow, Rumsfeld got the Chiefs to join him in raising doubts about the previously agreed U.S. proposal, forcing Ford to backtrack and leaving the secretary of state with no negotiating instructions. As one of his assistant secretaries, Morton Abramowitz, noted, "I remember very vividly, he beat the pants off Kissinger." The master diplomat himself agreed that Rumsfeld "in effect permitted and indeed encouraged the bureaucratic process to run into the sand."[18]

Rumsfeld used his first annual report as secretary to propound his views. He declared a basic objective of ensuring "essential equivalence with the USSR" and noted that the momentum of Soviet offensive and defensive programs would make Soviet capabilities seem superior to those of the United States. To prevent that outcome, of course, he defended Ford's budget request for a 14.7 percent increase in defense spending, 7 percent real growth above expected inflation. He also demonstrated his verbal fussiness by including a full-page discussion of the word "détente," explaining its derivation from pistol triggers, denying that it connoted "any hint" of "friendship, trust, affection, or assured peace," and declaring that "it is also a hope and an experiment."[19]

In public speeches and internal debates, Rumsfeld argued that the United States needed to spend more to avoid inferiority to the USSR. When Kissinger countered that talk about the trends only added to the perception of growing weakness, Rumsfeld retorted, "We have been slipping since the sixties from superiority to equivalence, and if we don't stop, we'll be behind."[20]

Within the Defense Department, he worked to improve morale and increase budgets. One of his first acts was to order the lights to be turned back up in the Pentagon, where they had been dimmed as part of an energy conservation policy. One of his first budgetary successes—duly leaked to the press—was when he got Ford to reverse a decision to cut the planned DOD budget by $7.5 billion. He persuaded the president to restore one third of the cut—as well as to endorse future increases in Pentagon spending.[21]

In his short time in office, he did not try to make major changes in U.S. strategy or in the management of U.S. forces. He favored the modernization of each component of the U.S. nuclear triad (MX missile, Trident submarine and missile, and the B-1 bomber). Despite congressional action putting off a final decision on the bomber until after the 1976 elections, he authorized the signing of the initial production contracts and even personally piloted one of the test aircraft in an effort to dramatize support.

He spent much of his time traveling both at home, giving speeches in support of Ford's policies, and abroad, to the usual conferences. In his first seven months in office, he went to NATO twice, Hawaii for a Korean conference, the Middle East, and made the first visit to Africa by a Pentagon chief. He went to Kenya to arrange the first U.S. sale of jet fighters to that nation, part of an effort to strengthen friendly governments against Soviet enticements.

His legacy after fourteen months was a defense budget growing once again and a broad consensus that the United States had to match the Soviet Union in nuclear forces. He also shepherded a new generation of weapons through another year of development.

With Jimmy Carter's election, Rumsfeld left government and took a position as CEO of the G. D. Searle pharmaceutical company, an Illinois firm founded by one of his original campaign supporters. He proved an aggressive, hands-on CEO. He sold off twenty-five unprofitable divisions, greatly expanded some others, and produced substantial profits. He also earned the title of "the axman" for his willingness to fire and transfer employees.[22] After the company was sold in 1985, Rumsfeld retreated from active management and served on various corporate and civic boards. From 1990 to 1993, he was again a CEO, this time of General Instrument Corporation.[23]

He suffered setbacks in the 1980s. President Reagan named him a special envoy to work on Middle East peace following the debacle of the Marine barracks bombing in Beirut, but he was unable to make any dents in the entrenched policy positions of the Middle East. He set up an exploratory committee to run for president in 1988, but dropped out after only a few months. He remained essentially in the political wilderness until 1998.

Then he regained prominence when asked to head a congressionally-mandated "Commission to Assess the Ballistic Missile Threat to the United States." The Republican-controlled Congress hoped such a panel would make the case in favor of its signature program of missile defense and allow it to prevail against Clinton administration hesitation. Rumsfeld deftly guided the commission's inquiry and secured support of the Democratic as well as Republican members on a report that concluded that the United States might have little or no warning before certain other countries could deploy ballistic missiles.[24]

His actions as head of the commission foreshadowed his handling of intelligence regarding Iraq. In both cases, he pressed the intelligence community with questions that exposed its uncertainty and then secured acknowledgment that the threat could be worse than previously thought.

Shortly before the 2000 election, he was named chairman of another special commission, this one on the military aspects of space policy. As that commission was moving toward unanimous conclusions endorsing U.S. superiority in space, with the means both to deter and to defend against hostile acts, Rumsfeld himself had to withdraw in order to take his bigger assignment back at the Pentagon.

Second Tour

Rumsfeld wasn't George W. Bush's first choice for secretary of defense. Former Senator Dan Coats (R-Ind.) was the presumptive nominee because of his ideological credentials as a Christian conservative and his well-regarded performance on the Armed Services Committee. But Coats reportedly blew his job interview with Bush because he lacked managerial experience and had no interest in getting into operational details. Bush instead wanted another CEO type, in keeping with his own Harvard Business School background.[25]

Rumsfeld had briefed Bush about missile defense during the campaign, and was later asked his views on the defense leadership, but he never received a direct job offer from the president-elect. That came in late December from his former protégé, Dick Cheney.[26] Bush presented his designee to the press as part of an experienced team that would help him meet the challenges of the twenty-first century. He specifically endorsed Rumsfeld for his knowledge of and dedication to missile defense. He also said he wanted the new secretary to improve military morale. He said Rumsfeld had "a broad mandate to challenge the status quo." Those were his only marching orders from the president-elect.

In his campaign for the presidency, Governor Bush criticized the Clinton administration for sending troops on so many peacekeeping missions and promised "an immediate review of our overseas deployments." He promised military personnel "better pay, better treatment, and better training." He promised deployment of a national anti-ballistic missile system "at the earliest possible date." And he pledged "an immediate, comprehensive review of our military"—structure, strategy, and spending priorities—with the hope that the United States might "move beyond marginal improvements" and "skip a generation of technology."[27] Bush did not even propose as much of an increase in defense spending as his Democratic rival, Vice President Al Gore. But he implied that more would be forthcoming, particularly to carry out his centerpiece program of national missile defense. To an officer corps increasingly willing to identify openly with the Republican Party, Bush and his running mate, Dick Cheney, promised, "Help is on the way."

The notion of radical change drew upon the sharp critique of current policy set forth the by National Defense Panel, the alternative opinion on military strategy required by Congress in the mid-1990s. A bipartisan group of members and defense intellectuals were pushing rapid U.S. embrace of the "Revolution in Military Affairs" (RMA) instead of the traditional evolutionary approach. They argued that the United States had the ability, since there was no near-term military peer competitor, to jump ahead to the next generation of computer-netted, precision weaponry, thereby saving the costs of maintaining large forces equipped with only slightly better systems.

Rumsfeld had not been part of the RMA clique. In fact, he cautioned senators at his confirmation hearing, "We cannot allow the effectiveness of our military forces to degrade while we are modernizing and transforming." But he noted the "ongoing technological revolution" and declared that "the U.S. defense establishment must be transformed to address our new circumstances."[28] "Transformation" then became the buzzword, the overarching term, for the changes he sought in military strategy, structure, weapons, and organization. Indeed, almost anything that was new, and everything that was costly, plastered itself with that label.

His other initial objectives included using offensive and defensive means to deter states from acquiring weapons of mass destruction and the means of delivery; improving the readiness and sustainability of U.S. forces; modernizing command, control, communications, intelligence and space capabilities; and reforming DOD structures, processes and organization.[29] He mentioned terrorism as one of the new threats the U.S. needed to defend against, as had Governor Bush during the campaign, but gave it no special emphasis or priority. He was confirmed by a voice vote shortly after the new president's inauguration.

Back in the Pentagon, Rumsfeld renewed his hard-charging style, making decisions, giving orders, and firing off his short memos, dubbed "snowflakes." Two of his "rules" made clear how he would lead DOD. "The secretary of defense is not a super general or admiral," one went. "His task is to exercise civilian control over the department for the commander in chief and the country." Another declared: "Reserve the right to get into anything, and exercise it."[30] At first he had to rely on his personal staff, for the lengthy vetting and confirmation processes took several months before he had his full complement of civilian subordinates. As deputy secretary, he made a surprising choice—not the usual business manager, but the intellectual anchor of the Cheney Pentagon and one of the leading foreign policy neoconservatives, Paul Wolfowitz. The two provided a heavy policy component to DOD leadership, leaving management and budgeting largely to others.

Revolution and Counterrevolution

Like Robert McNamara forty years earlier, Rumsfeld launched a series of studies by outsiders, mainly retired officers, industry executives, and think tank experts. He wanted bold, new ideas. With so few of his own people in office to help him, he also turned to a small group of aides who shared his political priorities. Determined not to be limited by the oldthink of those who served under the previous administration, he sought out in-house iconoclasts like Andrew Marshall and think tank zealots who favored exploiting advanced technology and disparaged what they labeled "sunset systems."

He considered the senior military leadership to be tainted by its service to the Clinton administration and institutionally incapable of radical change. Indeed, he froze them out of the review process, leaving the Chiefs and the Joint Staff sitting on their carefully prepared PowerPoint slides. They were ready to give advice because, by law, the new secretary had only until September 30 to give Congress his comprehensive strategic reassessment, called the Quadrennial Defense Review (QDR).[31]

Instead, Rumsfeld followed his own timetable, listening to his chosen experts. He shocked the Pentagon careerists by not asking for an immediate spending increase, as promised in the campaign and as requested by the Chiefs, when Bush sent his first budget proposals to Capitol Hill. He wanted more time to make longer-range choices. Those actions reaffirmed that he was in charge and that Pentagon business was no longer as usual.

The members of the old order launched their predictable counter-revolution in May 2001. Senior officers had complained to their overseers on Capitol Hill, who themselves felt excluded from the review process. When these gripes reached the daily press, after weeks of simmering in the defense trade press, Rumsfeld launched a public relations offensive. He scheduled special closed-door sessions with key congressional committees and increased his sessions with the Chiefs. He had his staff tally the numbers and then bragged about them. "I've met with [JCS Chairman General Hugh Shelton] about 1.3 times per day," he told the *Washington Post*. And he boasted of 170 meetings with 44 different general and flag officers in his first four months in office, as well as 70 meetings with 115 members of Congress.[32]

That was the quantity. The quality was different. "In meetings between the Rumsfeld team and military officers," one witness said, "you could cut the tension with a knife. None of the unformed guys know what to expect from the new SecDef."[33] By mid-July, there were press reports of bitter clashes between the Rumsfeld civilian team and the uniformed military. A senior aide berated a roomful of officers, "Can't you come up with anything new?" Rumsfeld himself openly rejected a major QDR panel's recommendations and told them to "go back."[34]

The secretary was willing to drop the planning criterion of two major, nearly simultaneous wars, but that did not resolve the issue of the size of the various armed forces. The civilians were reportedly ready to propose a 10 percent reduction in military personnel, including force structure cuts of two of ten active Army divisions, sixteen of sixty-one Air Force fighter squadrons, and one or two of twelve Navy carrier battle groups. When even the idea of those cuts met fierce resistance within the Pentagon and in Congress, Rumsfeld surrendered. He decided not to order specific reductions, but to require certain capabilities and set a budget ceiling, then let the services decide whether or how to make any man-power or program cuts. Wolfowitz tried to justify the retreat: "I think the secretary believes in the whole idea of freedom to manage, of giving people the responsibility for managing their organizations to certain goals."[35]

With Congress, he also made avoidable mistakes in those early months. He started by trying to muzzle the military by requiring a week's notice of all meetings on the Hill. He delayed sending budget increase proposals until July, and they fell far short of expectations. Wanting to wait until he had finished his review, he stiff-armed congressional efforts to give him advice and even extra money. When he decided to end B-1 bomber operations at three bases, without notifying the affected congressional delegations in advance, Congress retaliated by voting against the planned move. At one point Senate Majority Leader Trent Lott (R-Miss.) summoned Rumsfeld to a "Come to Jesus Meeting" with senior Republicans, where the defense secretary had to listen to a long list of grievances. Some Senators called Rumsfeld arrogant, and Lott himself put a temporary hold on all pending DOD nominees, thus delaying their confirmation by the Senate. The secretary did not change his approach.[36]

When White House budget officials denied half his request for new money, allowing only $18 billion of the $35 billion plus-up for fiscal year 2002, he accepted it quietly, thus angering both military leaders who had long been pointing out their shortfalls and congressional defense advocates who had been expecting more and were ready to fight for it. One of the leading conservative Republican magazines, *The Weekly Standard,* openly called for him and Wolfowitz to resign.[37]

Rumsfeld should have known better. One of his own "rules" quoted former Senator Pat Moynihan, "Stubborn opposition to proposals often has no other basis than the complaining question, 'Why wasn't I consulted?'" Another said, "Politics is human beings; it's addition rather than subtraction."[38] The secretary had a bold plan and he believed that he had to act boldly to achieve it. He repeatedly said, "Change is hard," without really applying that to his own leadership style.[39]

By August 2001, Rumsfeld was in retreat. His bold vision was in tatters, his attempts to transform the Pentagon stymied, his own leadership skills widely doubted. He confessed to a reporter, "I was not in the rhythm of the place." He also said he had learned a lesson. "It would be foolhardy to try to micromanage from the top . . . every aspect of everything that is going on."[40] Washington pundits speculated that he would be the first Bush cabinet member to leave the administration, and likely soon.

On September 10, he summoned DOD workers to the inner courtyard of the five-sided building to hear his warning about "a serious threat, to the security of the United States of America." The dangerous adversary, he said, was not overseas, but close to home. "It's the Pentagon bureaucracy," he declared. "Not the people, but the processes." He went on to complain about the "bloated bureaucracy," of innovation stifled by "institutional inertia," of "redundant staffs." The sharp words could have been the valedictory of a valiant warrior, leaving the battlefield after too many defeats.

Triumph as Secretary of War

On September 11, however, Rumsfeld was himself transformed from secretary of defense to secretary of war. All bureaucratic and congressional opposition vanished for many months. He had a blank check in budget and policy accounts to go after the terrorists and to craft the strategy and war plans to win what he labeled the global war on terrorism. His newfound prestige and buttressed authority also allowed him to impose his innovative planning process on the once-reluctant Pentagon.

He was in his office when American Airlines flight 77 struck the western side of the Pentagon. He raced outside to help in the rescue efforts, until persuaded to go inside to get to work on the military response to the terrorist attacks. He spoke with the president and recommended increasing the defense condition (DefCon) level from 5 to 3. The vice president told him that the president had authorized shooting down any hostile aircraft heading toward Washington. Rumsfeld then worked with the incoming JCS chairman, Gen. Richard Myers, to fashion rules of engagement for such operations.[41]

There were no war plans for action against al Qaeda in Afghanistan. The previous administration had limited itself to cruise missile strikes. Clinton's authorization to capture or kill Osama bin Laden lay dormant because of the lack of "actionable intelligence." Dick Clarke's counterterrorism proposals had been put into a nine month review that had laid a plan on Condoleezza Rice's desk only the day before. Rumsfeld admitted that there were few targets and major strikes might take sixty days to plan. Bush demanded quicker options. "Start the clock," he said. "I don't want to put a million-dollar missile on a five-dollar tent."[42]

Few in the Bush administration considered terrorism an urgent threat before September 11. Candidate Bush had included it in his Citadel speech and Rumsfeld had listed it in his confirmation priorities. But the defense secretary had refused to fill the Pentagon post specifically created by Congress to oversee and champion special operations forces, so it had remained empty since January 20. The strategic review had listed defending the United States as the first criterion for force sizing, but it was discussed mainly in terms of missile defense and nuclear, biological, and chemical threats. The QDR was hastily revised prior to its September 30 submission to Congress to highlight defense of the nation against terrorism as well as other threats.[43]

Months before, in March 2001, Rumsfeld had drafted his own set of guidelines for the use of force and walked the president through them. He did the same after September 11 and again before the Iraq war. His criteria were less restrictive than Weinberger's and put greater emphasis on the foreign policy context of military action. The wording was personal to Rumsfeld and somewhat informal. "If people could be killed, ours or others, the U.S. must have a darn good reason," he wrote. The operation must be "in the U.S. national interest," but was not limited to "vital" interests. The action should be "achievable at acceptable risk," with clear goals and acknowledgement of the risks of casualties. While not specifically endorsing preventive war or preemptive action, as Bush would later do, Rumsfeld did make the case for "early action" during the pre-crisis period. He also called for weighing both the risks of action and of inaction, though he concluded by warning, "It is a great deal easier to get into something than it is to get out of it."[44]

He became much more aggressive on combating terrorism, repeatedly arguing that the United States should be "leaning forward, not back." He also said that "if we're going to do something, it should be decisive; it should not be token. It should be serious, purposeful, and probably you have to include people on the ground."[45]

When the central command (CENTCOM) commander, Gen. Tommy Franks, offered a two-division war plan, however, Rumsfeld asked for a smaller force. He called in the special operations commander (SOCOM) commander and pushed for actionable plans. He transferred some Special Forces to work with CIA paramilitary forces. Operation Enduring Freedom, launched on October 7, called for only about one thousand U.S. troops inside Afghanistan, and they were used in innovative ways, including calling in air strikes by men on horseback. Despite fears of failure about a month into the operation, key Afghan towns fell to coalition forces in early November. And Rumsfeld was able to tally up the rapidity of the U.S. triumph: the air campaign had been launched within twenty-six days of the September 11 attacks; U.S. forces were on the ground in Afghanistan within thirty-eight days of September 11; and the Taliban were overthrown within sixty-three days. Remarkable success by any measure.[46]

Rumsfeld insisted on briefing the press three times a week on the war, earning a reputation for straight talk—and for honest avoidance. "I could answer that. I won't," he said frequently. He became a national celebrity. The president joked that he was "a matinee idol." He was satirized on "Saturday Night Live." He got a standing ovation after a briefing on Capitol Hill.[47] He used that public support to strengthen his power over the Pentagon.

Meanwhile, he was preparing for another Middle East war against Saddam Hussein's Iraq. He and Wolfowitz had joined other conservatives in signing a 1998 manifesto calling for the ouster of the Iraqi dictator. "In the near term, this means a willingness to undertake military action as diplomacy is clearly failing," the joint letter to President Clinton declared.[48] "Regime change" had been the declared policy of the United States for several years, but little had been done to bring it about. The $97 million voted by Congress for Iraqi insurgents never seemed to have any impact.

The president was also committed to getting rid of Saddam Hussein. In the campaign, he had threatened air strikes if the Iraqi leader were caught developing weapons of mass destruction. He also declared, "At some point in time the forces of good will take—will handle Saddam Hussein; I'm confident of that." At his first NSC meeting on January 30, 2001, Bush raised the topic of Iraq and ordered Powell to draw up a new sanctions regime and Rumsfeld to "examine our military options."[49]

In the early hours after the September 11 attacks, Rumsfeld reportedly asked his aides to get information to "judge whether good enough [to] hit S.H. at same time [as Bin Laden]." Wolfowitz raised the issue repeatedly at a Camp David meeting a few days later, until he was told to pipe down. Indeed, for several months Wolfowitz had downplayed the significance of bin Laden while pressing for action against Iraq. Bush told Rice after the Camp David meeting, "We won't do Iraq now; we're putting Iraq off. But eventually we'll have to return to that question."[50] But the president's September 17 directive on Afghanistan also ordered the Pentagon to begin planning military options against Iraq.[51]

On November 21, with the Taliban overthrown, Bush pulled Rumsfeld aside and asked him to start planning possible action against Iraq. He summoned General Franks and began the process of revising Op Plan 1003 Victor. The existing plan called for 500,000 troops, which Rumsfeld rejected out of hand. "He's less strong, so we don't need the old plan," he said. Rumsfeld raised the possibility of a force of 150,000 that would rely on speed rather than mass. Franks started with a 300,000 planning figure and cut it to 200-250,000 by the spring of 2002.[52]

His first revised plan was conventional in design, calling for ninety days of force preparation and movement, forty-five days of air attacks, and ninety days for major ground operations. Under pressure from Rumsfeld, he devised a shorter "Running Start" plan in contrast to the long "Generated Start" approach. By June of 2002, Franks briefed a concept for the new plan. It had the advantages of being usable in the event of preemptive action by Saddam and before all forces were in the theater. It envisioned a fourty five-day buildup accompanied by air strikes and Special Forces operations, followed by ninety days of "decisive offensive operations," and another ninety days to "complete regime destruction." Franks planned an invasion force of 180,000 that could grow to 250,000 if needed. He also expected to draw down the force to only about 50,000 within eighteen months of the end of combat.[53]

Rumsfeld's continuous dialogue with Franks achieved his desired goal of reducing the size of the planned force, thus demonstrating some benefits of the transformation he had been pushing on the Pentagon. But it also allowed him to deny that he had ever formally rejected military requests for high troop levels. "I have a feeling that if you ask Gen. Franks . . . about the war plan, he would say that there is nothing he has asked for that he has not gotten," Rumsfeld declared ten days into the war, "The plan we have is his."[54] This was another example of Rumsfeld's skillful application of civilian control.

Rumsfeld dealt directly with Franks and even arranged for the CENTCOM commander to meet privately with the president so that the top officials would gain mutual confidence and have the chance to read body language. While the chain of command runs directly from the defense secretary to the combatant commanders, bypassing the Joint Chiefs unless the chairman is used as a relay point, Rumsfeld recognized the need to engage the Chiefs. But he did so only at the end of March 2002, when Franks briefed them, and October, when Rumsfeld took them to the White House to give their views directly to the president.[55]

Nevertheless, senior military leaders conveyed their concerns to the press. Some doubted the urgency of going after Saddam Hussein. Some feared that the U.S. military was already stretched too thinly to mount the kind of attack that would be necessary. Some resented Rumsfeld's effort to fight a "Desert Storm Lite" war plan. Some, remembering Weinberger's tests, urged seeking advance approval for combat from Congress. In the end, the pace of planning was deliberate, allowing more time to refine the war plans—and to give more time for diplomacy. And Bush did seek, and receive, supportive action by the UN Security Council and the U.S. Congress.[56]

Meanwhile, Rumsfeld made another of his famous lists in October 2002, noting the many things that could go wrong in the operation. The memo to the president started with fifteen items, growing to twenty-nine by the time combat began in March 2003. Among his concerns were the use of chemical weapons by Iraq to spark inter-ethnic conflict, severe disruption in oil supplies, and a long siege before toppling Fortress Baghdad. To avoid being too negative, he appended a note at the bottom of the memo, saying that a list could also be prepared showing potential problems if there were no regime change in Iraq.[57]

Throughout 2002, the Pentagon planners prepared a series of briefings for the president and NSC officials on a huge array of topics, from Iraqi oil infrastructure to targeting approval authority, from planning against WMD to planning for "catastrophic success." Significantly, among the briefings prepared but never given beyond DOD were "congressional contact plans" and "post-conflict governance."[58]

While the war against Saddam Hussein was surprisingly rapid and successful, the aftermath became confused and painful. Rumsfeld had ordered Franks not to plan for the post-conflict "Phase IV" because he wanted no distractions from the war itself. He ignored a massive planning effort by the State Department because he wanted to retain control over the situation until it had clearly stabilized, and he distrusted some of State's personnel. What he did allow was late and insufficient.[59]

He was not alone in minimizing the need for postwar planning. Other officials, notably Deputy Secretary Wolfowitz and Vice President Cheney, had predicted that U.S. forces would be welcomed as liberators, not occupiers. Despite what Rumsfeld himself had warned about Afghanistan—that the locals would resist a large U.S. military presence, as they had the Soviet forces in the 1980s—he did not anticipate a similar outcome in Iraq. More than a year after the fall of Baghdad, Deputy Secretary Wolfowitz acknowledged the planners' misjudgment. "We had a plan that anticipated, I think, that we could proceed with an occupation regime for much longer than it turned out the Iraqis would have patience for. We had a plan that assumed we'd have basically more stable security conditions than we've encountered," he told a Senate committee.[60]

Donald Rumsfeld at a Pentagon press conference.
Department of Defense

Rumsfeld also shared the Bush administration's congenital opposition to what they called "nation-building." During the 1990s, several Republican critics blasted the Clinton administration for using military forces for humanitarian interventions, and then, as Rice sneered, using troops to escort children to school. Rumsfeld also wanted to reduce the number of military personnel assigned to what he considered nonmilitary tasks, including peacekeeping. Even during the war in Afghanistan to overthrow the Taliban, he told the press, "I don't think [that] leaves us with a responsibility to figure out what kind of government that country ought to have. I don't know people who are smart enough from other countries to tell other countries the kind of arrangements they ought to have to govern themselves."[61]

Although numerous DOD and at least three NSC groups looked at postwar issues, they never developed an integrated plan until shortly before the war. On January 20, Bush signed National Security Presidential Directive (NSPD) 24, establishing a Pentagon-run Office of Reconstruction and Humanitarian Affairs (ORHA) to plan and implement plans for administering postwar Iraq. Retired Army Lt. Gen. Jay Garner was named to head ORHA, but his small staff was hastily recruited and then denied entry into Iraq until Baghdad fell. Even then, ORHA lacked personnel and simple office equipment. After only one month in country, Bush appointed a civilian former ambassador, Paul Bremer, to head the Coalition Provisional Authority (CPA), the civilian buffer between the people and the military, and Garner was sent home. The DOD retained control since Ambassador Bremer was required to report through Rumsfeld—and the links between the civilians and the remaining U.S. military were few.[62] Throughout the planning for war and subsequent conflict, Rumsfeld retained tight control. Through Franks, he ran the war; through Garner and then Bremer, he ran the mission of securing peace. Powell and the State Department acquiesced to the logic of unity of command, despite their more detailed planning and genuine nation-building experience. When controversies arose over inadequate planning and the mistreatment of prisoners, Rumsfeld had to take responsibility. The so-called transfer of sovereignty on June 30, 2004—an action more symbolic than real, since U.S. troops remained in large numbers—also transferred nominal control to the new U.S. embassy in Baghdad. But the Pentagon could not escape a crucial role nor the criticism that inevitably accompanied it. And the man who triumphed in directing a successful war remained ensnared by the problems of building a durable peace.

Apogee of Civilian Control

Rumsfeld's operating style stayed the same throughout the ups and downs of his leadership—combative, questioning, assertive, dominating. In a tense meeting in the Situation Room in the fall of 2001, *Newsweek* reported, Rumsfeld pounded on the table and delivered a prolonged monologue. When he stopped, Cheney remarked, "You guys should have known him thirty years ago, before he mellowed."[63]

Same man, same job, same style. Rumsfeld pushed himself hard and those around him at least as hard. Up early, busy late. He made decisions with the same aggressiveness and speed with which he played squash, his frequent form of recreation while in the Pentagon. His preferred approach toward subordinates was "withering cross-examination" or "the wire-brush treatment," also labeled "death by a thousand questions."[64]

A former aide linked his style to his favorite sport. "It's the wrestler in him. It's how he thinks. It's all about positioning and sizing you up. It's there every time you meet him. He's friendly; he's got that toothy grin going. But then it's like a light switch is thrown, and it's war. Even in a group of people, he'll go around the table and take each man on, one at a time. It's like he's testing himself."[65] Rumsfeld himself admitted, "I tend to be impatient, so there's no question that from time to time I help people understand the difference between good work and poor work." Another time, he acknowledged, "I have a certain impatience about things. I like to get things done . . . so I do get to the point where I lean forward on things and talk to people."[66]

Though brusque, Rumsfeld's style had purpose—to keep him informed and also in control. He especially wanted to impose civilian control over the U.S. military because he believed that the Clinton administration had deferred too often to military opinion while, paradoxically, appointing senior officers who were now suspect for having found favor with that administration. He sought to promote a new generation of less conventional officers who would support his revolutionary programs for military transformation. His elevation of Air Force Gen. Richard Myers from vice chairman to chairman of the JCS suggests satisfaction with that officer's performance, but his naming a retired Special Forces general to head the Army and a Marine Corps general to command NATO was more indicative of his nontraditional approach. He even began interviewing candidates for two- and three-star positions on the Joint Staff, in some cases rejecting the officers proposed by their military superiors.[67]

He also tried—but had to back off—more radical changes. He endorsed cutting the term of the service chiefs from four years to two, thus giving the secretary a mid-term chance to replace senior officers, therefore making them more supportive of administration policies. He also suggested merging the Joint Staff with OSD, or at least eliminating Joint Staff offices that dealt with the press and Congress. While seeking to shorten the terms of the most senior officers, he proposed allowing the civilian leadership to extend the tours of favored officers beyond their normal retirement deadlines. This was in the name of flexibility, but it also clearly served the goal of control.[68]

The Army came in for unusually sharp criticism—and punishment—by Rumsfeld. Despite the far-reaching changes in tactics and weaponry being pursued by the Chief of Staff, Gen. Eric Shinseki, Rumsfeld and his top aides considered the Army mired in "old think." Their meetings were "a dialogue of the deaf," a senior officer commented. The Army had successfully resisted efforts to cut its strength during the QDR maneuverings in the summer of 2001, prompting Rumsfeld to storm out of one meeting on the topic. In January 2002, the defense secretary cancelled the Army's Crusader artillery program and tried to make General Shinseki a lame duck for his remaining eighteen months in office by announcing his successor. When Army Secretary Tom White tried to defend the Crusader decision in public, the defense secretary charged that he was insufficiently supportive. "Your body language was wrong," Rumsfeld complained. A year of backbiting later, Rumsfeld fired White.[69]

General Shinseki further alienated Rumsfeld in February 2003 when he told a congressional hearing that the United States would probably need "several hundred thousand" troops to occupy Iraq after the defeat of Saddam Hussein. Wolfowitz called such estimates "wildly off the mark." When he retired in June, Shinseki pointedly warned against leadership "filled with mistrust and arrogance." Everyone knew he was complaining about Rumsfeld.[70]

Rumsfeld came into conflict with others in the executive branch as well as with Congress in a long-running battle for bureaucratic control and supremacy. He clashed repeatedly with Colin Powell and the State Department in what many observers saw as worse than the legendary Shultz-Weinberger disputes. Some of the disagreements were over policy—whether to negotiate with North Korea, whether to go the United Nations before waging war in Iraq, whether to grant POW status to those captured in Afghanistan. But the two departments and their leaders also fought vicious turf battles. Notably, the DOD won the right to control the entities set up to manage postwar Iraq, first the ORHA and then the CPA.

In public, the two cabinet officers minimized their disagreements, despite the background leaks by their subordinates telling a different story. At one point in the summer of 2001, Rumsfeld sparred with reporters on the subject. In response to one question, he asked, "Are you trying to find some daylight between Colin and me?" When another reporter asked, "Do you always agree on everything?" Rumsfeld replied, "Except for those few cases where Colin is still learning."[71]

The defense secretary even clashed with the White House. He successfully undercut an NSC office set up to coordinate counterterrorism policy and expressed incredulity when Condoleezza Rice was formally named to coordinate postwar Iraq matters. He even contradicted the president when told that he was supposed to be reviewing possible changes in the *posse comitatus* law that forbids most military operations to enforce domestic law. He strongly resisted any efforts to saddle the DOD with homeland defense responsibilities, despite his own rhetoric in the QDR. "The Department of Defense's task is one that deals with external threats coming into the United States" he told the press. "We don't do borders. We don't do coastlines."[72] His principle seemed to be: avoid what you don't want, and tightly control what you have.

His control mania extended to minutiae. At times, Rumsfeld could be downright pedantic. He bristled at briefings filled with acronyms. In one of his famous "snowflakes," he complained that the Joint Staff was "just a lot of people spinning their wheels doing things we probably have to edit and improve." He ordered DOD personnel to stop using the term "CINC" for the combatant commanders, because only the president was truly the commander in chief. He ordered a halt to the use of the phrase "National Command Authorities," in use since the Cold War days when subordinates might not always know precisely who had survived a nuclear attack. Instead, Rumsfeld said the term should be replaced by "the president" or more usually "the secretary of defense." He also decried the use of impersonal terms for senior officials. "The White House doesn't do anything. The White House is a building. The Pentagon doesn't do anything either. But I am secretary of defense and I damned well can do things."[73]

After the victory in Afghanistan, Rumsfeld found his relations with Congress much improved. It did not hurt, of course, that he was asking for large increases in defense spending, which most congressional defense experts also favored, and which skeptics were reluctant to oppose. As the war in Iraq approached, however, senior Republicans complained to Bush's chief of staff that Rumsfeld was displaying disrespect and excessive secrecy toward Congress on military matters.[74] The impetus for the complaints was the war plan for Iraq, but the feeling was more widespread that the defense secretary was not treating Congress as a partner in crucial national security policy matters. When Rumsfeld came under pressure to resign after he acknowledged formal responsibility for the system that permitted abuse of Iraqi prisoners, few in Congress rushed to his defense.

Continuous Revolution

Rumsfeld largely ignored criticism because he was embarked on a special mission that he knew would generate opposition. But he sought to put in place a process that not only achieved a one-time transformation in the U.S. military but that also made likely continuing reforms for decades to come. He entered the Pentagon determined to make major improvements, but success in war spurred him to fight for additional radical change.

This rejection of the status quo and this imperative for change, some-times perhaps simply to do things differently, is the key to Rumsfeld's approach. The press and public fundamentally misinterpreted one of the "snowflakes" leaked in October 2003–leaked perhaps with his permis-sion, since it sends such a strong message. The October 16 memo, sent to only four people–his deputy secretary and under secretary for policy, and the chairman and vice chairman of the JCS–spawned headlines sug-gesting Rumsfeld's doubts about the war on terrorism, for it acknowl-edged "mixed results" against al Qaeda and "slower progress" against the Taliban and declared that "we lack metrics to know if we are winning or losing the global war on terror."[75]

But the real thrust of the memo was to demand new ways of thinking about and dealing with the challenge of terrorism. "It is not possible to change DOD fast enough," Rumsfeld wrote; "an alternative might be to try to fashion a new institution." He asked: "Does DOD need to think through new ways to organize, train, equip and focus to deal with the global war on terror? Are the changes we have made and are making too modest and incremental? My impression is that we have not yet made truly bold moves, although we have made many sensible, logical moves in the right direction, but are they enough?"

Whether because of age or experience, Rumsfeld was clearly impa-tient. He sought revolutionary change for the Pentagon, and fought for it, because he seemed to believe that anything less would be fatally insuffi-cient. This approach is the same he showed in private business, when he revamped the Searle company. A Princeton classmate who worked with Rumsfeld at that time noted that he subscribes to the maxim, "Don't cut off the tail of the dog one inch at a time."[76]

The vice chairman of the JCS, Marine Gen. Peter Pace, made the same point. "You have to understand the secretary in that he is very, very good at questioning the status quo."[77]

McNamara Redux?

Don Rumsfeld changed the Pentagon in large ways and small during his second tour. He might have made even more dramatic changes if he had not also made so many likely allies into opponents, or at best luke-warm supporters. As with so many great achievers, his virtues, seen from a different perspective, became his vices. His obsession with control alien-ated some subordinates and left him alone and apart within the Bush administration. His singlemindedness about success in war left him ill-prepared to manage peace. His tenacity became stubbornness, self-confi-dence turned to arrogance, and impatience blinded him to promising evolutions.

III

ROLES AND PERFORMANCES

13

Manager of the Pentagon

The Department is really run by intimidation, not by control, when you get right down to it. You have to intimidate people to get anything done.

–Deputy Secretary John Hamre[1]

One can slay only so many dragons each day.

–Robert McNamara[2]

The secretary of defense is up there on the bridge, enjoying the splendid view of the horizon and his authority to give orders. So he's signaling, "hard rudder left, hard rudder right"–and he thinks he's making some dramatic changes. What he forgets is that there are a lot of people down in the engine room who are simply getting seasick."

–Army Chief of Staff Gen. Creighton Abrams[3]

First among the prescribed duties of the secretary of defense is to "have direction, authority, and control over the Department of Defense."[4] Over the years Congress has added various conditions, limitations, and reporting requirements, but the secretary's principal task remains that of managing the huge organization centered in the Pentagon but sprawled across the globe.

Even with reductions after the end of the Cold War, the national defense establishment is still large in size and budget. The Pentagon counts 1.4 million military personnel on active duty, another 654,000 civilians, and 1.2 million men and women in the Guard and Reserves. Another two million military retirees and military family members receive benefits. The Defense Department has more than six hundred thousand individual buildings or structures in over six thousand different locations at home and in 146 countries abroad.[5] The budget requested for fiscal year 2005, which does not include possible costs for operations in Iraq and Afghanistan, was $401.7 billion.

These staggering figures make the DOD larger than any American business with a budget larger than the central government budget of any other nation—and higher than the total gross domestic product of all but a dozen countries in the world.[6] By comparison, Wal-Mart, the biggest U.S. company, employed 1.24 million people and had a budget of $248 billion in 2003.

Multiple, Simultaneous Processes

While any organization so large makes mistakes, employs cheats and shirkers, wastes money, and perpetuates inefficient behaviors, the Pentagon is generally recognized as having strong and effective management.[7] The systems in place provide top officials with an unusual degree of knowledge, oversight, and control of DOD activities. The challenge for the secretary of defense is to oversee and provide timely decisions for the many processes at work simultaneously, each ultimately reporting to him.

The primary means of managerial control is through the budget process. As former Secretary James Schlesinger said, "While several of the secretarial tasks are critical, in terms of visibility and impact, budget formulation is second to none in importance. The budget is where it all comes together."[8] The formulation of the budget follows a complex timetable of reports and reviews.

Even before the start of the budget cycle, each participant is aware of the existing, approved plan, which is reflected in the Future Years Defense Program (FYDP, pronounced "fid-ip"). This six-year management plan defines defense goals and outlines the operations and resources to achieve them. Each year's request has to fit within the allocated figures or it must justify and obtain approval for any deviation. The process is highly incremental. As former Vice Chairman of the JCS Gen. Robert Herres said, "We tie and untie our shoes yearly. We just did these things a year ago."[9]

Starting in the McNamara years, the Defense Department followed what was called PPBS, for Planning, Programming, and Budgeting System.[10] Each spring, the secretary would issue Defense Planning Guidance (DPG), setting priority objectives and capabilities which the armed forces should seek to achieve with their forthcoming budgets. The secretary also issued Contingency Planning Guidance for the use of existing forces.[11] While some of the DPG was necessarily highly classified, much of it usually appeared in unclassified form in the secretary's annual report.

The DPG triggered the development of Program Objective Memoranda (POMs) by each service in the spring and summer. These documents covered not only the forthcoming year's budget needs but also the total program requirements in later years. These had to be reconciled to fit within the assumed limits in FYDP. The military leadership commented on the emerging POMs with the JCS Chairman's Program Assessment (CPA).

During the summer, certain budget issues were identified for high level review by the Defense Resources Board (DRB), chaired by the deputy secretary. Decisions by the DRB were contained in Program Decision Memoranda (PDMs), which the services then used to prepare Budget Estimates Submissions (BES) for the DOD Comptroller, who conducted further reviews in the autumn, leading to final (PDMs), which could be appealed to the secretary by the services or the senior military commanders. By December, the budget proposals went to the White House for final review by the Office of Management and Budget (OMB) and perhaps the president. The overall budget is required by law to be submitted to Congress by the first week of February.

Starting with the fiscal year 2005 budget, Secretary Rumsfeld ordered several significant changes in the process. First, he renamed the process PPBE, for Planning, Programming, Budgeting, and Execution, and put a greater emphasis on tracking programs with metrics and cost models. Second, he made the budget review concurrent with the program review, since the two processes interacted with each other politically and budgetarily. Instead of the DRB, he substituted a new Senior Leadership Review Group (SLRG) to consider major budget issues. Third, he declared that the budgets should be built for two years at a time, with only a small number of Program Change Proposals (PCPs) allowed during alternate years. This meant that the POMs and BESs would not be developed in odd-numbered years. Finally, he replaced the DPG with something called Strategic Planning Guidance (SPG), a biennial document that would be "fiscally informed" and would later be supplemented by "fiscally constrained Joint Programming Guidance."[12]

Although biennial budgets have long been recommended to reduce paperwork in the Pentagon and the tortuous process in Congress, the first attempt in 1986 quickly reverted to a full-scale annual review. The DOD saw the need for too many changes and the appropriations committees on Capitol Hill insisted on annual money bills.

In this and other ways, Congress is reluctant to accommodate the bright ideas and management reforms offered by secretaries of defense. Within the DOD, for example, the budget is structured horizontally in terms of the administering agency (the services or defense agencies) and vertically in terms of eleven missions, called Major Force Programs (MFPs). These programs are further broken down into nearly 5,000

Program Elements (PEs). While the DOD since McNamara's time has presented its budget requests in terms of MFPs, Congress continues to appropriate funds by military department and in terms of personnel, operations and maintenance, procurement, and research and development.

This alphabet soup of documents, as confusing as it may be to outsiders, in fact works well in practice, providing the secretary tight control over the activities of the department, for they cover each program, project, or activity in the huge Pentagon budget. These materials provide the rationale for the programs, the associated costs, and the potential risks. They also enable Congress to make detailed inquiries into strategic, budgetary, and management issues before funds are authorized or appropriated.

The management challenge does not end when the budget is submitted, for then it must be defended on Capitol Hill. And after enactment, the funds must be allocated and expended, taking into account the cuts, adds, and conditions imposed by Congress. At any point in time, the DOD and its subordinate entities are juggling the decisions and paperwork for three different budgets: the current year with ongoing activities; the forthcoming year, as the budget is under consideration by Congress; and future years, with plans being reviewed and decided to build the next year's budget submission. Any changes affecting any of the various years can have significant ripple effects. As former Deputy Secretary Will Taft commented, "(W)e are always budgeting—we have biweekly budgeting."[13]

In addition to the process managed by the secretary and OSD, the uniformed military have their own parallel system, which takes guidance from the civilians and offers analyses and recommendations in turn. This additional alphabet soup includes the JCS chairman's periodic National Military Strategy (NMS); the short-term Contingency Planning Guidance (CPG) each year from the secretary of defense; the Joint Strategic Capabilities Plan (JSCP), which contains guidance to the combatant commanders and service chiefs for accomplishing military tasks and missions with current capabilities; and the annual Chairman's Program Assessment (CPA) that feeds into the PPBE cycle. Regional commanders also provide suggestions and requests for funds through the Integrated Priority Lists (IPLs) and contribute to other JCS and Joint Staff documents.[14]

For major weapons programs, there is a formal, highly regulated acquisition process separate and distinct from the budget process. It usually takes many years to turn a bright idea or technological breakthrough into a fielded weapon system because senior officials and congressional overseers want to avoid repeating past mistakes that led to cost overruns and performance shortfalls. Instead, programs must now pass a series of milestones and tests, as well as adjust to the funding changes imposed through the budget process. Only highly classified—so-called "black"—programs escape most of the strictures of the acquisition process.[15]

The personnel system provides the people to staff the various jobs, including the training and vetting of people for the senior positions. While previous secretaries took special care in interviewing candidates for the Joint Chiefs of Staff, particularly for chairman, Secretary Rumsfeld made a point of questioning even candidates for two- and three-star positions on the Joint Staff, and sometimes rejecting those preferred by senior officers. This allowed him to cultivate and reward those who shared his vision and determination to transform the services.

In addition to these major processes, there are many others, operating simultaneously and with significant impacts. The public relations process responds to media inquiries and works to create a favorable public view of the department and its activities. The legislative relations process is supposed to smooth the Pentagon's path up Capitol Hill, winning friends and budget support. The legal advisory process was particularly active in crafting the rules for conducting the war on terrorism and the treatment of captives in Afghanistan and Iraq, but it is always important in a department as subject to myriad laws and regulations as is the DOD.

Different subordinates run each of these processes, but each ultimately reports to the secretary and arguably has a claim on the secretary's limited time. And only the secretary can truly integrate and de-conflict the many processes.

Policymakers as Managers

Many secretaries were chosen because they had demonstrated management skills in industry or previously in the government. Those lacking such experience usually picked deputies with the necessary talents and deferred to them to run the department day-to-day, keeping only the most difficult or fundamental issues to handle personally.

In this usual pattern, the secretary is the public face of the department, the chief speechmaker, congressional witness, and White House adviser, while the deputy handles the routine briefings and paper flow. In practice, however, this delineation of authority is difficult to maintain. Recent presidents have sought to use the senior deputies as a decision group in the National Security Council system, the ones to listen to and task subordinate groups and the ones to frame tough choices for their principals to resolve. Nevertheless, inside the Pentagon the deputy does speak for the secretary and often does handle the bulk of process management.

Management means not only running the budget process, but also running the manifold other activities of the department. As James Schlesinger commented, "keeping the DOD a relatively harmonious whole . . . is easier said than done, for it cuts against the grain of some of his other responsibilities. Hard decisions tend to distract from harmony, particularly when there is overall budgetary pressure."[16]

The secretary and deputy rely on the staff of the Office of Secretary of Defense, which grew from three assistants and a few clerical personnel in 1947 to 2,056 in 2003. Of these, 1,873 are civilians and 483 military. These people are in addition to the 1,617 military and civilian personnel on the Joint Staff and the uniformed and civilian people working in the departments of the Army, Navy, Air Force, and the various defense agencies. The OSD personnel size has climbed by 82 people under Secretary Rumsfeld. These 2,056 people, including the senior officials who are under secretaries or assistant secretaries of defense, are the management and advisory team for the secretary. They are organized into thirty-four major offices, sixteen of which report directly to the secretary. They are tasked to develop and promulgate policies to support U.S. national security objectives; to oversee DOD plans and programs; to develop systems to supervise policy implementation and program execution; and to serve as the focal point for DOD participation in other security community activities. In short, they are extra sets of arms and legs, eyes and ears, and authoritative voices for the secretary and other senior officials.

The military departments are still large in size and important in function, but they have been drained of power by the increasing centralization of authority into OSD. The service secretaries are responsible for the recruitment, organization, supply, equipping, and training of their respective armed forces. The deployment and employment of the armed forces is through a different chain of command, running from the secretary of defense to the combatant commanders. While the services remain "separately organized" under basic law, they are required to operate "under the authority, direction, and control of the secretary of defense." Their only escape valve, enshrined into law by Congress, is the right to make recommendations directly to Capitol Hill, "after first informing the secretary of defense."[17]

Which weapons the services buy, which wars they plan for, how they are used in combat–all are decided ultimately outside of the services, by the secretary of defense in consultation with the senior military officers. Especially since the 1986 Goldwater-Nichols Act, OSD and the Joint Staff have worked to instill a sense of jointness in military operations in place of the service parochialism that had been historically dominant.

Despite the broad authority for the secretary of defense in standing law, Congress regularly exercises its Constitutional powers "to make Rules for the Government and Regulation of the land and naval Forces"[18] by writing detailed new laws and by giving clear guidance in committee reports. As a result, secretaries of defense frequently complain about the burden of congressional regulations and reporting requirements. In fact, they probably resent more the limitations on their discretion.

Other authors–from Blue Ribbon commissions to think tank studies to muckraking journalists–have assessed the management of the DOD and made recommendations for improvements. Most incoming secretaries have tried to make minor adjustments, such as creating new assistant secretary portfolios or mandating cuts in the size of OSD, but the basic organization of functions (and occasional dysfunctions) remains. My purpose is not to evaluate the various secretaries as managers, but rather to indicate how difficult their management responsibilities necessarily are.

Most secretaries have used their managerial authorities for collateral purposes, such as improving the standing of DOD programs with the press, Congress, and the public. It is not accidental that two secretaries who perceived their budgets to be in danger of major congressional cuts sought to trumpet their decisions to cancel a single weapons program. Caspar Weinberger ended the DIVAD artillery and Dick Cheney tried to kill the V-22 Osprey. Cheney tried to go further and kill the Navy's A-12 attack plane, but he ran afoul of procurement laws that gave cancellation authority to the program manager, not the secretary himself.[19] Don Rumsfeld signaled his dissatisfaction with Army transformation efforts by canceling the Crusader artillery.

Similarly, various secretaries have embraced outside commissions more to buy time than to obtain new ideas. Congress often mandated these studies to get a second opinion that could be used to counteract the institutional rigidity of the DOD. But, except for Goldwater-Nichols, few of these bright ideas gained enough support to be put into practice. Imposing structural or institutional change was a time-consuming, political capital-draining, high-risk endeavor that usually seemed less appealing than more modest, incremental adjustments.

Given the intricate and well-established processes within the Pentagon, secretaries of defense can often manage by exceptions–picking those symbolic or controversial issues that outsiders will use to judge their effectiveness and concentrating on making high quality decisions on them. They can also follow modern management techniques of offering broad visions and general guidance while leaving the details to subordinates.

Management Challenges

Recent secretaries have embraced the ideas of reform and have tried to implement changes in the processes by which the Pentagon manages itself. They took promising new technologies, such as for precision weaponry, and pushed a Revolution in Military Affairs. They recognized that the DOD was no longer the cutting edge in research and development, supplying "spin offs" to the private sector, but had become dependent on the "spin on" from industry, particularly in computers and communications. They advocated a Revolution in Business Affairs, with the DOD adopting best practices from commercial enterprises, including greater outsourcing of some activities while concentrating on what were considered core competencies. They have sought, with only limited success, authority to close and consolidate DOD's large domestic base infrastructure. They adopted numerous reforms in the acquisition process, especially downgrading the use of costly "milspecs" (military specifications) and increasing the use of commercial, off-the-shelf (COTS) items. And they tried to adapt the personnel system to an all-volunteer force of married people who grew unhappy at frequent moves and lengthy separations.[20]

These various reforms are ongoing, for few major changes are ideal, with no negative consequences. Imposing one-size-fits-all solutions has the advantage of simplicity and the disadvantage of rigidity. Allowing widespread discretion and exceptions is satisfactory to program managers and confusing to those seeking consistency and accountability. Since four of the last five secretaries had at least three years in office, with deputies who served nearly as long, they have had more opportunity to envision, decide on, and then succeed in implementing difficult but worthwhile changes in DOD management.

Congress is a necessary partner in these reforms, since it must write the laws and pay the bills. While members may fight to protect local contractors from disadvantageous changes, most accept the need to improve DOD processes. In 2003, for example, Congress approved far-reaching changes in the department's personnel rules–essentially setting up a new system separate from the longstanding rules and procedures of the civil service–despite concerns expressed by members with large numbers of civilian personnel in their districts. It had earlier created a similarly new system for the Department of Homeland Security, third largest in personnel after the DOD and Veterans Affairs. If these innovations can be implemented without major problems or perceived abuses, they may set a new standard for the rest of the federal government.

The DOD has been the initiator and test bed for many government management reforms, starting with PPBS budgeting under McNamara and continuing with acquisition reforms of recent years. Defense secretaries are even deemed to be talented managers after their Pentagon service–as seen in Jim Schlesinger's service as the first secretary of energy, Robert McNamara at the World Bank, and in the successful business careers of Don Rumsfeld, Dick Cheney, and Frank Carlucci. And while some former secretaries are considered unsuccessful, it is usually because they failed at some other task, in some relationship with their president, colleagues, or Congress, not because they failed to manage the complex Pentagon reasonably well. As Bing West concluded, "Heretical though it seems, there is probably too much emphasis on the role of secretary as internal manager. Defense does not lack for managers throughout the secretary's staff and the military; and history shows that no secretary has failed for poor management, while many have failed because they neglected other roles."[21]

14

War Planner

The upshot is that the secretary of defense regularly ignores the advice that comes up through the JCS system.

–James Schlesinger, 1985[1]

I would not dream of overruling a military commander.

–Caspar Weinberger, 1983[2]

You have to take seriously every request that comes in from your commanders in the field. And if you're not prepared to accept those requests for equipment, you ought to be prepared to change the mission or withdraw the forces.

–William Perry, October 3, 1995[3]

[The local commanders] will decide what they need and they will get what they need....To try to second-guess it from Washington, D.C., it seems to me is a difficult thing to do."

–Donald Rumsfeld, April 6, 2004[4]

With **"authority, direction, and control"**[5] over the Defense Department, the secretary is the link in the chain of command from the commander in chief, the president, to the armed forces. Through budget and program decisions, he shapes and sizes the forces. He signs the orders for overseas deployments and issues the key execute orders for military operations. He also guides the development of war plans.

The American political tradition enshrines the principle of civilian control. The Declaration of Independence specifically accused King

George III of imposing military rule on the colonies, declaring, "He has affected to render the Military independent of and superior to the Civil Power." Samuel Adams expressed a common sentiment in 1776 when he said, "A Standing Army, however necessary it may be at some times, is always dangerous to the Liberties of the People."[6]

The framers of the U.S. Constitution sought to guard against military domination of government by giving Congress explicit power to "make Rules for the Government and Regulation of the land and naval forces" and by limiting Army appropriations to two years.[7] For most of the next century and a half, the secretaries of war and the Navy played major roles in planning for military operations, and often in their execution.

When Congress wrote the National Security Act of 1947 and created the post of secretary of defense, it reiterated the importance of civilian control by requiring that the secretary be "appointed from civilian life" and forbidding selection of anyone who was "within ten years after relief from active duty as a commissioned officer of a regular component of an armed force."[8] The only exception among the twenty defense secretaries was George Marshall, for whom a special waiver had to be enacted by Congress.

Senior military officers were only advisers to the civilian president and defense secretary. Their titles reflected their restricted roles: Chiefs of *Staff* rather than commanders.[9] Only the officers in charge of deployed forces are truly combatant commanders. And while they usually communicate through the chairman of the JCS, only the civilian secretary can give them orders.

In writing the Goldwater-Nichols Act in 1986, Congress added specific language spelling out the chain of command—"from the president to the secretary of defense; and from the secretary of defense to the commander of the combatant command"—and allowing the transfer of forces from one command to another "only by the authority of the secretary of defense."[10] As a result of this section, the secretary or acting secretary has to sign each deployment order for U.S. forces, except for small numbers of people sent on temporary duty for non-operational support tasks. This is part of the system of civilian control.

Strategic Nuclear War Plans

Civilian control over nuclear weapons was incomplete prior to the late 1950s. Regardless of official doctrine, senior Air Force commanders like Gen. Curtis LeMay talked of preventive war and full-scale retaliation against civilian and military targets. Harry Truman was concerned enough about the possible use of these weapons that he refused to transfer them from civilian custody in the Atomic Energy Commission until the Korean War broke out in 1950. Throughout the following decade, the United States built a huge arsenal of nuclear weapons, from low-yield tactical warheads to multi-megaton city levelers, as well as a large array of delivery systems: ballistic and guided missiles, bombers, and even artillery. Each service built its own forces without regard to the capabilities of the others and each planned for enough power to destroy all major enemy targets by itself.

Strengthened by the 1958 defense reform law, Secretary Gates ordered the creation of a joint Air Force–Navy target planning staff and the development of a Single Integrated Operational Plan (SIOP) for the wartime use of strategic nuclear weapons. Secretary McNamara, shocked by the rigidity and destructiveness of the retaliatory plans, ordered revisions. He wanted to dispel the assumption of a spasm response and to create genuine alternatives for the president, including partial responses and strategic reserves as well as geographical withholds.

Wartime control of nuclear weapons was necessarily relaxed by various delegations of authority to assure the possibility of retaliation even after a surprise attack on Washington, but McNamara and his successors paid close attention to the details of targeting plans. They also tried to dictate nuclear strategy by their budgets. Accordingly, McNamara set numerical limits on the number of ICBMs to be built as well as on the number of missile-carrying submarines. Later secretaries set other numerical limits and approved or disapproved particular technologies, such as high accuracy guidance for hard targets and anti-ballistic missile systems. These decisions, for example, drove the United States to acquire a survivable retaliatory force that reduced the hair trigger on nuclear weapons or the incentive to strike preemptively. Various administrations also concluded detailed agreements with the Soviet Union that constrained their strategic forces in significant ways, thus further shaping likely nuclear war plans.

The "Lessons of Vietnam"

Non-nuclear war plans have been profoundly influenced in recent decades by the perceived lessons of the war fought in Southeast Asia. That conflict spawned a solid military consensus, especially on negatives, i.e., what not to do. Civilian views have been more varied: some side with the military critique, while others offer alternative strategies.

The military consensus is that civilians interfered too much in the conduct of the war, imposing conditions which increased U.S. casualties and prevented a possible and maybe even likely military victory. To regain a broader range of military discretion, the U.S. Army embraced and articulated the concept, derived from Soviet military thinking, of an operational level of war in between grand strategy and tactics on the battlefield. While civilians, with military advice, were supposed to set overall strategy, they were then supposed to turn over operational details to the professional military.

Many officers, especially aviators, still get angry when recalling stories about how Lyndon Johnson supposedly picked bombing targets in Vietnam. In fact, Johnson and McNamara exerted tight civilian control over air operations for broad strategic reasons—to avoid Soviet or Chinese intervention by limiting attacks near the Chinese border or against Soviet military advisers or supply ships. The president and his defense secretary did not pick targets of their choosing; they deselected some targets recommended by senior military officers because of their strategic concerns. But it did not help that they excluded a military officer in the key Tuesday lunch discussions of bombing targets until October 1967, when the Rolling Thunder strikes on the North had been going on for two and a half years.[11]

Besides non-involvement by civilians in operational details, the military consensus holds that civilian leadership should commit U.S. forces only for the defense of "vital" interests and only with the determination and political support to achieve victory. Many U.S. officers complain that the civilian leadership gave up too early and left those in uniform to suffer the consequences of defeat and public alienation.

This "never again" view, also labeled the "Vietnam syndrome," was probably best codified in Secretary Weinberger's 1984 speech on the use of force. He called for combat only when vital interests were at stake, thus ruling out lesser engagements. "We don't do windows," many officers argued. Weinberger said that the United States should not commit forces unless it had "the clear intention of winning," a sharp critique of any limited war that ends without the total defeat of the enemy regime. He demanded that force should be a last resort and that "there must be some reasonable assurance we will have the support of the American people and their elected representatives in Congress." Prior support would presumably require irrefutable threats and a commitment to persevere until victory. He also insisted that troops should be sent into combat only with clear political and military objectives, thus implying that neither Vietnam nor Lebanon had such clarity.

Every subsequent administration has felt obligated to make some reference to the substance of the Weinberger tests in justifying its own use of force. George H. W. Bush reassured the nation just before launching the 1991 Desert Storm attacks that they were necessary and justified. He also maintained an arm's length relation to operational details up to the point when he ordered a cease-fire. Bill Clinton promulgated national security strategy documents that recognized the need to act decisively and successfully to protect vital interests, but carved out categories of "important" and "humanitarian" interests for more limited military roles. He and his successor also claimed that the military operations they authorized had clear and attainable objectives. George W. Bush echoed the Vietnam lessons in his 2000 campaign and later insisted that his attacks against Saddam Hussein were a "war of necessity," not a "war of choice."

General Colin Powell, who worked with Weinberger in the preparation of his criteria, promulgated formal "joint doctrine" differentiating between "war" and "military operations other than war" that still might involve combat. Decisive victory was required only in "war." The U.S. military also took lessons from its tragic involvement in Lebanon in the 1980s to add notions of "endstates" and "exit strategies" to the Weinberger doctrine.

Even while professing adherence to the notion of heeding military advice, various secretaries of defense have nevertheless inserted themselves closely into military planning. In 1990, Cheney sought alternative ideas from a specially created team and pushed his ideas on the combatant commander. He and Secretary of State Baker also reviewed target lists. Perry and Cohen also challenged some of the military plans submitted for their approval and insisted on revisions. The Kosovo conflict air strikes were reviewed not only by U.S. officials, but also by senior NATO leaders in a process that many participants have greatly derided. Rumsfeld had numerous exchanges with General Franks during the development of the Iraq war plans.

Under Rumsfeld, the pendulum seemed to swing back toward open and unapologetic civilian assertiveness in the details of war plans. He even revised the process to guarantee an early role for his office in their development, as outlined below.

Capabilities-Driven Plans

Secretary Rumsfeld ordered a new approach to war planning and budgetary programming that emphasized a top-down system of specifying required joint capabilities instead of the bottom-up process of service-specific programs. He argued that strategy and planning had been subordinated to resourcing efforts, and that more could be accomplished with greater front-end attention to broad requirements without regard to the individual services. He urged the services to compete with ideas and programs to achieve the required capabilities. He instituted a new system of providing "strategic policy guidance" to shape both budgets and operational plans.

Whether or not this approach is accepted and effective—a test only later administrations can answer—it is consistent with the pattern of many secretaries of defense, who picked capabilities to determine strategy. McNamara, Schlesinger, and Brown had strong interests in nuclear strategy, for example, and used their programmatic decisions to reshape strategy and war planning. Brown and Perry emphasized breakthrough technologies that led to precision weapons and stealthy aircraft. McNamara and Weinberger increased non-nuclear capabilities for both deterrent and war-fighting objectives. Aspin supported major programs for nonlethal weaponry, in part to make military interventions more tolerable at home and more successful abroad. Rumsfeld recognized the enormous value of special operations forces and sought to increase their size and utility. He also pushed, with the president's strong support, the deployment of missile defenses and development of an effective anti-satellite (ASAT) capability, which reflected the administration's view that the militarization of space was an important interest and capability for U.S. armed forces.

Deliberate Planning Process

The defense secretary also presides over an elaborate process for the development of possible war plans. In every region there are nations with which the United States has formal or strongly implied defense commitments, or deployed forces which could be threatened by regional aggressors or political instability. There have always been assumed enemies or rogue states who have to be deterred or defeated by U.S. forces. Defense officials have routinely ordered preparation of plans to deal with these plausible contingencies. These have been developed through what is called the deliberate planning process, as distinct from the "crisis action" planning.

Prior to Secretary Rumsfeld, these deliberate war plans were periodically reviewed and refined by the regional combatant commanders and then put "on the shelf." The basic law from 1947 tasks the Joint Chiefs of Staff with "preparation of strategic plans and provision for the strategic direction of the military forces"–though "subject to the authority and direction of the president and the secretary of defense."[12]

For many years, the defense secretary had to request a briefing in order to learn just what the military intended to do in order to defend various allies and respond to possible Soviet or Chinese aggression. In 1980, Secretary Brown tried to interpose closer civilian supervision by issuing detailed Planning Guidance for Contingency Planning and ordering the new under secretary for policy to review any JCS directives for new or revised contingency plans before they were sent to the field and again after the revised plans were approved by JCS. The under secretary at that time, "Blowtorch Bob" Komer, later complained that the plans he saw were thin on strategy and less realistic in the absence of civilian review. He also faulted the plans for being routine and unimaginative.[13]

When the Reagan administration heeded military complaints about civilian "meddling" and reverted to the prior pattern of briefings on request, Komer pushed for and won congressional support for specific language permitting closer civilian oversight. The Goldwater-Nichols Act gave the under secretary for policy authority to "assist the secretary of defense–in preparing written policy guidance for the preparation and review of contingency plans; and in reviewing such plans."[14]

Secretary Rumsfeld took this a step further by revising the deliberate planning process to require OSD review at the start, during, and at the end of the development of each major war plan. He also began issuing "fiscally constrained and prioritized" guidance for the commanders and budgeters.

To outside observers, U.S. grand strategy may appear to bounce from one set of buzzwords to another, reflecting the special concerns of top officials. Each administration in practice insists on a new and different lexicon to describe essentially similar policies. But to the insiders, words have consequences, and different words lead to significantly different policies and programs.

With the end of the Cold War, for example, Secretary Cheney and General Powell declared they were redirecting U.S. military capabilities to a regional focus, to respond to plausible scenarios. They spoke of "forward presence" and "reconstitution" to defend overseas deployments of U.S. forces and to justify manpower levels and R&D programs to hedge against a revitalized Russian threat.[15]

The Clinton administration wound up supporting an equivalent strategy, but only after its bottom-up review. The president and the military then spoke enthusiastically of "peacetime engagement" rather than mere "forward presence." The military also embraced missions other than war as a way to "shape" the overseas environment. They justified continued large budgets by declaring a strategy requiring the capability to respond to the full spectrum of crises.[16] Their chief planning criterion was the capability to fight two major conflicts almost simultaneously, usually pointing to Iraq and North Korea.

Secretary Rumsfeld and the G. W. Bush administration revised their rhetoric after September 11, 2001, to make homeland defense the top priority. And when forced by Congress to submit a National Military Strategy, the administration adopted new terminology for longstanding missions. Key military objectives became to protect the United States; prevent conflict and surprise attacks; and prevail against adversaries. The sizing criteria became, after defending the homeland, "deter forward in and from four regions"; "swiftly defeat adversaries in [two] overlapping campaigns"; "win [one] decisive campaign to achieve enduring result" [presumably regime change]; and fight "limited lesser contingencies." The bumper sticker for the strategy was "protect, prevent, prevail."[17]

Rumsfeld revised the war planning process to phase with the changed budget process. The key impact was expected to be more civilian influence and oversight of regular military planning.

Crisis Action Planning

Military planning in crisis situations has also been changed in recent years, both by experience and to suit the style of Secretary Rumsfeld. The normal procedure is for the regional commander to suggest or the Joint Staff to trigger planning by sending a warning order that forces might be needed, for example, to evacuate Americans from a trouble spot or to provide humanitarian assistance or military support to a friendly nation. The frequency of such operations in the Clinton administration, however, prompted a revised policy process to plan better for what were euphemistically called "complex contingency operations." This was spelled out in Presidential Decision Directive (PDD) 56 in 1997. It called for interagency planning from the start, so that non-DOD personnel and activities could be integrated and coordinated with military operations. Since, in fact, the backbone of military plans is the Time-Phased Force Deployment Data (TPFDD), the assignment of particular cargoes in a considered sequence of airlift and sealift, planners wanted to be sure that both civilian and military cargoes were scheduled to avoid situations where civilian participants and their necessary gear arrived in different places days apart.

The Clinton administration also initiated a requirement that every deliberate war plan contain a thoroughly-vetted Annex V, a political-military plan that could provide for diplomatic activities, coordinate with international organizations and NGOs, provide supporting civilian personnel such as police, and so forth.

The Bush administration chose to ignore many of these innovations by its predecessor, disestablishing the NSC subgroup which had oversight over such planning and not insisting on full interagency coordination for military operations. This also fit Secretary Rumsfeld's proclivity for Pentagon-centered and Pentagon-controlled planning and execution, most evident in his rejection of interagency planning until shortly before launching the war against Saddam Hussein. While an Annex V remains a requirement for deliberate war plans, it is largely developed by uniformed planners. In the development of war plans for Afghanistan and Iraq, Rumsfeld set the pattern of frequent reviews, close oversight, and constraining decisions.

Military Veto?

There is substantial evidence that civilian leaders feel obligated to accept military advice, not just merely consider it. Dick Betts has found that, since World War II, with only one exception, presidents never authorized military operations when more than one of the Joint Chiefs was strongly opposed.[18] The single exception was in Lebanon in 1983, when President Reagan overruled military objections and ordered U.S. participation in the UN force there. When Gen. John Vessey was later asked why the Chiefs didn't protest more vigorously or even consider resigning, he replied that they thought the president might be right. "None of us marched in and told the president that the U.S. is going to face disaster if the Marines didn't withdraw. Those of use who were concerned . . .

realized we might be wrong. There was always this underlying hope that this might work out."[19]

Some presidents may accede to military opposition for the same reason—that the professionals might be right. Others may fear the political costs of rejecting that advice. In any event, presidents in recent decades have acted as if they granted the JCS a veto over military operations.

Senior military officials, not surprisingly, strongly deny that they have, or would ever exercise, a veto over military operations. They insist on their unwavering acceptance of civilian control. Nevertheless, in practice it seems as if their veto potential has led numerous presidents and secretaries of defense to defer to military wishes by accepting proposed terms and conditions of the employment of forces. Thus, George H. W. Bush doubled the number of troops planned for Desert Storm and thereby secured military support for that war. And in December 1992 he agreed at the last minute to the military commander's request to double the number of troops sent into Somalia and to change their assigned mission, dropping the requirement that they "disarm" the clashing clans.

Bill Clinton, faced with the military's routine option of "250,000 troops, six months, and $10 billion," when asked to consider a mission they disliked, decided against early intervention in Bosnia, ruled out all but token relief in Rwanda, postponed deployments into Bosnia until the Dayton Peace Accord was signed, and initially ruled out ground forces for Kosovo.

Even George W. Bush and Donald Rumsfeld accepted military recommendations to delay action in Iraq for several months to permit a better buildup, to increase the size of the planned force, and to go to the Congress and the United Nations for support. And when insurgent attacks increased in Iraq in 2004, Rumsfeld echoed his predecessors by promising to send whatever troops might be requested by the local commander. "If they want more troops, we will sign deployment orders," he declared.[20] These actions suggest that the military retained enormous influence over the size and shape and occurrence of military operations even under the tight civilian control of the Bush administration.

The defense secretary has broad authority to oversee, and even meddle in, war plans, though prudence and politics usually require him to give significant weight to professional military advice. What Eliot Cohen calls an "unequal dialogue"[21] is the inevitable, but desirable, result.

15

Diplomat

*In alliance relations, quite frequently the secretary of defense must play
a larger role than does the secretary of state.*

–James Schlesinger[1]

*Long before September 11, the U.S. government had grown increasingly
dependent on its military to carry out its foreign affairs. . . . The military
simply filled a vacuum left by an indecisive White House, an atrophied
State Department, and a distracted Congress.*

– *Washington Post* reporter Dana Priest[2]

The secretary of defense is not merely an adviser on foreign policy,
sitting as a member of the National Security Council, but also an active
diplomat, traveling abroad, hosting distinguished visitors, meeting with
prime ministers and heads of state, negotiating important agreements,
and in many ways and on many issues acting as an alternate foreign minister. Some have embraced that role, while others have endured it with
reluctance; none could avoid it.

Until the mid-1970s, defense secretaries typically took no more than
four overseas trips per year. Most of these were to Europe for NATO-
related meetings and, starting with McNamara, to Vietnam. The peacetime issues they handled were usually narrow military topics—equipment
modernization, training exercises, and troop deployments. They were not
the point men for broader foreign policy questions, such as relations with
the Soviet Union or China.

Frequent Fliers

After Vietnam, however, defense secretaries began traveling more widely and more often, and to places like Japan and South Korea, the Middle East, and Central America. On several occasions, presidents used secretarial visits for major foreign policy initiatives and for sensitive negotiations. Secretary Cheney went to the Middle East in 1990 to work out details of defense cooperation against Iraq. Secretary Perry averaged nineteen overseas trips per year during his tenure as he sought to build relations in peacetime that could be drawn upon in crises. Secretary Cohen only averaged between fifteen and sixteen trips per year, but they were of longer duration, covering several countries at a time. He, too, recognized the value of personal diplomacy as the basis for defense cooperation. Their activism was typical of the expanded role of defense secretaries as key foreign policy players. As Perry said, "Any future secretary who has the same view that most secretaries have had—that they ought to maintain working relationships with their counterparts . . . will have to deal as I dealt with sixty [nations] instead of twenty, and therefore will have to do more traveling."[3] Perry also insisted on visiting every regional commander twice a year. Donald Rumsfeld started out with a typical travel schedule in 2001, but it was redirected after the September 11 attacks. He has averaged only half a dozen trips per year, primarily to NATO conferences and to the Middle East.

Visits to key allies are unavoidable. Protocol requires contact, and with many nations the key issues of U.S. concern are security matters. Nations hosting large contingents of U.S. forces need consultations on financial aid arrangements and the local impact of military activities. NATO has two high level meetings each year requiring the attendance of the secretary. Key participants in allied military operations also expect frequent, face-to-face discussions at the ministerial level. Just to meet allied expectations demands a heavy travel schedule by the secretary.

Some secretaries have taken special personal interest in particular regions. Laird went to Japan, Brown to China, Perry to the former Soviet Union, and Cohen to Southeast Asia. Each saw his area of focus as one of emerging concern for the Defense Department and did not want to leave U.S. relations solely in the hands of the State Department.

The 1991 Gulf War taught Secretary Cheney and his successors that the Pentagon leader adds heft and seriousness to official visits. A secretarial visit or merely a Pentagon meeting with honor guard connotes a security relationship, a level of cooperation many foreign leaders find very attractive, for it raises their stature and that of their own armed forces.

Even lower level "mil-to-mil" contacts can be crucial supplements to regular diplomacy, particularly as a means to persuade foreign military leaders to cooperate on U.S. concerns and to accept civilian control from their own governments. The formal National Military Strategy documents of JCS Chairmen Shalikashvili and Shelton specifically stressed "engagement" with other nations as a major tool and objective. Secretaries Perry and Cohen both saw foreign exchanges as a key component of U.S. defense policy, solidifying political relationships and paving the way for crisis cooperation.

Presidents also have used their defense secretaries as the envoys of choice in particular crises. That is why Cheney was sent to obtain Saudi basing rights after the Iraqi seizure of Kuwait, why Aspin went to Korea in the early weeks of the Clinton administration, why Perry regularly dealt with the former Soviet republics on denuclearization issues, and why Cohen went to Indonesia with warnings about East Timor. They had presidential instructions and interagency guidance, but they were still the point men for key contacts.

While their foreign travel was coordinated with and acceptable to the State Department, defense secretaries always arrived as VIPs and often met with prime ministers and foreign ministers, not just defense ministers. They became conduits for policy discussions and signals—and their visits strengthened the notion that the U.S. military is one of the most accessible and helpful instruments of American policy.

Military Proconsuls

In addition to their own travel, defense secretaries oversee and direct the regional U.S. military commanders, the generals and admirals known as CINCs until Secretary Rumsfeld banned that title, reserving it solely for the president. The Pentagon divides the world into five regional commands: European (covering Europe, Russia, and most of Africa); Pacific (covering East Asia and Australia); Central (for the Middle East and Central Asia); Southern (covering Latin America south of Mexico and most of the Caribbean); and the new, post-9/11 Northern Command (covering Canada, Mexico, the United States, and Cuba). In addition to these geographical commands, there are functional commands for transportation, strategic nuclear weapon forces, space, joint forces training, and special operations.

The regional combatant commanders are tasked with developing war plans for likely contingencies in their areas and also to develop and carry out peacetime plans, under the rubric of "engagement," for training exercises, port visits, and commander travel. They submit proposals to the budget process called Integrated Priority Lists (IPLs). SOCOM, the special operations command, has its own budget line, a gift from Congress to protect its funding from raids by the services.

In recent years, the regional commands and their four-star commanders have become the most visible and active arm of U.S. diplomacy. In many nations these officers are viewed as proconsuls, the symbols of the American imperium and the most authoritative voice of U.S. policy. They come with all the trappings of power—large staffs and budgets, a long-distance aircraft and a fleet of helicopters, instant secure communications, and a protective security entourage equivalent to that for most heads of state. And they are treated accordingly by the host nations. By contrast, most U.S. ambassadors and even the assistant secretaries of state from Washington have to travel on scheduled commercial flights, unless they can hitch on military planes. They neither bring nor receive the pomp and circumstance that accompanies the regional commanders.[4]

Budgets for the regional commands surged at least 10 percent during the 1990s. By 2000, Central Command had a budget of $55.2 million; the Pacific Command topped $57 million; and the Southern Command jumped to $112 million, much of that for efforts to combat drug trafficking. Even the smallest command in terms of personnel, Southern, has a staff of over 1,100 people—more than work on Latin American issues in State, Commerce, Treasury, Agriculture, and the Pentagon itself combined.[5]

As Dana Priest commented, "the CINCs grew into a powerful force in U.S. foreign policy because of the disproportionate weight of their resources and organization in relation to the assets and influence of other parts of America's foreign policy structure—in particular the State Department, which was shriveling in size, stature, and spirit even as the military's role expanded."[6] She also notes that the Clinton administration assigned new jobs to the military that previously had been done by civilian agencies, including anti-drug trafficking, de-mining, humanitarian disaster relief, and anti-terrorism.[7]

In the competition for overseas influence, the Pentagon greatly outweighs and often out-performs the Department of State (DOS). Even before the war in Iraq in 2003, the Defense Department had over 340,000 military and civilian personnel stationed abroad or afloat. The State Department had only 6,800 people posted abroad. Indeed, the entire Foreign Service, from the most junior consular officer to senior ambassadors, has only 10,600 people—fewer than the number of colonels and Navy captains (11,329) in the U.S. armed forces.[8] The DOD has almost as many people assigned to our embassies as does the DOS—6,900 compared to 7,200. At many missions, State Department personnel are outnumbered by people from the more than thirty U.S. government agencies that assign people abroad. In Washington, too, the DOD outguns the DOS. There are 2,056 personnel in the office of the secretary of defense and 991 officers and civilians on the Joint Staff—nearly ten times the 370 people assigned to the office of the secretary of state.

The Pentagon has more means of persuasion than State. It has the aircraft to fly people or equipment to desired destinations. It can act quickly and decisively, unlike choreographed diplomacy. It has the money to spare on travel and special purchases, unlike the penny-pinching State

Department. It can threaten with an aircraft carrier or reward with the sale of new jet fighters. Traditional U.S. foreign aid takes years to program and reams of paperwork to administer, with outcomes more distant and usually less visible than what the military can do in a matter of days.

Nor can the State Department tell the regional commanders what to do. Each command has an ambassador-rank political adviser (PolAd) who is supposed to help provide a foreign policy perspective. Some commanders have kept their PolAds close at hand, drawing on their expertise, while others have shunted them off to oblivion. Secretaries of defense maintain tight control over their commanders, overseeing and limiting their contact with State Department officials.[9] This means that military concerns and military perspectives often become the dominant influences shaping U.S. diplomacy. Whether they seek such an expanded role or not, defense secretaries wind up as alternate foreign ministers. And when State and Defense clash over policy, as often occurs, Defense is often the victor by default.

Some regional commanders have embraced this diplomatic role enthusiastically and quite successfully. Dana Priest gives several vivid examples, particularly of Marine Gen. Tony Zinni.[10]

Division of Labor

Who should be in charge of U.S. foreign policy? Who should meet with foreign emissaries and who should negotiate agreements abroad for the United States? The law is clear. Section 2656 of Title 22, section 38 of the U.S. Code assigns the management of foreign affairs to the secretary of state.

> The Secretary of State shall perform such duties as shall from time to time be enjoined on or intrusted to him by the President relative to correspondences, commissions, or instructions to or with public ministers or consuls from the United States, or to negotiations with public ministers from foreign states or princes, or to memorials or other applications from foreign public ministers or other foreigners, or to such other matters respecting foreign affairs as the President of the United States shall assign to the Department, and he shall conduct the business of the Department in such manner as the President shall direct.[11]

But even this basic law indicates that the president can let others carry the ball on diplomacy. And that has often been the conscious or unconscious result. The Pentagon is the rich and agile heavyweight in the policy arena.

The law creating the job of secretary of defense and the National Security Council never defines "national security." In practice, the term means whatever officials choose to include within its elastic embrace. Foreign policy tends to mean things done to and with other nations and entities abroad, while national security includes economic and military measures done to strengthen and protect the nation. By that formulation, foreign policy is only a subset of the overarching term.

Although the regional commanders develop valuable, close ties to many of the governments in their Area of Responsibility (AOR), they are especially ill-suited to deal with several of the most severe disputes that threaten regional and global security and stability. Precisely because the commanders are expected to develop close and friendly ties to local governments, the AOR borders have been drawn between key disputants. The Pacific commander deals with India, while Pakistan is in the AOR of the Central Command. That command has all of the Middle East nations—except Israel. Egypt and much of East Africa are also under the domain of the Central Command, while the rest of North Africa and Southern Africa are part of the vast European Command. The new Northern Command includes Mexico and Cuba, but Guatemala and the rest of Central America and the Caribbean are part of the Southern Command.

The State Department has regional bureaus that encompass warring parties on the same continent, but the assistant secretaries are based in Washington and lack the ready access—and personal aircraft and entourage—of the regional commanders.

Some writers have lamented the inability of the State Department to measure up to the multiple demands of superpower foreign policy.[12] But the usual alternative posed is the small, talented, fast-acting NSC staff. The trouble with that, as the Iran-Contra investigators concluded, is that it gives too great an operational role to an ill-suited organization.

A better solution is not to exclude the DOD and its leader from diplomacy, but rather to accept and utilize their comparative advantages, all subject to the higher-level coordination out of the White House.

Foreign policy is only one aspect of national security, which also encompasses what we do at home as well as what we do abroad to protect ourselves and our interests. Defense secretaries in recent decades have usually had the breadth of knowledge and vision to play such a role. Many have promoted and been involved in activities far beyond the traditional and narrow view of their role in international affairs. And the personnel on the Joint Staff and OSD have the background and expertise to develop and carry out broad aspects of foreign policies.

The principal objection to granting the secretary of defense a nearly coequal role in "foreign policy" is that greater Pentagon influence would somehow militarize policy. That is a valid concern in the sense that defense planners are most comfortable in using the military instruments of policy. But those instruments range from weapons of war to psychological demonstrations of capabilities to friendships with foreign officers. Recent history has shown that the American military, supported by their civilian superiors, has been generally reluctant to support the use of force abroad. Military officers, thanks in part to broad-gauged Professional Military Education (PME), nowadays bring educational and policy experience equal to their civilian superiors.[13] Today's top officers are not at all martinets.

A positive advantage of giving the Pentagon a coequal role in policymaking is that military thinking is highly pragmatic, seeking results and conclusions with little regard to external perceptions and ideology. Although military advice tends to be binary ("us" vs. "them"), it also favors clearcut choices and eschews ambiguity and temporizing. "Hope is not a strategy" is a common—and quite sensible—military maxim.

By bringing a deliberate and rational approach to policymaking, the secretary of defense and his department strengthen the policy process in significant ways. The DOD brings resources, capabilities, experience, and a pragmatic mindset. The tight civilian control of military activities is also consistent with the requirements of democratic foreign policy.

16

NSC Adviser

Mr. President, here's what I think. That's the Pentagon's view on it.
Colin has a different view, and I want you to hear it. Colin, tell
the president why you're all screwed up.

−Colin Powell quoting Dick Cheney at a 1990 NSC meeting[1]

My sense of all the Cabinet officers I've worked with has been they are
very reluctant−and this may be because it's the Defense Department−to put
the president of the United States in a position where he potentially will
have to overrule the secretary of defense.

−Under Secretary Walt Slocombe[2]

I can't recall any daylight between the secretary of defense and the JCS.

−Clinton administration official, 1993–2000[3]

One of the most important but least explored roles of the secretary of
defense is as one of four statutory members of the National Security Council, the body that advises the president on the full range of defense and
foreign policy issues. The JCS chairman is the designated military adviser
to the secretary, the president, and the NSC as a whole, and he partici-
pates in meetings, but his role is supposed to be advisory and thus somewhat secondary to the defense secretary.

While the secretary personally is a member of the NSC, he also has
influence through his subordinates, who staff the numerous committees
that consider issues and formulate decision papers for the senior offi-

cials. The deputy secretary is a member of the next most important group, called in recent years the Deputies Committee, although the under secretary for policy sometimes attends with or in place of the deputy, since that office is the key point of interagency contact. When the DOD needs to coordinate with other departments, or when they raise issues which require DOD advice or participation, one or more of those top three officials get involved.

Most defense secretaries enjoy their NSC role. They get substantial time with the president, unlike most of their cabinet colleagues. They deal with some of the most important issues facing the nation. They represent and speak for their department, buttressed by thorough and superior staff work. They defend its interests and prerogatives. They offer capabilities, from transport and obedient workers to precision weapons and super secret intelligence, which are the envy of all other policymakers. Their ideas carry the added weight of the institution they command. They are freer than their colleagues to offer advice untainted by diplomatic niceties or domestic political pressures.

Offsetting these advantages is the fact that senior officials lose control of their calendars when they get summoned to frequent White House meetings to discuss the problem of the day. In a major crisis, one like Kosovo or Iraq that involved decisions on the use of force stretching over several weeks, most other matters get sidelined, deferred, or ignored. Such crises "suck all the oxygen out" of other issues, senior officials say.[4]

In the Clinton and G. W. Bush administrations, cabinet members had White House meetings—either full NSC sessions with the president or "Principals Committee" discussions in his absence—at least once or twice a week. These single-issue events were supplemented by weekly breakfasts and lunches among the two statutory cabinet members of NSC, the secretary of defense and the secretary of state, and the national security adviser. Each official brought his or her own special list of issues for discussion at these meals, and they often proved valuable for surfacing developing issues or smoothing coordination of other matters. The G. W. Bush administration also instituted daily secure telephone conference calls among the "big three."[5]

Recent presidents have used the NSC for substantive discussions, exploring issues and possible options, though they frequently reserved final decisions until after the meeting. This allows time for reflection and avoids open rejection of one official's recommendation in favor of another's. Clinton made a point of calling Cohen or Albright if he was going to go against that cabinet member's advice.[6]

In recent years, the defense secretaries have worked hard to be sure that there is "no daylight" between them and the JCS chairman. They want the Pentagon to speak with one voice, the better to prevail in interagency disputes. In practice, the secretary usually meets or talks to the chairman daily–and in a crisis, their staffs understand the importance of coordinating the point papers being sent to their superiors. Although the two officials may say the same things, they have two seats at the table and thus implicitly two votes on whatever issue is being discussed. This dual representation extends throughout the interagency process. Until Goldwater-Nichols, even high-ranking Joint Staff officers were back-seaters at Situation Room meetings, with the front chair held by a DOD civilian. Sometimes the secretary, like Cohen, let the chairman take the lead. Under Secretary Rumsfeld, the civilian was usually forceful and outspoken.

In some administrations, notably Reagan's and G. W. Bush's, there have been bitter disputes between the Defense and State Departments and their respective leaders. Sometimes these reflect a clash of personalities and operating styles as well as disagreements on the substance of policy. In fact, it is reasonable and should not be surprising when two such institutions have differing perspectives and recommendations.

Diplomats are used to ambiguity and compromise. They see foreign relations in shades of gray while military officials tend to see binary categories: friend or foe, peace or war, offense or defense. The State Department wants its diplomacy to be backed by the threat of force, but the Pentagon wants to make only credible threats that the national leadership is willing to carry out, despite the costs and risks.

Each department wants to utilize and protect its assets. Thus, the Pentagon tends to resist the use of force unless and until it can be used with the greatest chance of success and the lowest risk of failure or casualties. Military planners like clear objectives and fixed priorities because it makes their tasks easier and avoids the problems of sudden change. The U.S. military resists "nation-building" because it diverts soldiers from training and availability for serious combat against tougher foes.

Secretary Rumsfeld and Secretary Powell had reasonable differences on many policy questions. Each had plausible arguments, for example, on dealing with North Korea or the role of the United Nations in Iraq. It is normal in Washington for sharp differences to be leaked to the press, which has always considered conflict newsworthy. What is less common is for the White House to tolerate the public impression of disunity. President Reagan tolerated the Shultz-Weinberger feuding because he didn't want to choose between friends. President George W. Bush permitted open disagreement between Powell and Rumsfeld because he valued the debate and the fact that it allowed him to make the decisions, rather than being given only a single, consensus recommendation.

After all, the NSC exists to serve the president and his preferred operating style. If he values debate, it will happen. If he prefers unity and consensus, his advisers will try to obtain it without referring so many issues for his personal review. A wise secretary of defense accommodates his boss.

Ultimately, any defense secretary depends for his success on his relationship with the president. His advice will be heeded and his recommendations adopted when the president is comfortable with his personal style and confident in his leadership and control over the Pentagon. Cheney, Perry, Cohen, and Rumsfeld had such relationships, while Aspin did not.

In the NSC, the defense secretary represents his department, reflecting its views, insisting on its prerogatives, and providing information only it possesses. When others ask for options—how many troops would it take to solve the problem of the moment?—the secretary and the chairman can be encouraging or discouraging in their responses. If they say, as officials frequently did in the Clinton administration, that it would take "250,000 troops, six months and $10 billion," they can preclude action which they dislike. No one else can authoritatively counter their views.

Secretary Rumsfeld has been more successful than many of his predecessors in pushing military planners to accept and try alternative approaches—for example, fewer troops than they preferred in Iraq and extraordinary use of special operations forces in Afghanistan. He also preserved Pentagon autonomy in major policy initiatives, such as planning and execution of stability operations after the fall of Saddam Hussein. With the NSC banished from an operational role since the Iran-Contra scandal, the DOD has an enormous bureaucratic advantage in maintaining its control and initiative.

What was unusual in the G. W. Bush administration was the powerful role of Vice President Cheney. Although he gave his advice in private, his staff was quite active in the policy process. While his immediate predecessors, Gore and Quayle, had staffs of six to eight career detailees from other agencies to support them on NSC matters, Cheney increased his NSC staff to fifteen, including five political appointees. Such a sizable staff allowed his representatives to sit in on all important lower level meetings and to prepare materials that gave the vice president much greater leverage over the policy process. Since Cheney seemed to be in lockstep with Secretary Rumsfeld most of the time, the Pentagon had even more influence than its assets might otherwise dictate. Cheney could also speak with the expertise as a former secretary of defense, thus reinforcing the views of Rumsfeld and the chairman.

Bush's first-term national security adviser, Condoleezza Rice, worked as a junior NSC staffer in the early 1990s. Despite her close advisory relationship to the president, she was seen as less able to influence, much less discipline, her more experienced and celebrated cabinet colleagues, Rumsfeld and Powell. These facts also served to strengthen Secretary Rumsfeld in his role as an NSC adviser.

Any secretary of defense plays a powerful role in NSC deliberations because of the resources and capabilities of his department. The DOD can fly a presidential envoy halfway around the globe in a few hours. The DOD can deploy several hundred men, armed to intimidate or armed to fight, almost anywhere within a day. If the question is, how do we pay for this? DOD can usually, albeit reluctantly, find the answer in its $400 billion budget.

But the secretary also is strong because of U.S. ethics on the use of force. Americans have always believed that they fight only when provoked; only for the most noble, even universal, goals; only according to the standards of civilized society and the rule of law. If a secretary is willing to advocate the use of force, he usually has those powerful moral convictions on his side of the argument. By contrast, if he is reluctant, he forces all around the table to be willing to justify risky or questionable actions.

Ideally, the interagency process should not be one of voting between alternative positions that reflect the buildings in which they were prepared. Instead, it should be people from those buildings, steeped in the expertise and traditions of their institutions, on a shared journey to discover a solution to the problem the nation faces. The system works best when secretaries of defense are willing to go beyond dogged reiteration of their institutional talking points and search for common ground.

17

Successes and Failures

If he wasn't breaking china, he wouldn't be doing his job.

–Dick Cheney (on Don Rumsfeld)[1]

Despite their impressive prior experiences, defense secretaries tend to confuse priorities among their roles and spend too much time and energy on the wrong issues. More than any other cabinet member, a defense secretary is bushwhacked–caught off balance by a crisis that pertains to one role while he is concentrating on another role.

–F. J. West[2]

No one pattern of leadership explains the successes or predicts the failures of secretaries of defense. Men of similar backgrounds and personality have had quite different results in office. Some officials who were enormously effective for several years nevertheless ultimately lost the confidence of the president.

Business experience is valuable for someone who must manage the large, diverse, even sprawling Department of Defense. Several of the early secretaries and two of the most powerful–McNamara and Rumsfeld–applied their chief executive mindsets and techniques quite effectively to that role, but several of them failed to handle the political demands of the office, especially in public and congressional relations.

Military experience seems useful, but far from necessary, perhaps because most secretaries who served in uniform did so in the lower ranks. Brown, Cheney, and Cohen all did reasonably well in office, earning the respect of those around them, despite their lack of military service. On the other hand, Perry was strongly influenced by his time as an enlisted man, which made him particularly sensitive to quality of life issues for those in uniform.

Political experience is also valuable, but insufficient. Some who went directly from Capitol Hill into the Pentagon maintained their friendships and built a bulwark of support for their policies and programs. Laird, Cheney, and Cohen were especially good at that, but Aspin was a surprising failure. Rumsfeld had congressional experience, but by the time he went to the Pentagon the second time he had only disdain for the legislative branch and its role.

Technical expertise can be quite helpful to a Pentagon leader, allowing him to better assess the recommendations of subordinates, but it can also lead to intellectual arrogance. Brown and Perry made good use of their scientific backgrounds, but Schlesinger was too academic for his own good.

Close, personal ties to the president are particularly important, but several secretaries succeeded despite a more distant relationship—notably McNamara (at first with Kennedy), Laird, Carlucci, and perhaps Rumsfeld with Bush. And even strong friendship did not prevent Harry Truman from dumping Louis Johnson, or Lyndon Johnson from replacing McNamara. Nor did it keep Clark Clifford from turning against Johnson's Vietnam War. Reagan was much closer to Weinberger than to George Shultz, but he could never bring himself to choose one adviser's basic approach over the other's.

Luck, of course, plays a part. The firefighters were distracted from their preferred course by the necessity of dealing with recurring, high-visibility problems. Louis Johnson wound up on the wrong side of history when the Korean War broke out just as he was imposing further drastic budget cuts on the Pentagon. Aspin was the most available scapegoat for the failures in Somalia. Rumsfeld was rescued from an uphill battle to transform the DOD by the need to become an active secretary of war.

Timing affects a secretary's performance as well. Those brought into office at midterm or later have only a few months to master their duties before the electoral calendar imposes a lockdown on bold initiatives and careerists start dragging their heels on some issues, hoping to run out the clock on unwelcome policies. Those named at the start of an administration have the greatest opportunity to set a course and complete it.

It also helps to be in the Pentagon when the budget is going up rather than down. Those secretaries who had to impose budget restraint—Louis Johnson, Wilson, Schlesinger, and Aspin—found it harder to pursue other goals, or to keep the defense advocates in Congress happy. The exceptions were Laird, who managed a reduction in the Vietnam War effort by granting more operational latitude to the military leaders, and Cheney, who cut the budget less than Congress wanted while also letting the military fight the Gulf War largely as it preferred. On the other hand, rising budgets made it easier for other secretaries—notably McNamara,

Weinberger, and Rumsfeld–to appease the opponents of their management and policy reforms.

To be successful, a secretary of defense needs to simultaneously manage three key relationships–with the president, with Congress, and with the senior military leadership. If any one of the three lose faith or trust in him, he is doomed for failure, or at least for greatly reduced effectiveness. The president wants and needs someone who can provide helpful advice while running the Pentagon in ways that cause no embarrassment for the White House. Congress expects due deference to its views and prerogatives, and competent management of defense activities. The senior military leadership demands respect for their professionalism and expects clear guidance and timely decisions, even when contrary to their advice.

The notable failures are obviously Forrestal, Louis Johnson, Schlesinger, and Aspin, for each lost the support of both the president and Congress and had to be sacrificed. McNamara suffered the same ultimate fate, but only after he had succeeded in reshaping the Pentagon's processes and strategy.

The men deemed most successful by these standards are McNamara, Laird, Weinberger, Cheney, Perry, and Rumsfeld. Each maintained, at least for most of his tenure, a close relationship with the president, adequate relations with key officials in Congress, and (except for McNamara) excellent relations with the military leadership. Each performed his various institutional roles with skill. Each achieved much of what he set out to accomplish in policy terms. Each helped the president to accomplish key foreign policy goals. Each set standards for future leaders that could well be followed.

To prepare to command the Pentagon, an aspirant obviously needs issue expertise, a broad knowledge of defense policy matters and a penchant for strategic analysis. He or she also needs an inquiring mind and a talent for asking questions until full and truthful answers are obtained. The future secretary needs to know how to prioritize, to discern which matters are truly significant and which are marginal, so as to avoid being a prisoner of the inbox. And then he or she needs to know how to cultivate allies and balance the many cross pressures–from the White House, Congress, and the rest of the Pentagon–while maintaining personal integrity.

This nearly impossible job is difficult and sometimes defeating. It is probably the most challenging in the federal government other than the presidency. Yet some secretaries have risen to the challenge, have performed the myriad roles well, and have earned the respect of those who follow in their wake. Others have done nearly as well as the few cited here, but these deserve special recognition for their accomplishments. They demonstrate differing patterns of leadership, different paths to success. They give future secretaries of defense alternative models to try to emulate.

Appendix A

Secretaries of Defense

Name	Term of Service	Months	Background	Military Service	Operating Style
James Forrestal	9/17/47–3/28/49	18	Investment banker	Navy WWI	Revolutionary
Louis Johnson	3/28/49–9/19/50	18	Lawyer	Army WWI	Firefighter
George Marshall	9/21/50–9/12/51	12	Army officer	Career	Team Player
Robert Lovett	9/17/51–1/20/53	16	Investment banker	Navy WWI	Team Player
Charles Wilson	1/28/53–10/8/57	56	Industrialist	None	Team Player
Neil McElroy	10/9/57–12/1/59	26	Industrialist	None	Team Player
Thomas Gates	12/2/59–1/20/61	14	Investment banker	Navy WWII	Team Player
Robert McNamara	1/21/61–2/29/68	85	Industrialist	Air WWII	Revolutionary
Clark Clifford	3/1/68–1/20/69	11	Lawyer	Navy WWII	Firefighter
Melvin Laird	1/22/69–1/29/73	48	Politician	Navy WWII	Firefighter
Eliot Richardson	1/30/73–5/24/73	4	Lawyer	Army WWII	Team Player
James Schlesinger	7/2/73–11/19/75	29	Economist	None	Revolutionary
Donald Rumsfeld	11/20/75–1/20/77	14	Politician	Navy	Firefighter
Harold Brown	1/21/77–1/20/81	48	Physicist	None	Team Player
Caspar Weinberger	1/21/81–11/23/87	82	Lawyer	Army WWII	Revolutionary
Frank Carlucci	11/23/87–1/20/89	14	Government official	Navy	Team Player
Richard Cheney	3/21/89–1/20/93	46	Politician	None	Team Player
Les Aspin	1/20/93–2/3/94	12	Politician	Army	Firefighter
William Perry	2/3/94–1/24/97	36	Mathematician	Army	Team Player
William Cohen	1/24/97–1/20/2001	48	Politician	None	Firefighter
Donald Rumsfeld	1/20/2001–		Businessman	Navy	Revolutionary

Appendix B

Foreign Travel by Secretaries of Defense

Secretary	#/yr	Principal Areas Visited
Forrestal	1*	Canada
Johnson	3*	Europe, Asia
Marshall	2*	Canada, NE Asia
Lovett	2*	Europe
Wilson	3*	Europe, Asia
McElroy	1*	Asia
Gates	1*	Europe
McNamara	4	NATO Members, Vietnam
Clifford	4*	NATO Members, Vietnam
Laird	4	Vietnam, NATO Members, NE Asia
Richardson	0	–
Schlesinger	4	NATO Members, NE Asia
Rumsfeld	6*	NATO Members, Africa
Brown	6.2	NATO Members, Middle East, NE Asia
Weinberger	7.2	NATO Members, Middle East, Central America, Asia
Carlucci	11*	Data incomplete
Cheney	8.6	Middle East, Europe
Aspin	8*	Europe, Asia
Perry	19	NATO Members, Russia, US troop deployments
Cohen	15.5	Europe, Middle East, NE & SE Asia
Rumsfeld**	6	Europe, Middle East

*Total number of trips during term of office
**Figure for first 3 years in office
Source: OSD

Notes

1. The Nearly Impossible Job

1. Francis W. West Jr., "Secretaries of Defense: Why Most Have Failed," *Naval War College Review* 34 (March-April 1981), 86.
2. James Schlesinger, "The Office of Secretary of Defense," in Robert J. Art, Vincent Davis, Samuel P. Huntington, eds., *Reorganizing America's Defense: Leadership in War and Peace* (Washington: Pergamon-Brassey's, 1985), 262.
3. The latest information in all these categories is available at www.defenselink.mil.
4. The DOD's $401 billion budget is larger than the GDP of all other countries except France, Italy, Germany, United Kingdom, Russia, Spain, Australia, India, Japan, China, Canada, South Korea, Mexico, and Brazil.

2. The Cemetery for Dead Cats

1. Letter to Robert Sherwood, August 27, 1947, quoted in Walter Millis, ed., *The Forrestal Diaries* (New York: Viking, 1951), 299.
2. Francis W. West Jr., "Secretaries of Defense: Why Most Have Failed," *Naval War College Review* 43 (March-April 1981), 91.
3. Clark Clifford, *Counsel to the President* (New York: Random House, 1991), 146.
4. June 4, 1946, in Millis, 167.
5. Clifford, 148–49.
6. Clifford, 155.
7. Public Law, 80–253.
8. Clifford, 158.
9. Carl W. Borklund, *Men of the Pentagon* (New York: Praeger, 1966), 15.
10. Borklund, 59.
11. Townsend Hoopes and Douglas Brinkley, *Driven Patriot: The Life and Times of James Forrestal* (New York: Knopf, 1992), 359–60.
12. Clifford, 160.
13. In a post-resignation trip to Florida intended to provide rest and relaxation, Forrestal searched the closets and looked under the beds for hidden microphones and then whispered to his host, "The Russians are after me, the FBI is watching me, the Zionists are after me." Clifford, 174.
14. Thomas D. Boettcher, *First Call: The Making of the Modern U.S. Military, 1945–1953* (Boston: Little, Brown, 1992), 172.
15. Boettcher, 172–73.
16. Walter S. Poole, *The Joint Chiefs of Staff and National Policy,* vol. 4, *1950–1952* (Washington: Office of Joint History, Office of the Chairman of the Joint Chiefs of Staff, 1998), 9.
17. Boettcher, 229.

18. Poole, 33.
19. Doris M. Condit, *History of the Office of the Secretary of Defense,* vol. 2, *The Test of War, 1950–1953* (Washington: Historical Office, Office of the Secretary of Defense, 1988), 37.
20. Borklund, 102.
21. Richard M., Leighton, *History of the Office of the Secretary of Defense.* vol. 3, *Strategy, Money, and the New Look* (Washington: Historical Office, Office of the Secretary of Defense, 2001), 13.
22. Borklund, 148.
23. Borklund, 143.
24. Leighton, 10.
25. Borklund, 143.
26. Borklund, 143.
27. Borklund, 144.
28. Leighton, 6.
29. Roger R. Trask and Alfred Goldberg, *The Department of Defense, 1947–1997: Organization and Leaders* (Washington: Historical Office of the Secretary of Defense, 1997), 21.
30. Trask and Goldberg, 73.
31. Borklund, 161, 164, 179.
32. Stephen E. Ambrose, *Eisenhower,* vol. 2, *The President* (New York: Simon & Schuster, 1984), 434.
33. Robert J. Watson, *History of the Office of the Secretary of Defense.* vol. 4, *Into the Missile Age, 1956–1960* (Washington: Historical Office, Office of the Secretary of Defense, 1997), 130.
34. Watson, 735.
35. Watson, 735.

3. McNamara: The Numbers of Power

1. Henry L. Trewhitt, *McNamara* (New York: Harper & Row, 1971), 83.
2. Carl W. Borklund, *Men of the Pentagon: From Forrestal to McNamara* (New York: Praeger, 1966), 209.
3. Robert S. McNamara, *In Retrospect: The Tragedy and Lessons of Vietnam* (New York: Random House/Times Books, 1995), 14.
4. McNamara, 22.
5. Deborah Shapley, *Promise and Power: The Life and Times of Robert McNamara* (Boston: Little, Brown, 1993), 85.
6. Shapley, 85–86.
7. David Halberstam, *The Best and the Brightest* (New York: Ballantine, 1993), 10.
8. McNamara, 6.
9. Shapley, 3–4.
10. Shapley, 29.
11. Shapley, 33.
12. Quoted in James M. Roherty, *Decisions of Robert S. McNamara: A Study of the Role of the Secretary of Defense* (Coral Gables: University of Miami Press, 1970), 67.
13. Speech to the Nation, January 17, 1961.
14. Roherty, 67; McNamara, 23.
15. McNamara, 23.
16. Quoted in Roherty, 69.
17. Halberstam, 224.
18. Quoted in Shapley, 127.
19. Geoffrey Piller, "DOD's Office of International Security Affairs: The Brief Ascendancy of an Advisory System," *Political Science Quarterly* 98, no. 1 (Spring 1983), 65.
20. Kennedy also routinely calls Bundy "Mac" and even Treasury Secretary Dillon "Doug," but never Rusk "Dean." See Ernest R. May and Philip D. Zelikow, *The Kennedy Tapes*

(Cambridge: Harvard University Press, 1997), especially meetings of October 27, 1962, pp. 523, 526, 552, 619.

21. Dean Rusk, as told to Richard Rusk, *As I Saw It* (New York: W.W. Norton, 1990), 521.
22. Quoted in Shapley, 127.
23. Roger Hilsman, *To Move a Nation* (Garden City: Doubleday, 1967), 43.
24. Arnold Kanter, *Defense Politics: A Budgetary Perspective* (Chicago: University of Chicago Press, 1979), 79.
25. Quoted in Shapley, 103.
26. Quoted in Roherty, 67–68.
27. Shapley, 268.
28. Shapley, 359.
29. Quoted in Trewhitt, 17.
30. Roherty, 90, 198n53.
31. Douglas Kinnard, *The Secretary of Defense* (Lexington: University Press of Kentucky, 1980), 81.
32. Thomas D. White, "Strategy and the Defense Intellectuals," *Saturday Evening Post*, May 4, 1963.
33. Quoted in H. R. McMaster, *Dereliction of Duty* (New York: HarperCollins, 1997), 20.
34. Quoted in Fred Kaplan, *The Wizards of Armageddon* (New York: Simon & Schuster, 1983), 256.
35. Quoted in Kaplan, 254.
36. Quoted in Shapley, 233.
37. Richard A. Stubbing with Richard A. Mendel, *The Defense Game* (New York: Harper & Row, 1986), 269; Kanter, 34, 55.
38. Shapley, 99.
39. Jack Raymond, *Power at the Pentagon* (New York: Harper & Row, 1964), 284–85.
40. Raymond, 179–81.
41. Roherty, 94.
42. Quoted in Roherty, 93.
43. Quoted in Roherty, 93.
44. McMaster, 11–12.
45. Kanter, 35; Kinnard, 82; Shapley, 325.
46. Roherty, 192n3.
47. Kanter, 31.
48. Quoted in Kanter, 75.
49. Clark A. Murdock, *Defense Policy Formulation: A Comparative Analysis of the McNamara Era* (Albany: State University of New York Press, 1974), 82, 99.
50. Kanter, 88.
51. Congress and the Nation, 1945–1964 (Washington: Congressional Quarterly, 1965), 311.
52. Shapley, 106.
53. Shapley, 201–2.
54. Stubbing, 275–79.
55. Shapley, 228–29.
56. Kaplan, 270–72.
57. White, "Strategy."
58. Kaplan, 258.
59. Kaplan, 273.
60. Quoted in Kalpan, 316.
61. Kaplan, 323, 325.
62. Trewhitt, 252.
63. Kaplan, 329.
64. John McNaughton, quoted in Kaplan, 334.
65. Shapley, 322–5.
66. Quoted in McMaster, 354n75.

67. Piller, 64.
68. Trewhitt, 164.
69. Hilsman, 55.
70. Trewhitt, 166–7.
71. Trewhitt, 168.
72. Shapley, 270; Trewhitt, 254.
73. May and Zelikow, 133.
74. Shapley, 176–77, 264.
75. Shapley, 286; Trewhitt, 260.
76. Raymond, 280.

4. Schlesinger: The Independence of Ideas

1. Quoted in Douglas Kinnard, *The Secretary of Defense* (Lexington: The University Press of Kentucky, 1980), 161.
2. Gerald Ford, *A Time to Heal* (New York: Harper & Row and Reader's Digest Association, Inc., 1979), 324.
3. Kinnard, 161, 168; Henry Kissinger, *Years of Renewal* (New York: Simon & Schuster, 1999), 181.
4. James Schlesinger, "Quantitative Analysis and National Security," *World Politics* 15, no. 12 (Jan. 1963), 295–315.
5. Leslie H. Gelb, "Schlesinger for Defense, Defense for Détente," *New York Times Magazine,* August 4, 1974.
6. Gelb, "Schlesinger for Defense."
7. Kinnard, 161–162; Richard A. Stubbing with Richard A. Mendel. *The Defense Game* (New York: Harper & Row, 1986), 312.
8. Gelb, "Schlesinger for Defense."
9. Stubbing, 312.
10. Quoted in Stubbing, 313.
11. James Schlesinger, Oral History Interviews, Historical Office of the Secretary of Defense, February 7, 1991, p. 15.
12. James Schlesinger, "The Office of Secretary of Defense," in Robert J. Art, Vincent Davis, Samuel P. Huntington, eds., *Reorganizing America's Defense: Leadership in War and Peace* (Washington: Pergamon-Brassey's, 1985), 261. Italics in original.
13. Schlesinger, Oral History Interviews, February 7, 1991, p. 3.
14. Schlesinger, Oral History Interviews, July 12, 1990, pp. 23, 26.
15. Schlesinger, Oral History Interviews, July 12, 1990, p. 38.
16. Schlesinger, "Office," 262.
17. Gelb, "Schlesinger for Defense."
18. Schlesinger, Oral History Interviews, July 12, 1990, pp. 23, 40.
19. Ford, 320, 131.
20. Ford, 321.
21. Walter Isaacson, *Kissinger* (New York: Simon & Schuster, 1992), 623.
22. Isaacson, 623.
23. Isaacson, 622.
24. Henry Kissinger, *Years of Upheaval* (Boston: Little, Brown, 1982), 1192.
25. Schlesinger, Oral History Interviews, February 7, 1991, p. 16.
26. Schlesinger, Oral History Interviews, February 7, 1991, p. 16.
27. Kinnard, 265.
28. Kinnard, 166; Mark Perry, *Four Stars* (Boston: Houghton Mifflin, 1989), 248–52.
29. Perry, 257.
30. Stubbing 332; Ford, 323.
31. Kinnard, 163–5; Stubbing, 314–15.
32. Quoted in Schlesinger, "Office," 260.
33. Stubbing, 323, 325.

34. Stubbing, 325.
35. Stubbing, 326.
36. Schlesinger, "Office," 266, 259.
37. This section draws extensively on Fred Kaplan, *The Wizards of Armageddon* (New York: Simon & Schuster, 1983), especially pp. 357–76.
38. Quoted in Kinnard, 176.
39. Kaplan, 372–73.
40. Kaplan, 374.
41. Ford, 279.
42. Isaacson, 650–51.
43. Ford, 284.
44. Schlesinger, "Office," 259.
45. Kinnard, 157–58.
46. Stubbing, 330–31, Kinnard, 173–4.
47. Stubbing, 318–19.
48. Kinnard, 180–181.
49. Stubbing, 319; *Congress and the Nation*, vol. 4, *1973–1976* (Washington: Congressional Quarterly, 1977), 161.
50. Kissinger, *Years of Upheaval*, 1155–58.
51. Ford, 329–30; Kinnard, 186–88.
52. Schlesinger, Oral History Interviews, July 12, 1990, p. 42.

5. Weinberger: The Power of Tenacity

1. Robert C. McFarlane, *Special Trust* (New York: Cadell & Davies, 1994), 325.
2. McFarlane, 286–87.
3. Lou Cannon, *President Reagan: The Role of a Lifetime* (New York: Simon & Schuster, 1991), 84; Helene Von Damm, *At Reagan's Side* (New York: Doubleday, 1989), 136.
4. Caspar W. Weinberger, *Fighting for Peace: Seven Critical Years in the Pentagon*, (New York: Warner Books, 1990), 1–3.
5. Nicholas Lemann, "The Peacetime War: Caspar Weinberger in Reagan's Pentagon," *The Atlantic*, October 1984, 71ff.
6. Von Damm, 128, 130.
7. Hedrick Smith, *The Power Game: How Washington Works* (New York: Ballantine Books, 1988), 204–5.
8. Senate Committee on Armed Services, "Nomination of Caspar W. Weinberger to be Secretary of Defense," 97th Cong., 1st sess., January 6, 1981, 7.
9. David A. Stockman, *The Triumph of Politics: Why the Reagan Revolution Failed* (New York: Harper & Row, 1986), 107–9.
10. Smith, 576.
11. Cannon, 162.
12. Stockman, 290–94; Edwin Meese III, *With Reagan: The Inside Story* (Washington: Regnery Gateway, 1992), 178.
13. Alexander M. Haig Jr., *Caveat: Realism, Reagan and Foreign Policy* (New York: Macmillan, 1984), 87.
14. George P. Shultz, *Turmoil and Triumph: My Years as Secretary of State* (New York: Charles Scribner's Sons, 1993), 141.
15. Weinberger, 29.
16. Weinberger, 30–31, 90.
17. McFarlane, 287.
18. Mark Perry, *Four Stars* (Boston: Houghton Mifflin, 1989), 282–83.
19. Perry, 304.
20. James R. Locher, III, *Victory on the Potomac: The Goldwater-Nichols Act Unifies the Pentagon* (College Station: Texas A&M University Press, 2002), 244.
21. Adm. William J. Crowe Jr., *The Line of Fire* (New York: Simon & Schuster, 1993), 118.

22. Crowe, 126–28.
23. Quoted in Locher, 238.
24. McFarlane, 223.
25. Quoted in Smith, 207.
26. Smith, 209.
27. Smith, 209.
28. Smith, 208.
29. McFarlane, 325.
30. Locher, 234.
31. Locher, 242.
32. Quoted in Lemann, "The Peacetime War."
33. Smith, 162.
34. Locher, 240.
35. Lemann, "The Peacetime War."
36. Colin L. Powell, *My American Journey* (New York: Random House, 1995), 294.
37. Locher, 240.
38. Smith, 163.
39. Richard A. Stubbing with Richard A. Mendel, *The Defense Game* (New York: Harper & Row, 1986), 394, 393.
40. Smith, 530, 535.
41. Haig, 87; Stubbing, 385.
42. Fred Kaplan, *The Wizards of Armageddon* (New York: Simon & Schuster, 1983), 387–88.
43. Ronald Reagan, *An American Life* (New York: Simon & Schuster, 1990), 665; Cannon, 328–29.
44. Shultz, 650.
45. The full text is reprinted in Weinberger, 433–45.
46. Weinberger, n111. He attributed this to his belief that too few helicopters had been sent in the 1980 rescue attempt of U.S. hostages in Iran.
47. David C. Martin and John Walcott, *Best Laid Plans: The Inside Story of America's War Against Terrorism* (New York: Touchstone Book by Simon & Schuster, 1988), 274.
48. Weinberger, 388–90, 397, 402.
49. Stubbing, 379; Lemann, "The Peacetime War."
50. Weinberger, 222–23, 255; Cannon, 313.
51. Cannon, 203.
52. Weinberger, 205.
53. McFarlane, 187. Although his father was Jewish, he was raised as an Episcopalian.
54. Weinberger, 397–98; McFarlane, 187.
55. Weinberger, 144; Martin and Walcott, 93.
56. John H. Kelly, "Lebanon: 1982–1984." http://www.rand.org/publications/CF/CF129?CF-129.chapter6.html.
57. Kelly, "Lebanon;" Weinberger, 151–52.
58. Reagan, 465.
59. Smith, 569.
60. Strobe Talbott, *Deadly Gambits: The Reagan Administration and the Stalemate in Nuclear Arms Control* (New York: Knopf, 1984), 44, 47, 49.
61. David Callahan, *Dangerous Capabilties: Paul Nitze and the Cold War* (New York: Harper Collins, 1990), 436–37, 439.
62. Callahan, 442.
63. Cannon, 630–31.
64. Lawrence E. Walsh, *Firewall: The Iran-Contra Conspiracy and Cover-up* (New York: W.W. Norton & Company, 1997), 415.
65. Walsh, 493.
66. Weinberger, 353.
67. Cannon, 310.

6. Laird: The Power of Politics

1. Quoted in Richard Nixon, *RN: The Memoirs of Richard Nixon* (New York: Grosset & Dunlap, 1978), 289.
2. Robert M. Gates, *From the Shadows* (New York: Simon & Schuster, 1996), 46.
3. Seymour M. Hersh, *The Price of Power: Kissinger in the Nixon White House* (New York: Summit, 1983), n71.
4. Melvin R. Laird, Oral History Interviews, Historical Office of the Secretary of Defense, August 18, 1986, p. 8.
5. Laird, Oral History Interviews, September 2, 1986, p. 3.
6. Laird, Oral History Interviews, August 18, 1986, pp. 8–9.
7. Laird, Oral History Interviews, August 18, 1986, pp. 6–7.
8. John Ehrlichman, *Witness to Power: The Nixon Years* (New York: Simon & Schuster, 1982), 94, 305.
9. Henry Kissinger said he usually disregarded the president's late night calls, with single sentence demands for radical action and an immediate hang-up.
10. Walter Isaacson, *Kissinger* (New York: Simon & Schuster, 1992), 116.
11. Henry Kissinger, *White House Years* (Boston: Little, Brown, 1979), 44.
12. Kissinger, *White House Years*, 33.
13. Isaacson, 198.
14. Lawrence Korb, *The Fall and Rise of the Pentagon: American Defense Policies in the 1970s* (Westport: Greenwood Press, 1979), 93.
15. Richard A. Stubbing with Richard A. Mendel, *The Defense Game* (New York: Harper & Row, 1986), 312.
16. Korb, *Fall and Rise*, 92–93.
17. Laird, Oral History Interviews, September 2, 1986, p. 8.
18. Mark Perry, *Four Stars* (Boston: Houghton Mifflin, 1989), 216–17.
19. Laird, Oral History Interviews, September 2, 1986, pp. 11, 14.
20. Stubbing, 297.
21. Stubbing, 293.
22. Laird, Oral History Interviews, August 18, 1986, p. 27.
23. Stubbing, 292.
24. Laird, Oral History Interviews, August 18, 1986, pp. 27–28.
25. Clark Murdock, *Defense Policy Formation* (Albany: State University of New York Press, 1974), 170.
26. Laird, Oral History Interviews, September 2, 1986, pp. 2, 7.
27. H. R. Haldeman, *The Haldeman Diaries* (New York: Putnam, 1994), 86.
28. Laird, Oral History Interviews, September 2, 1986, p. 15.
29. Stubbing, 303, 306.
30. Korb, 87, 89.
31. Laird, Oral History Interviews, September 2, 1986, pp. 9–10; Stubbing, 298.
32. Kissinger, *White House Years*, 318–20.
33. Kissinger, *White House Years*, 318–21; Perry, 221; Hersh, 70–74; Nixon, 382–85.
34. Laird, Oral History Interviews, August 18, 1986, pp. 20–21.
35. Perry, 220.
36. Kissinger, *White House Years*, 275.
37. Kissinger, *White House Years*, 276; Hersh, 121.
38. Kissinger, *White House Years*, 303.
39. Kissinger, *White House Years*, 501, 1184.
40. Kissinger, *White House Years*, 394–97.
41. John Newhouse, *Cold Dawn: The Story of SALT* (New York: Holt, Rinehart & Winston, 1973), 38; Paul H. Nitze, *From Hiroshima to Glasnost* (New York: Grove Weidenfeld, 1989), 295.
42. Hersh, 90.
43. Korb, *Fall and Rise*, 122.

44. For the details of this embarrassing military spying operation, see Hersh 465–79, and Ehrlichman, 302–10.

7. Aspin: The Politics of Failure

1. David Halberstam, *War in a Time of Peace: Bush, Clinton, and the Generals* (New York: Scribner, 2001), 191.
2. Bob Woodward, "The Secretary of Analysis," *Washington Post Magazine*, February 21, 1993.
3. Warren Christopher, *Chances of a Lifetime* (New York: Scribner, 2001), 173.
4. Christopher, 173.
5. Woodward, "The Secretary of Analysis."
6. Woodward, "The Secretary of Analysis."
7. Senate Armed Services Committee, Confirmation hearing, January 7, 1993.
8. Interviews.
9. Rogelio Garcia, "Presidential Appointments to Full-Time Positions in Executive Departments During the 103d Congress," *CRS Report for Congress*, 94-453GOV, July 25, 1994.
10. Elizabeth Drew. *On the Edge: The Clinton Presidency* (New York: Simon & Schuster, 1994), 43; Colin Powell with Joseph E. Persico, *My American Journey* (New York: Random House, 1995), 564.
11. Drew, 45–47; George Stephanopoulos, *All Too Human* (Boston: Little, Brown, 1999), 126–28; Powell, 570–74; Richard Lacayo and Michael Duffy, "Bring on the Admiral," *Time Magazine*, Dec. 27, 1993; Michael Duffy and David S. Jackson, "Obstacle Course," *Time Magazine*, Feb. 8, 1993.
12. Drew, 359.
13. Drew, 141–42.
14. Powell, 563.
15. Eric Schmitt, "Aspin Overrules Navy Secretary, Saving Admiral," *New York Times*, October 5, 1993; Bill McAllister and Barton Gellman, "Aspin Reverses Ban on Married Marines," *Washington Post*, August 12, 1993.
16. Halberstam, 323–24.
17. Powell, 577–78.
18. Eric Schmitt, "Aspin Resigns from Cabinet; President Lost Confidence in Defense Chief, Aides Say," *New York Times*, December 16, 1993.
19. Interviews.
20. Interviews. Note that Secretary Rumsfeld talked of merging the Joint Staff with his own OSD staff, thereby achieving the same civilian control and dominance that Aspin had wanted.
21. Interviews.
22. Michael Gordon, "Pentagon Seeking to Cut Military But Equip It for 2 Regional Wars," New York Times, September 2, 1993; Ashton B. Carter and William J. Perry. *Preventive Defense: A New Security Strategy for America* (Washington: Brookings, 1999), 194.
23. Eric Schmitt, "Aspin Dismisses General as Head of Plane Project," *New York Times*, May 1, 1993.
24. *Congress and the Nation,* vol. 4, *1993–1996* (Washington: Congressional Quarterly, 1998), 291.
25. Drew, 142; Powell, 576–77; Interviews; Ivo H. Daalder, *Getting to Dayton* (Washington: Brookings, 2000), 12–15.
26. Daalder, 17.
27. Tim Weiner, "Raid on Baghdad," *New York Times*, June 27, 1993.
28. Drew, 319; interviews.
29. Drew, 319–23; Powell, 584, 586.
30. John Lancaster, "Aspin Lists U.S. Goals in Somalia," *Washington Post*, August 28, 1993.
31. Drew, 317, 327–31.

32. Drew, 332–34.
33. Interview.
34. Powell, 578.
35. Interviews and Leon V. Sigal, *Disarming Strangers* (Princeton: Princeton UP, 1998), 56–61, 77–80.
36. Strobe Talbott, *Russia Hand* (New York: Random House, 2002), 97–100.
37. Fred Barnes, "You're Fired," *The New Republic,* January 10 and 17, 1994, 13.
38. Interviews.
39. Interviews.
40. Drew, 361–68.

8. Cohen: The Politics of Defense

1. Dana Priest, "An 'Outsider' Set to Take Over Pentagon," *Washington Post,* Jan. 22, 1997.
2. David Halberstam, *War in a Time of Peace: Bush, Clinton, and the Generals* (New York: Scribner, 2001), 438.
3. Dana Priest, "An Outsider," Jan. 22, 1997.
4. Lloyd Grove, "The So-Long Senators," *Washington Post,* Jan. 26, 1996; John Donnelly, "The Evolution of William Cohen," *Boston Globe Magazine,* October 22, 2000.
5. "Remarks announcing the Second Term National Security Team and an Exchange with Reporters," December 5, 1996, *Public Papers of the President, William J. Clinton, 1996.*
6. Senate Committee on Armed Services, Nomination Hearing, Jan. 22, 1997.
7. Interviews; Madeleine Albright, *Madam Secretary* (New York: Miramax Books, 2003), 349.
8. Interviews.
9. Interviews.
10. Interviews.
11. Interviews. The NATO appointment for Ralston came when Cohen engineered an early retirement for Gen. Wesley Clark, who had frequently clashed with him over Kosovo operations.
12. Peter D. Feaver, *Armed Servants* (Cambridge: Harvard University Press, 2003), 217.
13. John Hamre, Oral History Interview, Historical Office of the Secretary of Defense, June 29, 2001, 5.
14. Quoted in James R. Locher, III, *Victory on the Potomac: The Goldwater-Nichols Act Unifies the Pentagon* (College Station: Texas A&M University Press, 2002), 239.
15. Oral History Interview, May 18, 2001, 12–13.
16. Oral History Interview, May 18, 2001, 17. Tyrer had started working for Cohen when he was eighteen, two decades before Cohen became secretary.
17. Interviews; Dana Priest, "An Ousider," Jan. 22, 1997; Donnelly, Oct. 22, 2000.
18. Locher, 284. The DOD argument that the $640 "toilet cover assembly" was designed of special materials so as to be unusually durable was blown away by cartoonists and comedians, who found it a convenient symbol of Pentagon extravagance.
19. *Congress and the Nation,* vol. 10, *1997–2001* (Washington: Press: 2002), 264–265.
20. Locher, 448.
21. Samantha Power, *A Problem from Hell* (New York: Perennial, 2002), 455, 235–236.
22. Confirmation hearing, Jan. 22, 1997.
23. Interviews and Statement of William S. Cohen to The National Commission On Terrorist Attacks Upon the United States, March 23, 2004, (later cited as the 9/11 commission), 21.
24. Dana Priest, *The Mission* (New York, W.W. Norton, 2003), 258–59.
25. Halberstam, 456.
26. Gen. Wesley K. Clark, *Waging Modern War* (New York: Public Affairs, 2001), 249.
27. Madeleine Albright, *Madam Secretary* (New York: Miramax Book, 2003), 394–95, 415; Peter D. Feaver, *Armed Servants* (Cambridge: Harvard University Press, 2003), 277–79.
28. Halberstam, 436–37. For Clark's list of grievances, see *Waging Modern War,* passim.
29. Cohen, Statement to 9/11 commission, 20.
30. Albright, 285–86; *Congress and the Nation, 1997–2001,* 822.

31. Cohen, Statement to 9/11 commission, 17.
32. Cohen, Statement to 9/11 commission, 2, 3, 5, 6.
33. Cohen, Statement to 9/11 commission, 10.
34. Interview; Steve Coll, *Ghost Wars* (New York: Penguin Press, 2004), 498.
35. Coll, 533.
36. Interviews.
37. Priest, *The Mission*, 225.
38. Priest, *The Mission*, 112.
39. Interviews; Donnelly, "William Cohen," Oct. 22, 2000.
40. Halberstam, 440.
41. See his own summary of his accomplishments in Statement to 9/11 commission, 17.

9. Brown: The Technology of Power

1. Quoted in Richard C. Stubbing with Richard A. Mendel, *The Defense Game* (New York: Harper & Row, 1986), 339.
2. Bernard Weinraub, "The Browning of the Pentagon," *New York Times Magazine,* January 29, 1978, 48; Stubbing, 338.
3. Jimmy Carter, *Keeping Faith: Memoirs of a President* (New York: Bantam, 1982), 55.
4. Senate Committee on Armed Services, *Nominations of Harold Brown and Charles W. Duncan,* 95th Cong., 1st sess., January 11, 1977, 7–8.
5. Weinraub, 44.
6. Weinraub, 46.
7. See Harold Brown, *Thinking About National Security* (Boulder: Westview Press, 1983).
8. Carter, 55.
9. Carter, 55–56.
10. Stubbing, 343–44, 349–50.
11. Zbigniew Brzezinski, *Power and Principle: Memoirs of the National Security Adviser, 1977–1981* (New York: Farrar, Straus, Giroux, 1983), 46.
12. Carter, 82.
13. Stubbing, 342.
14. Brzezinski, 44, 47.
15. Brzezinski, 45.
16. Brown, 204.
17. Stubbing, 364.
18. Mark Perry, *Four Stars* (Boston: Houghton Mifflin, 1989), 264, 266.
19. Weinraub, 59–60.
20. Quoted in Stubbing, 339.
21. Stubbing, 349.
22. Eisenstat diary, quoted in Nick Kotz, *Wild Blue Yonder: Money, Politics, and the B-1 Bomber* (Princeton: Princeton UP, 1988), 196.
23. Colin Powell L., *My American Journey* (New York: Random House, 1995), 237; Weinraub, 14.
24. Perry, 270–71.
25. Stubbing, 340.
26. Stubbing, 365.
27. Brown, 205.
28. Quoted in Stubbing, 340.
29. Stubbing, 341.
30. Stubbing, 343; Perry, 266.
31. Stubbing, 347; Lawrence J. Korb, "National Security Organization and Process in the Carter Administration" in Sam C. Sarkesian, ed., *Defense Policy and the Presidency: Carter's First Years* (Boulder: Westview, 1979), 131–32.
32. Kotz, 161, 163, 167, 170.
33. Stubbing, 350, 354.
34. Stubbing, 354.

35. Carter, 20.
36. Strobe Talbott, *Endgame: The Inside Story of SALT II*, (New York: Harper & Row, 1979), 58–59, 67.
37. See text of PD–59, July 25, 1980, declassified with redactions and obtainable from the Carter Presidential Library.
38. Hamilton Jordan, *Crisis: The Last Year of the Carter Presidency* (New York: Berkley Books, 1983), 43.
39. Jordan, 242, 237.
40. Jordan, 232.
41. Stubbing 345–46; Perry, 268.

10. Cheney: The Power of Decisiveness

1. Robert M. Gates, *From the Shadows: The Ultimate Insider's Story of Five Presidents and How They Won the Cold War* (New York: Simon & Schuster, 1996), 457.
2. George H. W. Bush and Brent Scowcroft, *A World Transformed* (New York: Knopf, 1998), 22.
3. Bush and Scowcroft, 22.
4. Richard Cheney, Oral History Interviews, Historical Office of the Secretary of Defense, December 6, 1994, 55.
5. David Halberstam, *War in a Time of Peace: Bush, Clinton, and the Generals* (New York: Scribner, 2001), 66.
6. Cheney, Oral History Interviews, December 6, 1994, 28–29.
7. Cheney, Oral History Interviews, December 6, 1994, 58.
8. Bush and Scowcroft, 35. Scowcroft had earned the award in Bush's first year.
9. Bush and Scowcroft, 23.
10. Cheney, Oral History Interviews, December 6, 1994, 55.
11. James A. Baker, III, *The Politics of Diplomacy: Revolution, War & Peace, 1989–1992* (New York: G. P. Putnam's Sons, 1995), 24.
12. Baker, 25.
13. Colin Powell with Joseph E. Persico, *My American Journey* (New York: Random House, 1995), 408, 327.
14. Powell, 405.
15. Cheney, Oral History Interviews, May 3, 1995, 33.
16. Adm. William J. Crowe Jr. with David Chanoff. *The Line of Fire: From Washington to the Gulf, the Politics and Battles of the New Military War* (New York: Simon & Schuster, 1993), 231.
17. Powell, 406.
18. Cheney, Oral History Interviews, December 6, 1994, 28.
19. Cheney, Oral History Interviews, December 6, 1994, 28–29.
20. Cheney, Oral History Interviews, December 6, 1994, 29.
21. Powell, 425.
22. Crowe, 314–318.
23. Don M. Snider, "Strategy, Forces and Budgets: Dominant Influence in Executive Decision Making, Post-Cold War, 1989–91," (Strategic Studies Institute, U.S. Army War College, Carlisle, PA.), 1993, 8; Lorna S. Jaffe, "The Development of the Base Force, 1988–1992," (Office of the Chairman of the Joint Chiefs of Staff, Joint History Office, 1993), 18; Senate Committee on Armed Services, Nomination of Richard B. Cheney, March 14, 1989, available from Lexis-Nexis; Baker, 70.
24. Quoted in Snider, 12; Jaffe, 18, 20; Powell, 439.
25. Snider, 24, 28.
26. Powell, 454–55; Jaffe, 30.
27. Snider, 29–30.
28. His action, based on production delays and cost overruns, was challenged in court and ruled improper, but the program remained cancelled. See James P. Stevenson, *The $5 Billion Misunderstanding* (Annapolis: Naval Institute Press, 2001).

29. Frederick Kempe, *Divorcing the Dictator: America's Bungled Affair with Noriega* (New York: G. P. Putnam's Sons, 1990), 309–14.
30. Kempe, 293.
31. Baker, 185.
32. Bob Woodward, *The Commanders* (New York: Simon & Schuster, 1991), 93, 83; Kempe, 363
33. Woodward, 96–101.
34. Woodward, 140–41, 160, 163, 167, 176, 183.
35. Woodward, 232.
36. Michael R. Gordon and Gen. Bernard E. Trainor, *The Generals' War: The Inside Story of the Conflict in the Gulf* (Boston: Little, Brown, 1995), 33–34.
37. Woodward, 330, 234, 238; Gordon and Trainor, 144–145.
38. Powell, 486.
39. Woodward, 290–95; Gordon and Trainor, 100–101.
40. Michael R. Beschloss and Strobe Talbott, *At the Highest Levels: The Inside Story of the End of the Cold War* (Boston: Little, Brown, 1993), 445, 74.
41. Baker, 560–61.
42. Powell, 544; Halberstam, 268; Baker, 649–50.
43. Gordon and Trainor, 44.
44. Patrick E. Tyler, "U.S. Strategy Plan Calls for Insuring No Rivals Develop," *New York Times*, March 8, 1992; Barton Gellman, "Keeping the U.S. First," *Washington Post*, March 11, 1992.

11. Perry: The Power of Decency

1. David Halberstam, *War in a Time of Peace: Bush, Clinton, and the Generals* (New York: Scribner, 2001), 328.
2. Strobe Talbott, *Russia Hand* (New York: Random House, 2002), 169.
3. Elizabeth Drew says that even after the initially announced successor, Vice Adm. Bobby Inman, withdrew, the White House considered Senators Lugar and Cohen and Nunn before settling on Perry. Drew, *On the Edge: The Clinton Presidency* (New York: Simon & Schuster, 1994), 372–72.
4. Drew, 373. George Stephanopoulos says that Inman was forced out because he failed to disclose background information that would likely have disqualified him anyway. Stephanopoulos, *All Too Human* (Boston: Little, Brown, 1999), 236. But his bizarre public behavior and emotional vacillation undercut his chances for confirmation.
5. *Public Papers of the President: William J. Clinton, 1994*, 122.
6. Statement to Senate Armed Services Committee, February 2, 1994.
7. Interviews and Halberstam, 328–29.
8. Interviews.
9. Senate Armed Services Committee, nomination hearing, p. 8 of downloaded text; interviews.
10. Ashton B. Carter and William J. Perry, *Preventive Defense: A New Security Strategy for America* (Washington: Brookings, 1999), 181, 183.
11. Carter and Perry, 177.
12. Carter and Perry, 194.
13. *Report on the Bottom-Up Review*, October 1993, 107–8.
14. For the year by year actions, see *Congress and the Nation*, vol. 9, *1993–1996* (Washington: Congressional Quarterly, 1998), 280, 301, 303, 312.
15. Roger R. Trask and Alfred Goldberg, *The Department of Defense, 1947–1997: Organization and Leaders* (Washington: Historical Office of the Secretary of Defense, 1997), 123.
16. Interviews.
17. Quoted in Richard Holbrooke, *To End a War* (New York: Random House, 1998), 210.
18. Quoted in Ivo H. Daalder, *Getting to Dayton* (Washington: Brookings, 2000), n169.
19. Halberstam, 391.
20. Samantha Power. *A Problem from Hell: America and the Age of Genocide* (New York:

HarperCollins/Perennial, 2002), 370–71.

21. Elaine Sciolino, "Top U.S. Officials Divided in Debate on Invading Haiti," *New York Times*, August 4, 1994; Halberstam, 278–82.

22. Television interview quoted by Ivo H. Daalder, *Getting to Dayton* (Washington: Brookings, 2000), 182.

23. Leon V. Sigal, *Disarming Strangers* (Princeton: Princeton University Press, 1998), 109.

24. Carter and Perry, 128–129.

25. Carter and Perry, 128–132.

26. Quoted in Power, 317.

27. Halberstam, 326, 330; Daalder, 69–79.

28. Carter and Perry, 98.

29. "Perrypatetic," *The Economist,* April 9, 1994; Dana Priest, *The Mission* (New York: Norton, 2003), 96; Interviews.

30. Carter and Perry, 93.

31. Carter and Perry, 23.

32. Interviews.

33. "The Clinton Administration National Security Council," (Oral History Roundtables, Sept. 27, 2000) Center for International And Security Studies at Maryland and The Brookings Institution, 22.

34. Strobe Talbott, *The Russia Hand* (New York: Random House, 2002), 145.

35. Carter and Perry, 31–32.

36. George W. Grayson, *Strange Bedfellows* (Lanham, MD: University Press of America, 1999), 95, 171.

12. The Rumsfeld Transformation

1. Quoted in James Mann, *Rise of the Vulcans: The History of Bush's War Cabinet* (New York: Viking, 2004), 58.

2. Quoted in Rowan Scarborough, *Rumsfeld's War* (Washington: Regnery, 2004), 84.

3. Henry Kissinger, *Years of Renewal* (New York: Simon & Schuster, 1999), 175.

4. Quoted in Scarborough, 136.

5. "Rumsfeld's Rules," *Wall Street Journal,* Jan. 29, 2001. For more biographical background, see Midge Decter, *Rumsfeld* (New York: Regan Books, 2003); Scarborough, 63–75.

6. Donald Rumsfeld, interview by John McWethy, *Primetime Thursday,* ABC, March 25, 2004.

7. Suzanne Nelson, "Stint on the Hill Offered Hints of Rumsfeld's Style," *Roll Call,* March 11, 2002; Decter, 41, 46.

8. Decter, 47.

9. He took no pay for the OEO job and thus circumvented the constitutional prohibition on taking a position created while he was a member of Congress. Mann, 10.

10. Decter, 49–51.

11. Scarborough, 74.

12. Mann, 14–16.

13. Gerald Ford, *A Time to Heal* (New York: Harper & Row, 1979), 186.

14. Joseph Kraft, "The Rising of Lowered Expectations," *New York Times Magazine,* August 3, 1975.

15. Mann, 61, 66–67.

16. John W. Finney, "Ford and Rumsfeld Endorse Brown to Continue as Head of Joint Chiefs," *New York Times,* Oct. 19, 1976; Elaine Sciolino and Eric Schmitt, "In Defense Post, Infighter Known for Working the Means to his End," *New York Times,* Jan. 8, 2001.

17. Mann, 67, 69; Senate Armed Services Committee, Rumsfeld Confirmation Hearing, January 11, 2001, Federal News Service transcript, 15.

18. Elaine Sciolino and Eric Schmitt, "In Defense Post," New York Times, Jan. 8, 2001; Mann, 68; Kissinger, 850.

19. Secretary of Defense, Donald H. Rumsfeld, "Annual Defense Department Report FY1977," Jan. 27, 1976, 2–3, 5, 6, 29.

20. Scarborough, 83.
21. Scarborough, 81; Reuters, "Ford is Reported Restoring Third of Defense Cuts," *New York Times*, Dec. 15, 1975.
22. Scarborough, 86; Decter, 81, 83.
23. Scarborough, 89.
24. Scarborough, 100–4.
25. Scarborough, 107–8.
26. Scarborough, 108–9.
27. George W. Bush, "A Period of Consequences," (speech, The Citadel, Charleston, SC, Sept. 23, 1999).
28. Thomas E. Ricks, "Rumsfeld, Bush Agendas Overlap Little, *"Washington Post*, Jan. 11, 2001; Senate Armed Services Committee, Opening Statement, Confirmation Hearing of Donald Rumsfeld, Jan 11, 2001.
29. Senate Armed Services Committee, Opening Statement, Confirmation Hearing of Donald Rumsfeld, Jan 11, 2001.
30. "Rumsfeld's Rules," *Wall Street Journal*, Jan. 29, 2001.
31. Rowan Scarborough, "Rumsfeld's 'Defense Inc.' Reasserts Civilian Control," *Washington Times*, April 24, 2001; Thomas E. Ricks, "Rumsfeld, Joint Chiefs Spar over roles in Retooling Military," *Washington Post*, May 25, 2001.
32. "Post Interview with Defense Secretary Donald H. Rumsfeld," *Washington Post*, May 20, 2001, http://www.washingtonpost.com/.
33. Quoted by George C. Wilson, "CEO Rumsfeld and his Pentagon Inc.," *National Journal*, March 17, 2001, 812.
34. Thomas E. Ricks, "Review Fractures Pentagon," *Washington Post*, July 14, 2001; Andrea Stone, "Rumsfeld Rejects Pentagon Report," *USA Today*, July 19, 2001.
35. Thomas E. Ricks, "Rumsfeld Mulls Two Options: Status Quo or 10% Military Cut," *Washington Post*, Aug. 9, 2001; Thom Shanker, "Defense Chief May leave Size of Field Forces Up to Services," *New York Times*, Aug. 17, 2001; Vernon Loeb, "Rumsfeld May Let Military Branches Decide Cutbacks," *Washington Post*, Aug. 17, 2001.
36. Scarborough, 121–122.
37. Robert Kagan and William Kristol, "No Defense," *Weekly Standard*, July 23, 2001.
38. "Rumsfeld's Rules," *Wall Street Journal*, Jan. 29, 2001.
39. Thomas E. Ricks, "For Military, 'Change is Hard,'" *Washington Post*, July 19, 2001.
40. Michael Duffy, "Rumsfeld: Older But Wiser?" *Time*, Aug. 27, 2001.
41. Prepared Testimony for 9/11 Commission, March 23, 2004, 11–12.
42. Ivo H. Daalder and James M. Lindsay, *America Unbound: The Bush Revolution in Foreign Policy* (Washington: Brookings, 2003), 100.
43. See "Guidance and Terms of Reference for the 2001 Quadrennial Defense Review," June 22, 2001, 8; "Quadrennial Defense Review Report," September 30, 2001, 18.
44. Rumsfeld interview by Bob Woodward, Oct 23, 2003, 28; "Guidelines for Committing Forces," reprinted in *New York Times*, Oct 14, 2002.
45. Daalder and Lindsay, 84; Rumsfeld, interview by Jim Lehrer, *News Hour*, PBS, March 25, 2004.
46. Scarborough, 3, 29–33; Rumsfeld testimony to 9/11 commission, 4.
47. Jonathan Weisman, "A Warrior in One Battle, Manager in Another," *USA Today*, Dec. 21, 2001.
48. Letter to President Clinton, released by the Project for the New American Century, January 26,1998, at http://www.newamericancentury.org/iraqclintonletter.htm.
49. George W. Bush, interview by Jim Lehrer, *Online News Hour*, PBS, Feb 16, 2000; Ron Suskind, *The Price of Loyalty* (New York: Simon & Schuster, 2004), 75.
50. Bob Woodward, *Plan of Attack* (New York: Simon & Schuster, 2004), 26.
51. David Martin, *CBS News*, citing notes taken by Rumsfeld aide Steve Cambone; Glenn Kessler, "U.S. Decision on Iraq Has Puzzling Past," *Washington Post*, Jan. 12, 2003; Woodward, *Plan of Attack*, 26.
52. Scarborough, 43–45.

53. Woodward, *Plan of Attack*, 134–35, 121, 98–99, 144–45, 148.
54. Donald Rumsfeld interview, ABC's *This Week*, March 30, 2003.
55. Woodward, *Plan of Attack*, 117–19, 207–8.
56. Dave Moniz and Jonathan Weisman, "Military Leaders Question Iraq Plan," *USA Today*, May 23, 2002; Thomas E. Ricks, "Military Sees Iraq Invasion Put on Hold," *Washington Post*, May 24, 2002; Thomas E. Ricks, "Some Top Military Brass Favor Status Quo in Iraq," *Washington Post*, July 22, 2002; David A. Fulghum & Douglas Barrie, Military Wants Congressional OK before Iraq Offensive," *Aviation Week*, August 12, 2002.
57. Woodward, Plan of Attack, 206.
58. Rumsfeld interview with Woodward, Oct 23, 2003, 7–8.
59. James Fallows, "Blind into Baghdad," *The Atlantic Monthly*, Jan/Feb. 2004, 68; Woodward, *Plan of Attack*, 282–85.
60. Daalder and Lindsay, 111; Robin Wright and Thomas E. Ricks, "U.S. Faces Growing Fears of Failure, Wolfowitz Concedes Errors as Damage Control Continues," *Washington Post*, May 19, 2004.
61. Daalder and Lindsay, 111–112.
62. Woodward, *Plan of Attack*, 283–84; Barbara Slavin & Dave Moniz, "How Peace in Iraq Became So Elusive," *USA Today*, July 22, 2003; Mark Fineman, Robin Wright, and Doyle McManus, "Preparing for War, Stumbling to Peace," *Los Angeles Times*, July 18, 2003.
63. Evan Thomas, "Chemistry in the War Cabinet," *Newsweek*, Jan. 28, 2002.
64. Thom Shanker and Eric Schmitt, "Rumsfeld Seeks Consensus Through Jousting," *New York Times*, March 19, 2003.
65. Quoted in Michael Duffy and Mark Thompson, "Secretary of War," *Time*, Dec. 29, 2003–Jan. 5, 2004.
66. ABC Primetime Thursday, March 26, 2004; Thomas E. Ricks, "Rumsfeld's Hands-On War," *Washington Post*, Dec. 9, 2001.
67. Vernon Loeb and Thomas E. Ricks, "Rumsfeld's Style, Goals Strain Ties in Pentagon," *Washington Post*, Oct. 16, 2002; Thomas E. Ricks, "Bush Backs Overhaul of Military's Top Ranks," *Washington Post*, April 11, 2002.
68. Greg Jaffe, "Rumsfeld Floats Plan to Cut Terms of Service Chiefs," *Wall Street Journal*, Nov. 5, 2002; Vince Crawley, "Proposals Aim to Extend Senior Officers' Careers," *Navy Times*, March 29, 2004; Scarborough, 127
69. Scarborough, 119, 120, 126, 130, 134, 140.
70. Scarborough, 139; Thom Shanker, "Retiring Army Chief of Staff Warns Against Arrogance," *New York Times*, June 12, 2003.
71. Evan Thomas, "Chemistry in the War Cabinet," *Newsweek*, Jan. 28, 2002.
72. Scarborough, 6–7; Donald Rumsfeld interview by Jim Lehrer, *News Hour*, PBS, March 25, 2004.
73. Rowan Scarborough, "Defense Secretary Criticizes Top Staff," *Washington Times*, Jan. 24, 2003; Evan Thomas, Michael Isikoff, and Tamara Lipper, "The Insider," *Newsweek*, April 5, 2004.
74. James G. Lakely, "GOP Veterans Rap Secrecy on Defense Issues," *Washington Times*, Jan. 14, 2003.
75. The memo was subsequently released to the press and can be found at http://www.defenselink.mil/news/Oct2003/d20031016sdmemo.pdf.
76. Mark Mazzetti and Richard Newman, "Rumsfeld's Way," *U.S. News & World Report*, Dec. 17, 2001.
77. "A Conversation with Peter Pace," Council on Foreign Relations, Washington, DC, Feb. 17, 2004.

13. Manager of the Pentagon

1. Oral History Interview, Historical Office of the Secretary of Defense, May 18, 2001, 9.
2. Quoted in James Schlesinger, "The Office of Secretary of Defense," in Robert J. Art,

Vincent Davis, Samuel P. Huntington, eds., *Reorganizing America's Defense: Leadership in War and Peace* (Washington: Pergamon-Brassey's, 1985), 260.

3. Quoted in Schlesinger, "The Office of Secretary of Defense," 263.
4. 10 USC 202(b).
5. The latest information in all these categories is available at www.defenselink.mil.
6. The DOD's $401 billion budget is larger than the GDP of all other foreign countries except France, Italy, Germany, United Kingdom, Russia, Spain, Australia, India, Japan, China, Canada, South Korea, Mexico, and Brazil.
7. The Bush administration gives it low marks, however, on financial management and on the use of electronic forms and procedures. See OMB report, February 2004.
8. Schlesinger, "The Office of Secretary of Defense," 259.
9. Quoted in Robert Art, "The Pentagon: The Case for Biennial Budgeting," Political Science Quarterly 104, no. 2 (1989): 197.
10. While PPBS works effectively to control the budget, many officials and analysts over the years have complained that "the first P is often silent." They argue that the budget process is frequently separated from the policy planning process and thus the cause of strategy-resource mismatches.
11. See the next chapter for discussion of the guidance for war planning.
12. See materials from Defense Acquisition University.
13. Quoted in Art, "The Case for Biennial Budgeting," 197. Achievement of true biennial budgeting would reduce this somewhat, but there are always likely to be numerous changes requiring high level DOD and congressional review.
14. These processes are also under revision in order to be in line with the new PPBE system.
15. In 2004, these "black" programs reportedly totaled $23.3 billion, the highest level since 1988. Dan Morgan, "Classified Spending on the Rise," *Washington Post,* Aug. 27, 2003.
16. Schlesinger, "The Office of Secretary of Defense," 260.
17. See *U.S. Code,* title 10, for each Service.
18. U.S. Constitution, art. 1, Sec. 8.
19. James P. Stevenson, *The $5 Billion Misunderstanding* (Annapolis: Naval Institute Press, 2001), 308, 320.
20. For one former secretary's view of these challenges, see Carter and Perry, ch. 6.
21. F. J. West Jr. "Secretaries of Defense: Why Most Have Failed," *Naval War College Review* 34 (March-April 1981): 92.

14. War Planner

1. James Schlesinger, "The Office of Secretary of Defense," in Robert J. Art, Vincent Davis, Samuel P. Huntington, eds., *Reorganizing America's Defense: Leadership in War and Peace* (Washington: Pergamon-Brassey's, 1985), 265.
2. Quoted in Schlesinger, "The Office of Secretary of Defense," 257.
3. Bill Gertz, "Perry Talks of Somalia Lessons," *Washington Times,* October 4, 1995.
4. News conference, April 6, 2004.
5. 10 *U.S. Code* 113(b).
6. Declaration of Independence; Richard H. Kohn, *Eagle and Sword* (New York: Free Press, 1975), 2.
7. U.S. Constitution, art. 1, Sec. 8.
8. 10 *U.S. Code* 113(a). Note that officers from the Reserves or National Guard are not precluded from such appointments, in keeping with the framers' belief in the militia and the practical political fact that even Members of Congress often maintain commissions in the reserves or guard.
9. The post of Commanding General of the Army had been eliminated by the 1903 reforms by Army Secretary Elihu Root that created a general staff headed by a chief of staff. When the U.S. Navy created a similar post a decade later, it chose the deliberately circumscribed title of Chief of Naval Operations.

10. 10 *U.S. Code* 162.

11. Mark Clodfelter. *The Limits of Air Power* (New York: Free Press, 1989), 84–88.

12. 10 *U.S. Code* 211 (b)

13. Robert W. Komer, "Strategymaking in the Pentagon," in Art, Davis, and Huntington, eds., *Reorganizing America's Defense*, 216–217.

14. 10 *U.S. Code* 134 (b) (2).

15. See this in Powell's *National Military Strategy of the United States,* January 1992.

16. See the National Military Strategy documents of General Shalikashvili in 1995 and General Shelton in 1997.

17. See 2004 *National Military Strategy.*

18. Richard K. Betts, *Soldiers, Statesmen, and Cold War Crises* (New York: Columbia University Press, Morningside Edition, 1991), 4, 233.

19. David C. Martin and John Walcott, *Best Laid Plans* (New York: Simon & Schuster, 1988), 147.

20. News conference, April 7, 2004.

21. See Eliot Cohen, *The Supreme Command* (New York: Simon & Schuster, 2002).

15. Diplomat

1. James Schlesinger, "The Office of Secretary of Defense," in Robert J. Art, Vincent Davis, Samuel P. Huntington, eds., *Reorganizing America's Defense: Leadership in War and Peace* (Washington: Pergamon-Brassey's, 1985), 259.

2. Dana Priest, *The Mission* (New York, W. W. Norton, 2003), 14.

3. Bradley Graham, "Exiting Perry Reflects on a Stressful Tenure," *Washington Post,* Dec. 6, 1996.

4. This section draws heavily on the reporting and analysis of Dana Priest. See *The Mission*, 70–76.

5. Priest, n71, 74.

6. Priest, 16–17.

7. Priest, 45.

8. Figures from the Department of State and Department of Defense.

9. Efforts in the Clinton Administration to improve DOD/DOS collaboration fell short when Sec. Cohen and Gen. Shelton refused to let Secretary of State Albright meet with the CINCs during their twice yearly conferences in Washington. Gen. Zinni also complained that OSD was a roadblock to better interagency coordination. Priest, 90.

10. Priest, 67 and elsewhere.

11. *U.S. Code*, title 22, ch. 38, Sec. 2656.

12. Leslie Gelb, "Why Not the State Department?" *The Washington Quarterly* (Autumn 1980), 25–40, reprinted in Karl F. Inderfurth and Loch C. Johnson, *Decisions of the Highest Order* (Pacific Grove, CA: Brooks/Cole Publishing Co., 1988).

13. Christopher P. Gibson and Don M. Snider, "Explaining Post-Cold War Civil-Military Relations: A New Institutionalist Approach," (Working Paper No. 8, John M. Olin Institute for Strategic Studies, project on U.S. Post Cold-War Civil-Military Relations, 1997).

16. NSC Adviser

1. Interview with General Colin L. Powell, The National Security Council Project, Oral History Roundtables, The Brookings Institution/Center for International and Security Studies at Maryland, Nov. 23, 1999, 57.

2. "The Clinton Administration National Security Council," The National Security Council Project, Oral History Roundtables, The Brookings Institution/Center for International and Security Studies at Maryland, Sept. 27, 2000, 22.

3. Interview with former senior official.

4. Several officials interviewed by the author used the same language to describe the almost exclusive attention given to major military crises.

5. Note the absence of the JCS chairman from some of these informal sessions. In the final year of the Reagan administration, secretaries Shultz and Carlucci met in person in Powell's White House office every morning they were all in town.
6. Interview with Samuel R. Berger, The National Security Council Project, Oral History Roundtables, The Brookings Institution/Center for International and Security Studies at Maryland, April 13, 2001, 78.

17. Successes and Failures

1. Dick Cheney, interview by John McWethy, *Primetime Thursday*, ABC, Mar. 25, 2004.
2. F. J. West Jr. "Secretaries of Defense: Why Most Have Failed," *Naval War College Review* 34 (March-April 1981):86.

Bibliography

Books

Albright, Madeleine. *Madam Secretary.* New York: Miramax Books, 2003.

Ambrose, Stephen E. *Eisenhower.* Vol. 2, *The President.* New York: Simon & Schuster, 1984.

Art, Robert J., Vincent Davis, and Samuel Huntington, eds. *Reorganizing America's Defense: Leadership in War and Peace.* Washington, DC: Pergamon Brassey's, 1985.

Baker, James A. III. *The Politics of Diplomacy: Revolution, War & Peace, 1989-1992.* New York: G. P. Putnam's Sons, 1995.

Beschloss, Michael R., and Strobe Talbott. *At the Highest Levels: The Inside Story of the End of the Cold War.* Boston: Little, Brown, 1993.

Betts, Richard K. *Soldiers, Statesmen, and Cold War Crises.* New York: Columbia University Press, Morningside Edition, 1991.

Boettcher, Thomas D. *First Call: The Making of the Modern U.S. Military, 1945-1953.* Boston: Little, Brown, 1992.

Borklund, Carl W. *Men of the Pentagon: From Forrestal to McNamara.* New York: Praeger, 1966.

Brown, Harold. *Thinking About National Security.* Boulder: Westview Press, 1983.

Brzezinski, Zbigniew. *Power and Principle: Memoirs of the National Security Adviser, 1977-1981.* New York: Farrar, Straus, Giroux, 1983.

Bush, George, and Brent Scowcroft. *A World Transformed.* New York: Knopf, 1998.

Califano, Joseph A. Jr. *The Triumph and Tragedy of Lyndon Johnson.* New York: Simon & Schuster, 1991.

Callahan, David. *Dangerous Capabilties: Paul Nitze and the Cold War.* New York: Harper Collins, 1990.

Cannon, Lou. *President Reagan: The Role of a Lifetime.* New York: Simon & Schuster, 1991.

Carter, Ashton B., and William J. Perry. *Preventive Defense: A New Security Strategy for America.* Washington: Brookings, 1999.

Carter, Jimmy. *Keeping Faith: Memoirs of a President.* New York: Bantam, 1982.

Christopher, Warren. *Chances of a Lifetime.* New York: Scribner, 2001.

Clark, General Wesley K. *Waging Modern War.* New York: Public Affairs, 2001.

Clifford, Clark. *Counsel to the President.* New York: Random House, 1991.

Clodfelter, Mark. *The Limits of Air Power.* New York: Free Press, 1989.

Cohen, Eliot. *The Supreme Command.* New York: Simon & Schuster, 2002.

Coll, Steve. *Ghost Wars.* New York: Penguin Press, 2004.

Condit, Doris M. *History of the Office of the Secretary of Defense.* Vol. 2, *The Test of War, 1950–1953* Washington: Historical Office, Office of the Secretary of Defense, 1988.

Congressional Quarterly. *Congress and the Nation, 1945–1964.* Washington: Congressional Quarterly, 1965.

———. *Congress and the Nation,* Vol. 4, *1973–1976.* Washington: Congressional Quarterly, 1977.

———. *Congress and the Nation,* Vol. 9, *1993–1996.* Washington: Congressional Quarterly, 1998.

———. *Congress and the Nation,* Vol. 10, *1997–2001.* Washington: Congressional Quarterly, 2002.

Crowe, Admiral William J., Jr., with David Chanoff. *The Line of Fire: From Washington to the Gulf, the Politics and Battles of the New Military War.* New York: Simon & Schuster, 1993.

Daalder, Ivo H. *Getting to Dayton.* Washington: Brookings, 2000.

Daalder, Ivo H., and James M. Lindsay. *America Unbound: The Bush Revolution in Foreign Policy.* Washington: Brookings, 2003.

Darman, Richard. *Who's in Control? Polar Politics and the Sensible Center.* New York: Simon & Schuster, 1996.

Decter, Midge. *Rumsfeld.* New York: Regan Books, 2003.

Drew, Elizabeth. *On the Edge: The Clinton Presidency.* New York: Simon & Schuster, 1994.

Ehrlichman, John. *Witness to Power: The Nixon Years.* New York: Simon & Schuster, 1982.

Enthoven, Alain, and K. Wane Smith. *How Much is Enough? Shaping the Defense Program, 1961–1969.* New York: Harper & Row, 1971.

Feaver, Peter D. *Armed Servants.* Cambridge: Harvard University Press, 2003.

Ford, Gerald R. *A Time to Heal.* New York: Harper & Row and Reader's Digest Association, Inc., 1979.

Freedman, Lawrence. *The Evolution of Nuclear Strategy.* New York: St. Martin's, 2nd ed. 1989.

Gates, Robert M. *From the Shadows: The Ultimate Insider's Story of Five President and How They Won the Cold War.* New York: Simon & Schuster, 1996.

Gordon, Michael R., and Gen. Bernard E. Trainor. *The Generals' War: The Inside Story of the Conflict in the Gulf.* Boston: Little, Brown, 1995.

Grayson, George W. *Strange Bedfellows.* Lanham, MD: University Press of America, 1999.

Haig, Alexander M., Jr. *Caveat: Realism, Reagan and Foreign Policy.* New York: Macmillan, 1984.

Halberstam, David. *The Best and the Brightest.* New York: Ballantine, 1993.

———. *War in a Time of Peace: Bush, Clinton, and the Generals.* New York: Scribner, 2001.

Haldeman, H. R. *The Haldeman Diaries.* New York: Putnam, 1994.

Hersh, Seymour M. *The Price of Power: Kissinger in the Nixon White House.* New York: Summit, 1983.

Hilsman, Roger. *To Move a Nation.* Garden City: Doubleday, 1967.

Holbrooke, Richard. *To End a War.* New York: Random House, 1998.

Hoopes, Townsend, and Douglas Brinkley. *Driven Patriot: The Life and Times of James Forrestal.* New York: Knopf, 1992.

Inderfurth, Karl F., and Loch C. Johnson. *Decisions of the Highest Order.* Pacific Grove, CA: Brooks/Cole Publishing Co., 1988.

Isaacson, Walter. *Kissinger.* New York: Simon & Schuster, 1992.

Jaffe, Lorna S. "The Development of the Base Force, 1988–1992," Office of the Chairman of the Joint Chiefs of Staff, Joint History Office, 1993.

Jordan, Hamilton. *Crisis: The Last Year of the Carter Presidency.* New York: Berkley Books, 1983.

Kanter, Arnold. *Defense Politics: A Budgetary Perspective.* Chicago: University of Chicago Press, 1979.

Kaplan, Fred. *The Wizards of Armageddon.* New York: Simon & Schuster, 1983.

Kempe, Frederick. *Divorcing the Dictator: America's Bungled Affair with Noriega.* New York: G. P. Putnam's Sons, 1990.

Kinnard, Douglas. *The Secretary of Defense.* Lexington: University Press of Kentucky, 1980.

Kissinger, Henry. *White House Years.* Boston: Little, Brown, 1979.

———. *Years of Renewal.* New York: Simon & Schuster, 1999.

———. *Years of Upheaval.* Boston: Little, Brown, 1982.

Kohn, Richard H. *Eagle and Sword.* New York: Free Press, 1975.

Korb, Lawrence J. *The Fall and Rise of the Pentagon: American Defense Policies in the 1970s.* Westport: Greenwood Press, 1979.

———. *The Joint Chiefs of Staff: The First Twenty-Five Years.* Bloomington: Indiana University Press, 1976.

Kotz, Nick. *Wild Blue Yonder: Money, Politics, and the B-1 Bomber.* Princeton: Princeton University Press, 1988.

Leighton, Richard M. *History of the Office of the Secretary of Defense.* Vol. 3, *Strategy, Money, and the New Look.* Washington: Historical Office, Office of the Secretary of Defense, 2001.

Locher, James R. III. *Victory on the Potomac: The Goldwater-Nichols Act Unifies the Pentagon.* College Station: Texas A&M University Press, 2002.

Mann, James. *Rise of the Vulcans: The History of Bush's War Cabinet.* New York: Viking, 2004.

Martin, David C., and John Walcott. *Best Laid Plans: The Inside Story of America's War Against Terrorism.* New York: Touchstone Books by Simon & Schuster, 1988.

May, Ernest R., and Philip D. Zelikow. *The Kennedy Tapes.* Cambridge: Harvard University Press, 1997.

McFarlane, Robert C. *Special Trust.* New York: Cadell & Davies, 1994.

McLellan, David S. *Cyrus Vance.* Totowa, NJ: Rowman & Allanheld, 1985.

McMaster, H. R. *Dereliction of Duty.* New York: HarperCollins, 1997.

McNamara, Robert S. *In Retrospect: The Tragedy and Lessons of Vietnam.* New York: Random House/Times Books, 1995.

Meese, Edwin III. *With Reagan: The Inside Story.* Washington: Regnery Gateway, 1992.

Millis, Walte, ed. *The Forrestal Diaries.* New York: Viking, 1951.

Murdock, Clark A. *Defense Policy Formulation: A Comparative Analysis of the McNamara Era.* Albany: State University of New York Press, 1974.

Newhouse, John. *Cold Dawn: The Story of SALT.* New York: Holt, Rinehart & Winston, 1973.

Nitze, Paul H. *From Hiroshima to Glasnost.* New York: Grove Weidenfeld, 1989.

Nixon, Richard. *RN: The Memoirs of Richard Nixon.* New York: Grosset & Dunlap, 1978.

Perry, Mark. *Four Stars.* Boston: Houghton Mifflin, 1989.

Poole, Walter S. *The Joint Chiefs of Staff and National Policy.* Vol. 4, *1950–1952.* Washington: Office of Joint History, Office of the Chairman of the Joint Chiefs of Staff, 1998.

Powell, Colin, with Joseph E. Persico. *My American Journey.* New York: Random House, 1995.

Power, Samantha. *A Problem from Hell.* New York: Perennial, 2002.

Priest, Dana. *The Mission.* New York, W. W. Norton, 2003.

Public Papers of the President: William J. Clinton, 1996. "Remarks announcing the Second Term National Security Team and an Exchange with Reporters," December 5, 1996.

Public Papers of the President: William J. Clinton, 1994. "Remarks Announcing the Nomination of William Perry to be Secretary of Defense and an Exchange with Reporters," January 24, 1994.

Raymond, Jack. *Power at the Pentagon.* New York: Harper & Row, 1964.

Reagan, Ronald. *An American Life.* New York: Simon & Schuster, 1990.

Rearden, Steven L. *History of the Office of the Secretary of Defense.* Vol. 1, *The Formative Years, 1947–1950.* Washington: Historical Office, Office of the Secretary of Defense, 1984.

Reeves, Richard. *President Kennedy.* New York: Simon & Schuster, 1993.

Regan, Donald T. *For the Record: From Wall Street to Washington.* San Diego: Harcourt Brace Jovanovich, 1988.

Roherty, James M. *Decisions of Robert S. McNamara: A Study of the Role of the Secretary of Defense.* Coral Gables: University of Miami Press, 1970.

Rusk, Dean, with Richard Rusk. *As I Saw It.* New York: W. W. Norton, 1990.

Safire, William. *Before the Fall.* Garden City: Doubleday, 1975.

Sarkesian, Sam C., ed. *Defense Policy and the Presidency: Carter's First Years*. Boulder, Co:
    Westview, 1979.
Scarborough, Rowan. *Rumsfeld's War*. Washington: Regnery, 2004.
Schlesinger, Arthur M. Jr. *A Thousand Days: John F. Kennedy in the White House*. Boston:
    Houghton Mifflin, 1965.
Schwarzkopf, Gen. Norman H. *It Doesn't Take a Hero*. New York: Linda Grey Bantam Books,
    1992.
Shapley, Deborah. *Promise and Power: The Life and Times of Robert McNamara*. Boston: Little,
    Brown, 1993.
Shultz, George P. *Turmoil and Triumph: My Years as Secretary of State*. New York: Charles
    Scribner's Sons, 1993.
Sigal, Leon V. *Disarming Strangers*. Princeton: Princeton University Press, 1998.
Smith, Hedrick. *The Power Game: How Washington Works*. New York: Ballantine Books, 1988.
Snider, Don M. "Strategy, Forces and Budgets: Dominant Influence in Executive Decision
    Making, Post-Cold War, 1989–91," Strategic Studies Institute, U.S. Army War College,
    Carlisle, PA, 1993.
Speakes, Larry. *Speaking Out: The Reagan Presidency from Inside the White House*. New York:
    Charles Scribner's Sons, 1988.
Stephanopoulos, George. *All Too Human*. Boston: Little, Brown, 1999.
Stevenson, James P. *The $5 Billion Misunderstanding*. Annapolis: Naval Institute Press, 2001.
Stockman, David A. *The Triumph of Politics: Why the Reagan Revolution Failed*. New York:
    Harper & Row, 1986.
Stubbing, Richard A., with Richard A. Mendel. *The Defense Game*. New York: Harper &
    Row, 1986.
Suskind, Ron. *The Price of Loyalty*. New York: Simon & Schuster, 2004.
Talbott, Strobe. *Deadly Gambits: The Reagan Administration and the Stalemate in Nuclear Arms
    Control*. New York: Knopf, 1984.
————. *Endgame: The Inside Story of SALT II*. New York: Harper & Row, 1979.
————. *Russia Hand*. New York: Random House, 2002.
Trask, Roger R., and Alfred Goldberg. *The Department of Defense, 1947–1997: Organization
    and Leaders*. Washington: Historical Office of the Secretary of Defense, 1997.
Trewhitt, Henry L. *McNamara*. New York: Harper & Row, 1971.
Vance, Cyrus. *Hard Choices: Critical Years in America's Foreign Policy*. New York: Simon &
    Schuster, 1983.
Von Damm, Helene. *At Reagan's Side*. New York: Doubleday, 1989.
Walsh, Lawrence E. *Firewall: The Iran-Contra Conspiracy and Cover-up*. New York: W. W.
    Norton & Company, 1997.
Watson, Robert J. *History of the Office of the Secretary of Defense*. Vol. 4, *Into the Missile Age,
    1956–1960*. Washington: Historical Office, Office of the Secretary of Defense, 1997.
Weinberger, Caspar W. *Fighting for Peace: Seven Critical Years in the Pentagon*. New York:
    Warner Books, 1990.
Woodward, Bob. *Plan of Attack*. New York: Simon & Schuster, 2004.
————. *The Commanders*. New York: Simon & Schuster, 1991.
Zumwalt, Elmo R., Jr. *On Watch*. New York: Quadrangle, 1976.

Articles and Other Materials

"Perrypatetic." *The Economist,* April 9, 1994.
ABC *Primtetime Thursday*. Interview with John McWethy, March 25, 2004.
Art, Robert. "The Pentagon: The Case for Biennial Budgeting." *Political Science Quarterly*,
    104, no. 2 (1989): 193-214.
Aspin, Les. *Report on the Bottom-Up Review,* October 1993, Department of Defense.
Barnes, Fred. "You're Fired." *The New Republic,* January 10 & 17, 1994, 13.
Berger, Samuel R. "Interview with Samuel R. Berger." The National Security Council Project,
    Oral History Roundtables, The Brookings Institution/Center for International and

Security Studies at Maryland, April 13, 2001.

Brookings Institution/Center for International and Security Studies at Maryland. "The Clinton Administration National Security Council," The National Security Council Project, Oral History Roundtables, Sept. 27, 2000.

Bush, George W. "A Period of Consequences." Speech at The Citadel, Sept. 23, 1999.

Cheney, Richard. Oral History Interviews. Historical Office of the Secretary of Defense, December 6, 1994; February 27, 1995; May 3, 1995.

Cohen, William S. Statement to The National Commission On Terrorist Attacks Upon the United States, March 23, 2004.

Crawley, Vince. "Proposals Aim to Extend Senior Officers' Careers." *Navy Times,* March 29, 2004.

Department of Defense. "Guidance and Terms of Reference for the 2001 Quadrennial Defense Review." June 22, 2001.

———. "Quadrennial Defense Review Report," September 30, 2001.

Donnelly, John. "The Evolution of William Cohen." *Boston Globe Magazine,* October 22, 2000.

Duffy, Michael. "Rumsfeld: Older But Wiser?" *Time,* Aug. 27, 2001.

Duffy, Michael, and David S. Jackson. "Obstacle Course," *Time,* Feb. 8, 1993.

Duffy, Michael, and Mark Thompson. "Secretary of War." *Time,* Dec 29, 2003 and Jan. 5, 2004.

Fallows, James. "Blind into Baghdad." *The Atlantic Monthly,* Jan/Feb 2004, 52–74.

Fineman, Mark, Robin Wright, and Doyle McManus. "Preparing for War, Stumbling to Peace." *Los Angeles Times,* July 18, 2003.

Finney, John W. "Ford and Rumsfeld Endorse Brown to Continue as Head of Joint Chiefs." *New York Times,* Oct. 19, 1976.

Fulghum, David A., and Douglas Barrie. "Military Wants Congressional OK before Iraq Offensive." *Aviation Week,* Aug. 12, 2002.

Garcia, Rogelio. "Presidential Appointments to Full-Time Positions in Executive Departments During the 103d Congress." *CRS Report for Congress,* 94-453GOV, July 25, 1994.

Gelb, Leslie H. "Schlesinger for Defense, Defense for Détente." *New York Times Magazine,* August 4, 1974.

Gellman, Barton. "Keeping the U.S. First." *Washington Post,* Mar. 11, 1992.

Gertz, Bill. "Perry Talks of Somalia Lessons." *Washington Times,* Oct. 4, 1995.

Gibson, Christopher P. and Don M. Snider. "Explaining Post–Cold War Civil-Military Relations: A New Institutionalist Approach." Working Paper No. 8, project on U.S. Post Cold–War Civil-Military Relations. John M. Olin Institute for Strategic Studies, Harvard University, 1997.

Gordon, Michael. "Pentagon Seeking to Cut Military But Equip It for 2 Regional Wars." *New York Times,* Sept. 2, 1993.

Graham, Bradley. "Exiting Perry Reflects on a Stressful Tenure." *Washington Post,* Dec. 6, 1996.

Grove, Lloyd. "The So-Long Senators." *Washington Post,* Jan. 26, 1996.

Hamre, John. Oral History Interviews. Historical Office of the Secretary of Defense, May 15, 2001; May 18, 2001; June 29, 2001.

Jaffe, Greg. "Rumsfeld Floats Plan to Cut Terms of Service Chiefs." *Wall Street Journal,* Nov. 5, 2002.

Kagan, Robert, and William Kristol. "No Defense." *Weekly Standard,* July 23, 2001.

Kelly, John H. "Lebanon: 1982-1984." http://www.rand.org/publications/CF/CF129?CF-129.chapter6.html.

Kessler, Glenn. "U.S. Decision on Iraq Has Puzzling Past," *Washington Post,* Jan. 12, 2003.

Kraft, Joseph. "The Rising of Lowered Expectations," *New York Times Magazine,* Aug. 3, 1975.

Lacayo, Richard, and Michael Duffy. "Bring on the Admiral," *Time,* Dec. 27, 1993.

Laird, Melvin R. Oral History Interviews. Historical Office of the Secretary of Defense, August 18, 1986; Sept. 2, 1986; Oct. 29, 1986.

Lakely, James G. "GOP Veterans Rap Secrecy on Defense Issues." *Washington Times,* Jan. 14, 2003.

Lancaster, John. "Aspin Lists U.S. Goals in Somalia." *Washington Post,* Aug. 28, 1993.

Lemann, Nicholas. "The Peacetime War: Caspar Weinberger in Reagan's Pentagon." *The Atlantic Monthly,* Oct. 1984.

Loeb, Vernon, and Thomas E. Ricks. "Rumsfeld's Style, Goals Strain Ties in Pentagon." *Washington Post,* Oct. 16, 2002.

Loeb, Vernon. "Rumsfeld May Let Military Branches Decide Cutbacks." *Washington Post,* Aug. 17, 2001.

Longley, Charles H. "McNamara and Military Behavior." *American Journal of Political Science.* 18, no. 1 (Feb. 1974): 1–21.

Mazzetti, Mark, and Richard Newman. "Rumsfeld's Way." *U.S. News & World Report,* Dec. 17, 2001.

McAllister, Bill & Barton Gellman. "Aspin Reverses Ban on Married Marines," *Washington Post,* August 12, 1993.

Moniz, Dave, and Jonathan Weisman. "Military Leaders Question Iraq Plan." *USA Today,* May 23, 2002.

Morgan, Dan. "Classified Spending on the Rise." *Washington Post,* Aug. 27, 2003.

Nelson, Suzanne. "Stint on the Hill Offered Hints of Rumsfeld's Style." *Roll Call,* March 11, 2002.

New York Times. "Ford is Reported Restoring Third of Defense Cuts," Dec. 15, 1975.

Pace, Peter. "A Conversation with Peter Pace." Council on Foreign Relations, Washington, DC, Feb. 17, 2004.

PBS Online News Hour. Jim Lehrer interview with Donald Rumsfeld, March 25, 2004.
———. Jim Lehrer interview with George W. Bush, Feb 16, 2000.

Piller, Geoffrey. "DOD's Office of International Security Affairs: The Brief Ascendancy of an Advisory System." *Political Science Quarterly* 98, no. 1 (Spring: 1983), 59–78.

Powell, Colin. "Interview with Gen. Colin L. Powell," The National Security Council Project, Oral History Roundtables, The Brookings Institution/Center for International and Security Studies at Maryland, Nov. 23, 1999, 57.

Priest, Dana. "An 'Outsider' Set to Take Over Pentagon," *Washington Post,* Jan. 22, 1997.

Project for the New American Century. "Letter to President Clinton." Jan. 26, 1998. www.newamericancentury.org/iraqclintonletter.htm.

Ricks, Thomas E., "Bush Backs Overhaul of Military's Top Ranks," *Washington Post,* April 11, 2002.
———. "For Military, 'Change is Hard,'" *Washington Post,* July 19, 2001.
———. "Military Sees Iraq Invasion Put on Hold," *Washington Post,* May 24, 2002.
———. "Review Fractures Pentagon," *Washington Post.* July 14, 2001.
———. "Rumsfeld Mulls Two Options: Status Quo or 10% Military Cut." *Washington Post,* Aug. 9, 2001.
———. "Rumsfeld, Bush Agendas Overlap Little. *Washington Post,* Jan. 11, 2001.
———. "Rumsfeld, Joint Chiefs Spar Over Roles in Retooling Military." *Washington Post,* May 25, 2001.
———. "Rumsfeld's Hands-On War." *Washington Post,* Dec. 9, 2001.
———. "Some Top Military Brass Favor Status Quo in Iraq." *Washington Post,* July 22, 2002.

Rumsfeld, Donald, "Rumsfeld's Rules." *Wall Street Journal,* Jan. 29, 2001.
———. "Annual Defense Department Report FY 1977," Jan. 27, 1976.
———. "Guidelines for Committing Forces." *New York Times,* Oct. 14, 2002.
———. Interview with Jim Lehrer, PBS NewsHour, March 25, 2004.
———. Inteview by Bob Woodward, Department of Defense transcript, Oct. 23, 2003.
———. News conference, April 6, 2004.

Scarborough, Rowan. "Defense Secretary Criticizes Top Staff," *Washington Times,* Jan. 24, 2003.

———. "Rumsfeld's 'Defense Inc.' Reasserts Civilian Control," *Washington Times,* April 24, 2001.

Schlesinger, James. "Quantitative Analysis and National Security." *World Politics* 15, no. 2 (Jan. 1963): 295–315.

———. Oral History Interviews. Historical Office of the Secretary of Defense, July 12, 1990, and Feb. 7, 1991.

Schmitt, Eric. "Aspin Resigns from Cabinet; President Lost Confidence in Defense Chief, Aides Say." *New York Times,* Dec. 16, 1993.

———. "Aspin Dismisses General as Head of Plane Project." *New York Times,* May 1, 1993.

———. "Aspin Overrules Navy Secretary, Saving Admiral." *New York Times,* Oct. 5, 1993.

Sciolino, Elaine, and Eric Schmitt. "In Defense Post, Infighter Known for Working the Means to His End." *New York Times,* Jan. 8, 2001.

Sciolino, Elaine. "Top U.S. Officials Divided in Debate on Invading Haiti." *New York Times,* August 4, 1994.

Shanker, Thom. "Defense Chief May Leave Size of Field Forces Up to Services." *New York Times,* Aug. 17, 2001.

———. "Retiring Army Chief of Staff Warns Against Arrogance." *New York Times,* June 12, 2003.

Shanker, Thom, and Eric Schmitt. "Rumsfeld Seeks Consensus Through Jousting." *New York Times,* March 19, 2003.

Slavin, Barbara, and Dave Moniz. "How Peace in Iraq Became So Elusive." *USA Today,* July 22, 2003.

Stone, Andrea. "Rumsfeld Rejects Pentagon Report." *USA Today,* July 19, 2001.

Thomas, Evan. "Chemistry in the War Cabinet." *Newsweek,* Jan. 28, 2002.

Thomas, Evan, Michael Isikoff, and Tamara Lipper. "The Insider," *Newsweek,* April 5, 2004.

Tyler, Patrick E. "U.S. Strategy Plan Calls for Insuring No Rivals Develop." *New York Times,* March 8, 1992.

U.S. Congress. Senate. Committee on Armed Services. *Nominations of Harold Brown and Charles W. Duncan* 95th Cong., 1st sess. January 11, 1977.

———. *Aspin Confirmation Hearing.* January 7, 1993, Federal News Service Transcript.

———. *Rumsfeld Confirmation Hearing.* January 11, 2001, Federal News Service Transcript.

———. *Cohen Nomination Hearing.* January 22, 1997, Federal News Service Transcript.

———. *Nomination of Richard B. Cheney.* March 14, 1989.

———. *Nomination of Caspar W. Weinberger to be Secretary of Defense.* 97th Cong., 1st sess., January 6, 1981.

Washington Post. "Post Interview with Defense Secretary Donald H. Rumsfeld," May 20, 2001. http://www.washingtonpost.com/.

Weiner, Tim. "Raid on Baghdad," *New York Times,* June 27, 1993.

Weinraub, Bernard. "The Browning of the Pentagon." *New York Times Magazine,* Jan. 29, 1978.

Weisman, Jonathan. "A Warrior in One Battle, Manager in Another." *USA Today,* Dec. 21, 2001.

West, F. J. Jr. "Secretaries of Defense: Why Most Have Failed." *Naval War College Review* 34 (March-April 1981) : 86–92.

White, Thomas D. "Strategy and the Defense Intellectuals." *Saturday Evening Post,* May 4, 1963.

Wilson, George C. "CEO Rumsfeld and His Pentagon Inc." *National Journal,* March 17, 2001, 812.

Woodward, Bob. "The Secretary of Analysis." *Washington Post Magazine,* Feb. 21, 1993.

Wright, Robin, and Thomas E. Ricks. "U.S. Faces Growing Fears of Failure, Wolfowitz Concedes Errors as Damage Control Continues." *Washington Post,* May 19, 2004.

Index

9/11 attacks, 169

Abrams, Creighton, 51–2, 181
Acheson, Dean, 11
Afghanistan, 170–71
Air Force, U.S., 31, 34–6, 52, 97, 109, 129, 138, 144, 176
Albright, Madeleine, 107–8, 111, 208
arms control, 38; ABM Treaty, 56–7; SALT, 50, 56–7, 72, 83, 87, 121, 130; INF, 72–3
Army, U.S., 7, 35–6, 52, 67, 97, 130, 191
Aspin, Les, 106, 142, 147–8, 150, 193, 214–15; appointment, 92; background, 91–2; and Congress, 92–6; defense management, 97; diplomatic activities, 100–101, 201; personality and operating style, 5, 51, 93, 96–7, 101, 103; and President Clinton, 92, 94, 98–102, 210; and U.S. military, 94–7; strategy, 97

Baker, James, 63, 136–7, 142, 144, 193
Berger, Samuel (Sandy), 100, 108, 111, 117
Betts, Dick, 196
Bosnia and the Balkans, 97–8, 106, 113, 145, 151–5
Bottom Up Review (BUR), 96, 97, 151, 195
Bremer, Paul (Jerry), 174
Brown, George, 51, 127, 132, 162
Brown, Harold, 193–4, 213–14; appointment, 122; background, 28, 121–2; and Congress, 125–7; defense management, 128–30; diplomatic activities, 132–3, 200; and NSC, 133–4; personality and operating style, 123–4, 127–8; and President Carter, 121–34; and U.S. military, 125

Brzezinski, Zbigniew, 108, 123–4
budgeting, 61–2, 67–8, 110–12, 123, 126–9, 139–42, 151, 163, 167–8, 181–5, 219n, 234n; PPBS, 26, 33–6, 182, 188, 234n; PPBE, 183–4
Bundy, McGeorge, 26
Bush, George H. W., 73, 135–7, 139–42, 145, 192, 197
Bush, George W., 112, 146, 165–6, 169–71, 192, 195, 197, 208–210

capabilities-driven plans, 193–4
Carlucci, Frank, 61, 119, 161, 188, 214
Carter, Jimmy, 53, 61, 64, 121–34, 153, 161–2, 165, 173, 175, 187–8, 193, 195, 213
CENTCOM (Central Command), 116, 170, 172
Chairman, Joint Chiefs of Staff (CJCS), 4, 30, 64, 79, 110, 127, 132, 137, 184, 207–209
Cheney, Richard, 92, 97, 161–2, 165, 175; appointment, 135–6; background, 135–7; and Congress, 138, 141–2; diplomatic activities, 144, 200–201; and NSC, 144–5, 207, 210; personality and operating style, 138–9, 146; and President G. H. W. Bush, 135–7, 139–42, 210; and U.S. military, 137–8, 140, 142–4
China, 11, 133, 155–6
Christopher, Warren, 92, 97–101, 148, 153
civil-military relations, 122, 172, 189–93, 235n
Clark, Wesley, 113–114, 155, 227n
Clements, William, 50, 60
Clifford, Clark, 5, 7, 9, 75, 214

Clinton, Bill, 171, 192, 196–7, 208; and
    Aspin, 92–96, 98–102; and Cohen,
    105–107, 111–12, 114, 117; and Perry,
    147–8
Coats, Dan, 165
Cohen, William, 65, 117, 193, 213–14, 227n;
    appointment, 106, 230n; background,
    105–6; and Congress, 105, 107, 109–
    110; defense management, 111–12;
    diplomatic activities, 116, 200–201;
    and NSC, 116–17; personality and
    operating style, 5, 110–111; and
    President Clinton, 106–107, 117, 208,
    210; and U.S. military, 108–110, 112–
    14
combatant commanders (CINCs), 152–3,
    169, 172, 177, 201–203
Congress, U.S., 7–8, 16, 32–3, 52–3, 94, 96,
    99–100, 109, 111, 126–7, 129–30, 136–
    8, 141–2, 149–51, 162, 167–8, 172, 177,
    183–4, 186–8, 190, 192, 195, 214–15,
    235n. *See also* House of Representa-
    tives and Senate
crisis action planning, 195–6
Crowe, William, 64–5, 137–8, 145
Cuba, Bay of Pigs, 32; missile crisis, 42

defense budget. *See* budgeting
Defense Department reorganization, in
    1949, 9–10; in 1953, 14; in 1958, 15–
    16, 29–30, 191; in 1986, 66, 111
Defense Planning Guidance (DPG), 145,
    182–3
deliberate planning process, 182–5, 194–5
diplomatic activities of SecDefs, 199–205
Dole, Bob, 65
Dugan, Michael, 144

EC-121 incident, 80
Eisenhower, Dwight D., 13–17, 29–30, 77
Ellsworth, Robert, 159
Europe. *See* NATO and Europe

failure rate of SecDefs, 3
Ford, Gerald, 45, 48–50, 57, 136, 160–62
foreign travel by SecDefs, 70, 100, 116, 133,
    144, 155–6, 164, 199–201, 217
Forrestal, James, 5, 7–10, 17, 21, 122, 215,
    219n; background, 7–8; and Congress,
    9; personality and operating style, 5;
    and President Truman, 9; and U.S.
    military, 8–9
Franks, Tommy, 170–74

Garner, Jay, 174

Gates, Robert, 135
Gates, Thomas, 16–17, 30, 36, 191
gays in uniform, 94–6
Global War on Terrorism (GWOT), 114–
    115, 159, 169, 178
Goldwater-Nichols Act, 16, 66, 111, 113,
    125, 148, 186, 190, 194, 209
Gore, Al, 98, 100, 107, 148, 165, 210
Gulf War, 142–4, 193, 214

Haig, Alexander, 59–61
Haiti, 100, 145, 152–3
Halberstam, David, 91, 117, 147
Hamre, John, 109–110, 181
Hartmann, Robert, 159
Herres, Robert, 182
Holum, John, 94
House of Representatives, U.S., 91–2, 107,
    114, 160–61. *See also* Congress

Inman, Bobby, 101–102, 148, 230n
Iran hostage rescue mission, 131–2
Iraq, 114, 142–4, 152, 162, 169–74, 176–7,
    208

Jackson, Henry M. (Scoop), 49, 56–7, 77,
    126, 130, 162
Johnson, Louis, 5, 10–12, 17, 75, 214–15
Johnson, Lyndon B., 26–7, 39–42, 192, 214
Joint Chiefs of Staff (JCS), 8, 13–16, 30–
    32, 64, 66, 79, 81, 125, 148, 167, 172,
    194, 196
Joint Staff, 85, 96, 108, 131, 155, 167, 172,
    175, 186, 195, 204, 209, 226n
Jones, David, 64, 66, 127, 131–2
Jones, James, 110

Kanter, Arnold, 34
Kaplan, Fred, 39
Kennedy, John F., 13; and McNamara, 23–
    7, 38, 40, 214
Kennedy, Robert F., 23
Kinnard, Douglas, xi
Kissinger, Henry, 48–50, 54–7, 61, 78–81,
    83–7, 136, 159, 162–3
Korean War and Korea policy, 11–14, 100,
    113, 133, 145, 152–3, 155, 214
Kosovo, 113–14, 208
Kuwait, 70, 92, 98, 142–4, 201

Laird, Melvin, 46; appointment, 77–8;
    background, 78; and Congress, 80–
    83; defense management, 83–4;
    personality and operating style, 5, 82–
    3, 89; and President Nixon, 77–80,

84–7, 214; and U.S. military, 81–2; and Vietnam, 78, 84–6
Lake, Anthony, 100–102, 148
leadership patterns, 4–5, 213–15
Lebanon, 71–2, 196
LeMay, Curtis, 29, 31, 190
Lemnitzer, Lyman, 32, 37
Lovett, Robert, 12–13, 17, 24–5

MacArthur, Douglas, 12–13
Mahon, George, 82, 121, 126
Marine Corps. U.S., 8, 95, 97, 110, 142
Marshall, George, 4, 7, 11–13, 17, 190
Mayaguez rescue, 54–5
McElroy, Neil, 15–17, 47
McFarlane, Robert (Bud), 59, 65
McNamara, Robert, 48, 52, 81–2, 93, 121, 128, 166, 178, 181, 188, 191–3, 213–15; appointment, 13, 16, 23–4; background, 24–5; and Congress, 32–33; defense management, 33–36; and foreign policy, 40–41; and NSC, 41–2; and nuclear strategy, 36–8; personality and operating style, 5, 28–9; and Presidents Kennedy and Johnson, 23–4, 26–7, 38–42; and U.S. military, 29–32; and Vietnam, 38–40
military proconsuls, 201–203
military veto over use of force, 196–7
missile defense, 68, 112, 163–5, 194
Moorer, Thomas, 51, 88

National Defense Panel (NDP), 111–12, 165
National Military Establishment, 4
National Security Act of 1947, 4, 8, 9, 190
National Security Council (NSC), 8, 63, 80, 98, 108, 207–11
NATO and Europe, 55–6, 87, 100–101, 113–14, 129, 132, 144–5, 156–7, 161, 199, 201, 227n
Navy, U.S., 7–8, 11, 16, 95, 97, 129
Nixon, Richard M., 45, 48, 77–80, 84–7, 161
nuclear weapons and strategy, 36–8, 53–55, 68, 130–31, 190–91
Nunn, Sam, 60, 92, 94–5, 153, 230n

Office of the Secretary of Defense (OSD), 16, 28, 138, 148, 150, 175, 184–7, 194, 204, 226n

Pace, Peter, 178
Packard, David, 83, 150
Panama, 126, 132, 142–3
Perle, Richard, 68, 72, 130

Perry, Mark, 81
Perry, William, 96–7, 106, 108, 111, 116, 127, 189, 193, 213–15; appointment, 147–8, 230n; background, 147–8; and Congress, 149–50; defense management, 150–51; diplomatic activities, 155–6, 200–201; and NSC, 156–7; personality and operating style, 149–50, 157–8; and President Clinton, 147–8; and U.S. military, 148–9
personnel selection, 82–3, 93, 109, 127, 139, 162, 175, 185
Pickering, Thomas, 116
Powell, Colin, 92, 94–6, 127, 137–41, 143–5, 152–3, 176, 193, 196, 207, 209
Priest, Dana, 199, 202–203

Quadrennial Defense Review (QDR), 111–12, 114, 167, 177

Reagan, Ronald, 57, 59–65, 70–73, 128, 142, 164, 209
Revolution in Military Affairs (RMA), 165–6, 187
Rice, Condoleezza, 169, 174, 176, 210
Richardson, Elliot, 47, 119
Rogers, William, 79, 84
Rumsfeld, Donald, 57, 61, 136, 188–9; appointment, 162, 165–6, 213–15, 226n; background, 159–64; and Congress, 160–62, 167–8, 176–7; defense management, 165–8, 177–8, 193; and NSC, 171, 176–7, 209–210; personality and operating style, 5, 21, 166–7, 174–7; and President G. W. Bush, 165–6, 169–71, 210; "Rules," 160, 166, 168; and U.S. military, 162, 167, 169–72, 175–6
Rusk, Dean, 24, 27–8, 41
Russia (and Soviet Union), 11, 15, 126, 140, 145, 156–7, 163

Schlesinger, James, 3, 93, 182, 185, 188–9, 193, 199, 214–15; appointment, 48; background, 45–7; and Congress, 49, 53, 56–7; defense management, 52–3; diplomatic activities, 54–6; nuclear strategy, 53–4; personality and operating style, 5, 45, 48; and President Nixon, 45, 48; and President Ford, 45, 48–50; and U.S. military, 50–52
Scowcroft, Brent, 135–7

Secretaries of Defense, background, 4, 216;
    firefighters, 5, 75; foreign travel, 217;
    leadership roles, 5, 185; legal
    provisions, 11, 29–30, 88, 113, 177, 181,
    186, 189, 194; list of, 216; revolution-
    aries, 5, 21–2; team players, 5, 119
Senate, U.S., 65, 92–3, 105, 112, 149, 166,
    168, 173. *See also* Congress
Shalikashvili, John, 95, 148, 152–5, 201
Shelton, Hugh, 111, 114–16, 167, 201
Shinseki, Eric, 176
Shriver, Sargent, 23
Shultz, George, 59–60, 63–5, 69, 161, 209,
    214
Slocombe, Walt, 207
Somalia, 97–100, 152, 214
span of control, 4
Special Operations Command (SOCOM),
    111, 201
State, Department of, 27–8, 40–41, 79, 202–205
Stockman, David, 61
Stubbing, Richard, xi, 82–3

Talbott, Strobe, 147, 156
Taylor, Maxwell, 32, 39
Tower, John, 65, 135
Truman, Harry S., 7–13, 214

use of force, 69–70, 98, 112–13, 145, 151–
    2, 170, 172, 191–3, 209, 211

Vance, Cyrus, 108, 123–4, 130
Vessey, John, 64, 196
Vietnam War, 33, 36; "Lessons," 69, 191–
    3; conduct, 38–40, 83–6, 192
Vinson, Carl, 33, 35

war planning, 36–40, 53–55, 68–70, 97–
    100, 112–16, 130–32, 142–5, 151–5,
    169–174, 189–197
Warner, John, 105, 145
weapons programs, 35–8, 123, 125–7, 129–
    30, 227n
Weinberger, Caspar, 109, 111, 128, 152, 170,
    172, 187, 189, 214–15; appointment,
    59–61; background, 60; and Congress,
    65–6; defense manage-ment, 61–2, 67–
    8; diplomatic activities, 70–73; and
    NSC, 209; personality and operating
    style, 5, 66–7; and President Reagan,
    59–60, 62–4, 71–3; and U.S. military,
    64–5; use of force tests, 69–70, 192
Welch, Larry, 138
West, F. J. (Bing), 3, 188, 213
Wheeler, Earle, 32, 82, 85
White, Gen. Thomas, 30, 38
Wilson, Charles, 13–15, 17, 47, 214
Wolfowitz, Paul, 140–141, 144, 146, 166,
    170–171, 173, 176

Zinni, Anthony, 116, 203

About the Author

Charles A. Stevenson, Ph.D., has observed the Office of the Secretary of Defense and its secretaries professionally since the 1960s. For twenty-two years he served as a defense and foreign policy adviser in the U.S. Senate. A longtime professor at the National War College in Washington, D.C., he now teaches at the Nitze School of Advanced International Studies at Johns Hopkins University. He lives in University Park, Maryland.